A rare, animated picture of McGonagall in a performance of what would seem likely to be "The Rattling Dublin Boy," his Irish comic song which always drew enthusiastic audience participation. Could well be the photograph referred to in Chapter 17 as "McGonagall Defying His Enemies."

NO POETS' CORNER
IN THE ABBEY

THE DRAMATIC STORY OF

WILLIAM McGONAGALL

by

DAVID PHILLIPS

1971

DUNDEE
DAVID WINTER & SON LTD.
15 SHORE TERRACE

LONDON
GERALD DUCKWORTH & CO. LTD.
3 HENRIETTA STREET

PREFACE

In this book I have attempted an imaginative study of William McGonagall. All the facts that I have been able to dig up are here, and drawing on my local knowledge I have tried to present these in appropriate settings, and with likely attendant scenes and characters where I thought such to be an advantage.

A cynic might justifiably remark that wild liberties could be taken in any account of McGonagall's life, since it could be said that he seemed to keep his facts for his doggerel and his imagination for his reminiscences (giving both 1825 and 1830 as dates of birth for instance). I have not taken liberties with the facts as recorded. What I have tried to do is, here and there, use the techniques of the novel to clarify, illumine, highlight the facts—and in the process, I hope, to bring something of McGonagall the man and his times to life.

If this succeeds as a story which throws some light on McGonagall, or as a study of him which is more readable than a bare pedantic copying of yellowing pages from dusty archives, then in either case I'll be happy; I meant the book to be both these things.

My grateful thanks to the Librarian and staff of Dundee Public Libraries for facilities and help concerning research—and most certainly also to William J. Smith of David Winter & Son Ltd., the Printers, whose whole idea it was; whose authoritative knowledge on McGonagall, enthusiasm and drive had propelled me half-way through the book before I had really made up my mind whether or not I could do it.

Thanks also to the staff of the General Register Office, Edinburgh, and to Messrs D. C. Thomson & Co. Ltd., Dundee.

D. PHILLIPS.

Dundee 1971.

FOREWORD

During the past 25 years since literary critics discovered William McGonagall as a writer of the world's worst bad verse, there has been an enormous international interest in his works. I have received letters from all over the world asking for more information on the Poet's life and, indeed, to quote an extract from a recent letter, "The story of his trip on foot to Balmoral Castle is so interesting that it only whets the reader's appetite for all the facts." His books of poems are to be found on many a bookshelf. On both sides of the Iron Curtain there is a treasured place for the volumes enshrining the worst poet in the history of literature. I have felt for some considerable time that the McGonagall story should be told with a sympathetic understanding and by a local author who could envelop himself into the life and character of the immortal William McGonagall. David Phillips is a well-known writer and has spent many months in the archives of the Dundee Public Library and elsewhere sifting and confirming all the information I had available in my own possession, including the historic documents written in McGonagall's own handwriting and making this story into a moving description of the poet's life. The story tells of how McGonagall hawked his poems in the streets and recited them in pubs and halls in Dundee only to be pelted with eggs and badly treated by his fellow Dundonians. David Phillips brings McGonagall to life in a story which contains humour, pathos and drama. The crowds gathering at Poets' Corner in Westminster Abbey pay daily homage to Chaucer, Kipling, Browning and Tennyson. Few will think of Sir William Topaz McGonagall. In my opinion he was a genius. Not only did he prophesy the Tay Bridge Disaster and his own immortaility, he even wrote his own epitaph.

> *I earnestly hope the inhabitants of the beautiful City of Dundee*
> *Will appreciate this little volume got up by me,*
> *And when they read its pages, I hope it will fill their hearts*
> *with delight,*
> *While seated around the fireside on a cold winter's night;*
> *And some of them, no doubt, will let a silent tear fall*
>
> *In dear remembrance of WILLIAM McGONAGALL.*

The tears may often be of laughter, but his works live on when those of real poets are forgotten.

WILLIAM J. SMITH.

LIST OF ILLUSTRATIONS

William McGonagall	Frontispiece
Balmoral Castle	16
Rev. George Gilfillan	39
Grassmarket, Edinburgh	42
Theatre Royal	55
Music Hall	58
Tay Bridge (after disaster)	103
Dion Boucicault	106
Burns Statue and Albert Institute	119
Sir Henry Irving	122
Letter from Buckingham Palace	135
Tay Whale	138
Paton's Lane	147
Lamb's Hotel	158

APPENDIX

Note on Spurious Autobiography	I
Letter to Alec Lamb	II
Letter to Lamb offering MSS.	III
Letter to Sir John Leng	IV
Letter to James Shand	V
Jack O' The Cudgel	VI

. . . but be as Kind and Condenscending
As to give me your Patronage.

CHAPTER ONE

THE picnic had been a great success. Although for most of the time the skies had remained overcast, this made the sudden shafts of sunlight the more dramatic in the way they picked out cottage and farm, unexpectedly glittered back from burn and loch in the Deeside valley far below. "Mr Landseer would have been enchanted with some of the wonderful effects of light and shade," the Queen had observed. Now she stood beside the tartan rug on which she had sat, and which the ever-attentive John Brown, her personal manservant, was now picking up to fold. Other servants were packing away equipment, loading the ponies in preparation for the descent to Balmoral. . . .

The little old lady in black who was Queen Victoria, Empress of India, had been as relaxed and happy as Brown had seen her for many a day; the tea, which he had prepared himself, having played its part.

"Really, Brown; tea made over a fire in the open is *most* refreshing; I cannot remember when I have enjoyed a cup of tea more. The wonderful mountain air, of course——"

"Aye. And the glass of whisky that was in it, your majesty!"

Now she was becoming a little petulant, with "Where is that girl?"

"The lassie will be busy getting things put away. We'll not have to dally, now, your majesty; I warn you there's rain and maybe worse on the way."

"But she must come and brush these crumbs off my dress." And she hadn't looked any the less petulant at his "Oh, just give yourself a shake like any other woman!" But she did knock off the crumbs herself, and soon the party was on the way down to the castle, she mounted on her pony with the faithful highlander at its head, as the skies darkened and the breeze died to a still, heavy sultriness.

They got back before the storm broke. Lightning leapt across the summits, great claps of thunder reverberated in the valleys, rebounded from rock walls. Grouse, ptarmigan, hares hid themselves in the heather; deer had gathered in groups to the sheltered sides of corries. . . . And in the now torrential downpour over many miles of moor and mountain, only one creature moved in the open; a little man limping hurriedly along the winding road that led steeply up Glenshee.

McGonagall's priest's hat was sodden; his unseasonable frock-coat was heavy with water; trousers clung with wetness; boots squelched. Clutching his coat-collar to him with one hand, jabbing and trailing a heavy walking-stick with the other, he stumbled wildly on, a little man with long black locks plastered to his ears, an out-of-key figure in the great wet wildness that afforded not even tree, hedge or wall as shelter. . . . But now, thank God! a big rock loomed round a bend of the stony road. Crouched in its lee he was glad to find the coppers-worth of bread and cheese he had bought in Alyth had remained dry; more important, so had the precious letter and the sheets of writing paper. He ate ravenously as the rain hissed and sang all round him. Then on, rain or not, for hadn't he told them in Dundee he would go through fire and water to present himself to her gracious majesty? And he was still a long, long way from Balmoral, and would have to be finding somewhere to sleep this night. Struggling to his feet he gasped as the storm whipped at his coat-tails and hat, drove needles of rain up his sleeves. Slithering down to the stippled puddles of the rutted, muddy road he stumbled on. . . .

"And how did you travel to Balmoral, Mr McGonagall?"

"On foot, Your Majesty, all the way from Dundee."

"And were you caught in that dreadful storm?"

"I was, Your Majesty; but nothing could turn me from my purpose."

"You are a man of courage as well as a poet, Mr McGonagall. Such fearful weather for the time of the year. We were very glad indeed we did not have to go out in it and could remain warm and comfortable in the Castle. I hope the staff are looking after you all right; you have only to mention anything you require. . . ."

Now the rain was trickling down his neck, but what of that? Every glaury step brought him nearer his objective. He pictured the scene inside the magnificent but cosy castle, Her Most Gracious Majesty, Queen of Great Britain and Empress of India, smiling attentively.

It would probably be best first of all to recite his "Requisition To The Queen" composed the previous year, 1877, at his tenement home in Dundee; Smith's Buildings, 19 Paton's Lane, just two or three months after the urge to write had first overwhelmed him. And he would also have to do the "Address To Shakespeare" and "Address To Burns" which he had sent to the Queen with the "Requisition"— which had brought in reply the Royal Letter now borne safely in the inside pocket of an inside coat. These were but short pieces; introductory; and Her Majesty would certainly want to hear his very first inspiration when the Muse had without warning descended upon him and would not be said nay, the address to the Reverend George Gilfillan. . . .

Lightning tore across the purple sky; thunder crashed after it in earth-shaking rage. A buoyancy, mostly light-headedness, born of a meagre diet, exhaustion, and the spectacularly unfamiliar lifted his face into the sheets of rain, and with near-jaunty thumps of his stick he stumped and lurched in a defiant march against the elements, roaring out his verses—

Most August! Empress of India, and of great Britain the
  Queen,
I most humbly beg your pardon, hoping you will not think it
  mean
That a poor poet that lives in Dundee,
Would be so presumptous to write unto Thee.

Most lovely Empress of India, and Englands generous Queen,
I send you an Address, I have written on Scotlands Bard,
Hoping that you will accept it, and not be with me to hard,
Nor fly into a rage, but be as Kind and Condescending
As to give me your Patronage.

Beautiful Empress of India, and Englands Gracious Queen,
I send you a Shakespearian Address written by me.
And I think if your Majesty reads it, right pleased you will be.
And my heart it will leap with joy, if it is patronized by Thee.

Most Mighty Empress of India, and Englands beloved Queen,
Most Handsome to be Seen.

11

I wish you every Success.
And that heaven may you bless.
For your Kindness to the poor while they are in distress.
I hope the Lord will protect you while living
And hereafter when your Majesty is . . . dead.
I hope Thee Lord above will place an eternal Crown! upon
your Head.
I am your Gracious Majesty ever faithful to Thee,
William Macgonagall, The Poor Poet,
That lives in Dundee.

Then, staggering round the next bend—Praise be; God had guided him right enough; a cottage!

Knock at the door fearlessly, yet modestly. A bit louder perhaps.

The country wife gaped in astonishment; behind her the comforting glow of lamp and firelight.

"Good lady——" the water pouring up his arm as he raised a hand to his pulped headgear; but she had turned to call her man. The shepherd came puffing his pipe to share her amazement. Rods of rain drove at McGonagall's bare head and seeped down his collar—

"Good people, with my hand on my heart I assure you before God—who surely guided me here—that I am neither burglar nor sheep-stealer only a poor honest soul seeking shelter."

"Where would ye be making for, then?"

"Good sir, I am bound for Balmoral to see Her Most Gracious Majesty; I am a poet, and proud to say I have Her Majesty's Patronage."

"A *poet*!" 'A poet?" they echoed.

"You'll better come in bye, anyway. That's been a terrible day; where have you come from?" Suddenly he was almost welcome; they felt compassion for the inadequate grotesque wanderer.

And "From Dundee; a poet from Dundee. . . . Wait now——"

"William McGonagall, at your service!" standing at attention in a widening pool of water.

"Och, we've heard of you, all right—mind of that bit in the *Weekly News* I read out to you, Jean?"

"Fine that; aye . . . give us your hat and coat, Mr McGonagall, and over to the fire with you——"

12

"Aye—this chair, man; and off with your boots. *McGonagall*, eh? Well now, well now."

"You'll take a bite of supper, Mr McGonagall? How far were you meaning to get the night?"

"He need go no further this night—there's a bed out bye in the barn you would be welcome to Mr McGonagall."

The wife swung the black kettle over the blaze and in minutes its musing song had changed to an urgent rattling of the lid.

Steam rising from his drying clothes and from a mug of tea, he told them of himself and his gift and how it had fallen upon him like an assassin. He recited a little, and would have liked to have repaid their kindness with a more full-blooded entertainment, only he could hardly keep his eyes open in the warm snugness of the kitchen. But he gladly, and with a courtly flourish, bestowed upon the shepherd a copy of the twopenny edition of his poems, with his compliments which delighted both host and hostess. Then he was shown out to the barn.

"A queer kind o' creature," said the wife as she cleared the table.

"Aye, that," pipe in mouth studying the thin paperback of verse.

"Is he really a poetry writer visiting the Queen?"

"Well, here's his book, isn't it? Och, but he's well-known in Dundee and round about. But poets are funny kind of creatures, not like other folk."

"But would the Queen send for the likes of him?"

"He has a letter from Balmoral that seems genuine enough, but maybe not an invitation exactly. . . . Aye, but there's some funny folk made welcome at Balmoral, just the same; and McGonagall seems a harmless enough creature."

"His coat . . ." re-arranging the steaming garment over the chair at the fire, "Yon old one of yours the bitch had the pups on is a king to it; look at the stains, he's been sleeping out I'd say."

"Well, never heed it now, woman; it's time we were in our bed. And rest assured you'll hear how the man fares at the castle, for isn't every scrap of gossip passed from servant-lass to cottar-wife like wildfire up and down the glens the length and breadth of the country-side——"

"Aye—and from footman to ghillie, and ghillie to shepherd over all the hills of Deeside. The *Weekly News* is not in it!"

"All right, all right then, wife; away to our bed then. And sleep easy—I'd say he has no knife——"

"Och, aye, aye, aye . . . a harmless creature."

*   *   *   *   *   *   *   *

Although in one of his accounts of this expedition McGonagall assures us

> . . . *the blankets and sheets*
> *Were white and clean,*
> *And most beautiful to be seen,*
> *And I'm sure would have pleased Lord Aberdeen*

—he slept badly, "dreaming I was travelling between a range of mountains, and seemingly to be very misty, especially the mountain tops. Then I thought I saw a carriage and four horses, and seemingly two drivers, and also a lady in the carriage, who I thought would be the Queen. Then the carriage vanished all of a sudden, and I thought I had arrived at Balmoral Castle, and in front of the Castle I saw a big Newfoundland dog, and he kept barkingy loudly and angry at me But I wasn't the least afraid of him, and as I advanced towards the front door of the Castle, he sprang at me, and seized my right hand, and bit it severely, until it bled profusely. I seemed to feel it painful, and when I awoke, my dear readers, I was shaking with fear, and considered it to be a warning or a bad omen to me on my journey to Balmoral. But, said I to myself—

> *Hence babbling dreams!*
> *You threaten me in vain.*

"Then I tried to sleep, but couldn't. So the night stole tediously away, and morning came at last, peeping through the chinks of the barn door. So I arose, and donned my clothes, and went into the shepherd's house, but the shepherd wasn't in. He'd been away two hours ago, the mistress said, to look after the sheep on the rugged mountains. . . ."

*   *   *   *   *   *   *   *

The kindly shepherd's wife made him sit down to a bowl of porridge "for it's a dreary road to Balmoral"; and at about ten a.m. he was on his way again, stopping often to look back and marvel at the rugged grandeur of the increasingly wilder and further-flung panorama as the road wound and rose more and more steeply up between boulders and heather to 2,199 feet at the summit of the

Cairnwell Pass. By noon he was down Glen Clunie and walking between the whitewashed houses of Braemar. Twelve miles then along the Deeside road to Balmoral, and he was stumping along making good enough time, although not now feeling too optimistic about his mission, his dream appearing to him now as an omen of ill.

For the first few miles the road was deserted; then he looked round at a whispering of leaves, a cracking twig. At the edge of the trees on his left a great stag stood motionless, head proudly high, alert; a glint of sunlight on its great spread of antlers; one foot raised. McGonagall, the frumpish buffoon from the smoky, stoury town, and the lord of the mountains in confrontation, so near he could see the velvet nose twitching. Then the stag threw its head up, and in one bound had cleared the road, seeming to almost brush the scruffily pretentious frock-coat with its coarse thick hair. A flurry of leaves and it had vanished into the trees on his right.

More cheerfully, and even in some excitement, he resumed his journey, looking back every so often to see if other deer crossed.

Then a carriage and pair approached from the direction of Balmoral. Would it be first the monarch of the glen and then Her Imperial Majesty herself? And yet at the same time as he strained his eyes he hoped it wasn't her, for how could he dare to try and stop the Queen's equipage? Yet better to see her in passing than maybe miss her altogether. The clip-clop of hooves again, the bumping of wheels; this wasn't Her Majesty either; a farmer in a pony-cart.

The scenery was pleasant, very pleasant, but lacked the ruggedness he had expected to continue here—until, looking back, he unexpectedly beheld the great massif of Lochnagar now rising above the heather and trees. He was standing raptly contemplating this and thinking of the great Lord Byron, when—

"Aye, she's a big one, sir. Big enough for you, sir? Man it's a grand day, sir."

The tinker was in rags, the tartan bag of the pipes under his arm bleached and dimmed with rain and sun, the ribbons on the heads of the drones but ragged strips tattered and split.

"You weren't thinking of going up there, sir; eh? Ha, ha. Aye, she's a big one; Queen O' Deeside they call her."

"Majestic enough, it cannot be denied, my good man; but for all its majesty what but rocks and heather beside the true Queen of

15

Deeside, and Great Britain," doffing his shapeless hat, "and Empress of India!' '

"Well put, sir! Are you meaning to go far, then?"

"Balmoral Castle, no less."

"Och, they'll not let you in there. Mind, they say the old body is kindness itself if you managed to get hold of her in the right mood; but you never get any further than the lodge gates; and a right snotty lot *there* I can tell you! Mind you, the cottar wives are awful good— when they have it. But if you have what they want in the way of pirns of thread and needles and such like they'll buy if they have the coppers at all——"

"My dear fellow—*I* am no pedlar; unless you might say I peddle my poetry.

"A poet? Is that right now? A poet and a musician!" patting the bag of the pipes; "Aye! Well met! Did you know a poet has poetry about that mountain, eh?"

"Lord Byron; I know his poetry well; *England, Thy beauties are tame and domestic*——"

"I know it—*I* know it; ah, but can you *sing* it; do you know the air of it, sir? Can you sing it?"

"If you'd ever been in Dundee you would know I could sing that and many another hundred——"

"I never go to Dundee! Too many relations in the Sidlaw Hills I don't get on with—I run away from them when I was a laddie. Tell you what, sir; you wouldn't have a wee bit baccy? And I'll give you a tune on the pipes—your pleasure; any air you name. Or I'll give you a song; I'll give you 'Dark Lochnagar.' Can you spare a crumb of tobaccy?" hopefully fumbling and bringing a clay pipe from a ragged pocket.

"Tobacco nor bread; I haven't a crumb of either, and that's the God's truth."

"Well, God bless you anyway, sir; I'll give you a song for luck to help you on your way," and the tinker leaned back, opened his mouth, took off his greasy cap, and launched into "Dark Lochnagar" —in which McGonagall couldn't resist joining after a few bars.

With a hand on each other's shoulder they brought the song to a rousing conclusion, their heads thrown back with the gusto of their rendering.

16

Balmoral Castle and the River Dee. Rebuilt in 1858 by Prince Albert as a Highland retreat for Queen Victoria. In 1878 McGonagall was given short shrift by the constable at the lodge after walking from Dundee through wild mountainous country in a thunderstorm hoping to be granted audience. Crathie Church can be seen to right.

"Good day to you now, sir, and good luck to you at the Castle."

"And good day to you; and God go with you on your travels."

They shook hands and went their separate ways, McGonagall's heart much lighter now. A little way on he heard the skirl of the tinker's pipes starting up, and looking back he saw him swaggering off to the tune of a stirring march.

He reached the lodge gates of the Castle just as the tower clock struck three. . . .

The Rich Man In His Castle, The Poor Man At His Gate . . .

In the castle drawing-room Queen Victoria sat in one of the tartan-covered chairs. Tartan hangings framed the windows; the little table at her side was draped with a cloth on which was worked scenes from a deer stalk. A door opened and kilted John Brown, still a strapping handsome figure in his fifties, entered.

She turned to him, passing a hand over her eyes with a little smile.

"A wee nap, your majesty? It'll do you good."

He walked over and picked up from the tartan carpet the golded ornately-bound volume which had fallen beside her chair, and set it on the table. "Aye; some of your English poetry would put most folk to sleep. . . . Are you ready for tea now, your majesty?"

The queen waved a hand in mild reproval; smiled, "Lord Tennyson is a very great poet, Brown, and I do love his verses. Yes; I'll have tea now."

Brown paused at the door with "You wouldn't have fallen asleep had I been reading Burns to you!"

"Now, Brown, it was the drive this afternoon. The air is very strong up here, Brown—like the tea you made at the picnic yesterday."

"Would your majesty have a wee drop in your tea just now, maybe?"

"No, no; certainly not! Off with you, Brown."

A little later, Brown, in a pony-cart, stopped at the lodge inside the gates. "Aye, she's at her cup of tea now, Sandy. Fell asleep reading poetry; she gets a lot of comfort out of her reading now.

Och, in spite of everything, she's just like any other old widow body; lonely, seekin' what comfort she can get——"

"Aye that, John. You've just missed a visitor by the way—AND a poet into the bargain. At least, a would-be-visitor and I'd say a would-be poet. But here's his wee book right enough."

"What did he want? You realise the need for care——"

"Och, he was harmless—one look at him told ye that. You never saw such a sight of a man. A wee, shuffling creature—yet proud in his way. . . . Well, he tried to make out the Queen would see him——"

"I tell you, Sandy, we can't be too——"

"Oh, but he had a letter right enough, with the seal on it. But not an invitation by a long chalk. A letter that had been sent him from London by Biddulph returning some verses he had sent there and telling him the Queen couldn't accept such. Mind, he was comical too. But he went away quite peaceable when he saw he wasn't getting in; away back home to Dundee—and on foot, by God!"

"Ah, well. But we must aye watch, Sandy. Well then, I'm away to Ballater. I'll not be that long. Let nobody in then, Sandy."

The spick-and-span equipage turned out of the gate and rattled off in the opposite direction to which McGonagall had taken.

As for the little man, he was presently straightening his shoulders and once again knocking on a cottage door.

CHAPTER TWO

IN his "Autobiography of Sir William Topaz McGonagall, Poet &
Tragedian, Knight of the White Elephant, Burmah" he gives this
account of his encounter with the lodge-keeper at Balmoral Castle
that summer afternoon.

". . . my heart wasn't full of glee, because I had a presentiment
that I wouldn't succeed." He told the "big burly-looking man
dressed in a suit of pilot cloth" that he expected to see the Queen
and be permitted to give an entertainment before her.

"I showed him Her Majesty's letter of patronage, which he read,
and said it was a forgery. I said, if he thought so, he could have me
arrested. He said this thinking to frighten me, but, when he saw he
couldn't, he asked me if I would give him a recital in front of the
Lodge as a specimen of my abilities. 'No, sir," I said; 'nothing so
low in my line of business. I am

NOT A STROLLING MOUNTEBANK

that would do the like in the open air for a few coppers. Take me
into one of the rooms in the Lodge, and pay me for it, and I will
give you a recital, and upon no consideration will I consent to do
it in the open air.'

"Just at that time there was a young lady concealed behind the
Lodge door hearkening all the time unknown to me. The man said,
'Will you not oblige the young lady here?' And when I saw the lady
I said, 'No, sir. Not if Her Majesty would request me to do it in
the open air, I wouldn't yield to her request.' Then he said, 'So I see,
but I must tell you that nobody can see Her Majesty without an introductory letter from some nobleman to certify that they are safe to be
ushered into Her Majesty's presence, and remember, if ever you come
here again, you are liable to be arrested.' So I bade him good-bye,
and came away without dismay, and crossed o'er a little iron bridge
there which spans the River Dee, which is magnificent to see. I went
in quest of lodgings for the night, and, as I looked towards the west,

I saw a farmhouse to the right of me, about half a mile from the highway. To it I went straightaway, and knocked at the door gently, and a voice from within cried softly, 'Come in!' "

The old man and woman sitting at the fire made him welcome; the old man, when he had heard his story, offering him lodging for two or three days, which would give him a chance of seeing the Queen passing—"and he was sure she would speak to me, as she always spoke to the gipsies and gave them money."

The old woman, blind from birth, chimed in with "Aye, and gold, not silver," telling him of the Queen's kindness to herself and other old women, giving them tea, and sugar, and bread, and the left-over meats; and how she found work for the men "all just to help needy folk, and I'm sure if you see her she will help you."

After a supper of porridge and milk he retired once more to a bed in a barn; but, he relates—

"NOT TO SLEEP, BUT TO THINK

of the treatment I had met with from the constable at the lodge . . . and I thought in particular what the constable told me—if ever I chanced to come the way again I would be arrested, and the thought thereof caused an undefinable fear to creep all over my body. I actually shook with fear, which I considered to be a warning not to attempt the like again. So I resolved that in the morning I would go home again the way I came. All night through I tossed and turned from one side to another, thinking to sleep, but to court it was all in vain, and as soon as daylight dawned I arose and made ready to take the road."

The astonished farmer told him it was only five a.m. and to go back to bed for another two or three hours and he's still have plenty of time to see the Queen at the roadside. But he was now far too scared that the constable would have him arrested if he saw him hanging about, and after the young girl of the house prepared brose for him—probably taken with a horn spoon from a wooden bowl— he was on his way, with cheese sandwiches and the assurance of a hearty welcome any time he cared to return.

After about six miles on the road he had to stop and attend to his burning, blistered feet; and ate the bread and cheese. Somewhere near Braemar he got a bed for threepence at the Miller's Lodging House and had more porridge and milk for which he paid twopence.

But the female lodging-house-keeper also threw in a basin of hot water for him to wash his feet. Next morning, after a refreshing sleep, he borrowed a teapot from the woman and made tea with tea and sugar he had left from a purchase at Alyth on the way up. He "infused the tea, and drank it cheerfully, and ate the remainder of my cheese and bread. I remember it was a lovely sunshiny morning when I left, resolved to travel to Blairgowrie, and lodge there for the night."

Despite sore feet, he was in a happy frame of mind going down Glenshee, no doubt feeling that he had now put a comfortable distance between the constable at Balmoral and himself. . . . But how long elapsed before he could write (the last lines from "Balmoral Castle")—

> Beautiful Balmoral Castle,
> With your green swards and flowers fair,
> The Queen of Great Britain is always welcome there
> For the young and the old
> Tries to do for her all they can,
> And the faithful Highlanders there
> Will protect her to a man,
> Which is most beautiful to see,
> Near by Balmoral Castle
> And the dark river Dee.

Anyway, on such a sunny summer day Glenshee was an inviting place—

> As I chanced to see trouts leaping in the
> River o' Glenshee,
> It helped to fill my heart with glee,
> And to anglers I would say without any doubt
> There's plenty of trouts there for pulling out.

On such a bonnie day there would be outings to the glen, and the girls in their summer blouses and straw hats, the young men in shirt sleeves with twinkling armbands would not pass the doggedly plodding figure in the creased frock-coat and battered hat without salutation as their horse-drawn brake rattled by—millworkers on a day-jaunt, merry with freedom and country air, melodeon music and song, bottled beer and tuppeny meat pies.

On he strode down to Blairgowrie, the road getting busier. Past a field where horses that had drawn the picnic brake grazed while the driver tended a fire on which was set the big tea dixie, and shrieks and cries of encouragement came from the flushed competitors and their supporters in the married women's race.

If his travel-weary habiliments proclaimed the down-at-heel actor (he *was* a down-at-heel *would-be* actor) or fair-seeking peddler of quack remedies who could only appear grotesque away from the contrived world of theatre and booth, gaudy stalls and exhortations of the market-place, his features at least were perhaps more in harmony with the surroundings than most of the holiday-makers. . . . Melancholy, a look in repose of peasant patience, an air inherited from his Irish peasant ancestry handed on from generations of acceptance of dependence on fullness or famine at the whim of nature. A face that told of long ages of hardship, deprivation—the life his parents left their native Ireland to escape. . . . A country face—certainly not that of the rubicund rustic or turnip-faced oaf; more with the look of a sacrificing mother who had sons lost to the sea or the wars; features that had in repose an inward preoccupation as if listening for the chilling cry of the banshee across a lifeless bog. There was, too, about it the look of an ancient, ancient experience, of a *different* kind of people of long, long ago; the hint of a leprechaun, perhaps? Except that there was no slightest trace of the leprechaun's impishness, no sign that earthy peasant humour ever quirked at the lip or winkled from the eye. William McGonagall, Poet and Tragedian, he styled himself, having no truck with Comedy; yet, such fame as he had was as a comedian. He was the comic who played nothing else but Hamlet and got laughs he didn't want.

Yet he remained an optimist through it all, seeming to have that quality of dogged persistence and the unwavering pursuit of ill-advised courses of action which later were to be consciously exploited by Buster Keaton.

So that now as he approached the village of Blairgowrie, a solemn leprauchan leaving behind the Glen of the Fairies as Glenshee may be translated, in spite of sore feet and only fourpence in his pocket, despite the fact that he had failed to gain audience with the Queen and thus compel his detractors to give him serious consideration as a poet; despite all this, the nearer he got to Blairgowrie the bolder

22

his step, the more assuredly he bore down on his stick, every now and then throwing up his head with a curious gesture that came near to arrogance. Blairgowrie would be busy with holiday-makers and fruit pickers and combinations of both with money to spend; he could sell quite a few copies of the slim twopenny edition of his "Poetic Gems."

Turning a corner he was looking down on two cyclists wobbling laboriously to the foot of the brae on their precarious high wheels. Their cricket caps, tight trousers and vests, and sweating concentration on remaining balanced made them look like outlandish insects cautiously probing a strange environment. They jumped off and became tired men wheeling unwieldy encumbrances.

"Aye, there. There's plenty of picking at Blair, but some are paying better nor——"

"Isn't it a grand day, gentlemen? Will you go far on these machines?"

"Depends on the braes! Of course the more we walk up the more to coast back down—have you come far yourself?"

"Balmoral Castle."

"Oh aye?" You been seeing the Queen? Heh, heh."

"I must confess that was my intention. However, I—I couldn't wait until she was available. Oh, the good people living nearby assured me that she would see me——"

"She didn't expect you then, eh? Heh, heh! Did you not write to say you were coming, then, heh, heh?"

"Aha! I should have thought of that; I should have!"

"Well, you'll know better next time. Aye . . . well good luck at the picking; we'll away on a bit."

"Pray, wait a moment. Would you care to take with you copies of my poems——"

"*Poems*? You're a poet?"

"William McGonagall, Poet and Tragedian. . . . Only twopence per copy, sirs."

"McGonagall . . . the name's familiar, somehow—but we've no money——. Left it with the landlady in the lodgings for safe keeping. . . . Tell you what, eh, Alec? We'll let you have a go on the machines for your books, eh?"

"Thank you, gentlemen; but no. God bless you just the same."

The berry capital, Blairgowrie, hummed, and sang, whistled, shouted—was raucous—with life.

Near a bell-tent down by the river a group of loudly-whooping young people danced a hectic reel to a fiddle and jew's harp; a woman fed a bairn; an old woman with a shawl round her sat at the tent door wagging her head in time; inside could be seen the form of an old man lying asleep, aye, or maybe drunk; there was a terrible amount of drinking went on at the berry-picking.

The square was a shifting pattern of strolling, swaggering, staggering men and women, threaded through with barefoot urchins.

The pub doors swung continuously to a non-stop traffic. Templar, nay, prohibitionist McGonagall, stalked by shaking his head at the triumph of alcohol. . . . But he must find lodging for the night. A respectable-looking young woman and a boy sat on a pub window. Could the lady direct him to a reasonable lodging-house?

There was one quite near—he would get in all right; all the berry-pickers camped or slept in barns. "You're not going in there to drink, are you mister?" He raised his hands in horror.

"Wish my man was like you; went in for five minutes, him and his brother about an hour ago; there'll be hellish little left of the berry money. I was going to ask you to tell them to come out; no decent woman would put her nose in *there*."

McGonagall explained that though he didn't take strong drink his business often enough took him into such places—and even though it didn't he would have gone in in such a cause.

"A fellow no bigger than yourself, mister; dark and a moustache; and a navy suit, and his brother dressed the same; he's dark too, they're alike except for the moustache; his brother's is bigger. George Dailly; his brother's Dan. . . ."

He pushed his way into a roaring hubbub of men, most of them dark and moustached and about his height. Thick skeins of smoke drifted under the low yellowed ceiling. After days of pure air the reek and stench of beer and sweat and urine clutched his throat and made him gasp. When he caught his breath again—

"Are the brothers Dailly here? Does anybody know the Daillys?"

A red-faced man with bulging bloodshot eyes turned to him.

"I've been talking to them; I know them. They're away now, though; went away, oh, twenty minutes ago. Out that other door.

24

They'll be across the road yet; ye'll catch them there." Digging McGonagall in the ribs. "They were giving the wife the slip, he was saying. Bit of a targer Dod's wife. . . ."

"The swine; the bloody swine!" when he told her. "I should have known. Leave me standing like a dummy; well I'm fed up of it, bloody fed—they've had a fine week of it! Well, come on," jerking away the hand her son had been picking his nose with, "we're going home! Thanks, mister."

Aye, that was drink. Wherever men earned a few coppers, there were the publicans rubbing their hands behind their counters.

They wouldn't get *his* coppers, although he was often enough in public-houses earning coppers as an entertainer.

From *Reminiscences* in *Poetic Gems*—

". . . I was taken into a public-house by a party of my friends and admirers, and requested to give them an entertainment . . . the money I received from them I remember amounted to four shillings and sixpence. . . . Of course, you all ought to know that while singing a good song, or giving a good recitation, it helps to arrest the company's attention from the drink. . . . Such, at least, was the case with me—at least the publican thought so—for—what do you think? He devised a plan to bring my entertainment to an end abruptly . . . he told a waiter to throw a wet towel at me . . . and I received the wet towel, full force, right in the face, which staggered me . . . and had the desired effect. . . . My dear friends, a publican is a creature that would wish to decoy all the money out of people's pockets that enter his house; he does not want them to give any of their money away for an intellectual entertainment. . . . Oh! my dear friends, be advised by me. Give your money to the baker, and the butcher, also the shoemaker and the clothier, and shun the publicans; give them no money at all . . . They would wish us to think only about what sort of strong drink we should make use of, and to place our affections on that only, and give the most of our earnings to them; no matter whether your families starve or not, or go naked or shoeless, they care not, so long as their own families are well-clothed from the cold, and well fed. My dear friends, I most sincerely entreat of you to shun the publicans as you would shun the devil, because nothing good can emanate from indulging in strong

25

drink, but only that which is evil. Turn ye, turn ye! Why be a slave to the bottle?"

But he had better secure a bed for the night; Blairgowrie was still twenty miles from Dundee.

"Fourpence, in advance," the lodging-house woman told him.

This left him with nothing. He paid her and went back into the streets to approach some of the more sober-looking groups in the square with "Poetic Gems."

Most grinned and shook their heads, some few took the book and looked at it before shaking their heads, some waved him away when they saw he was trying to sell something.

"Christ, look who's here!"

Suddenly he was the centre of a crowd of Dundonians who recognised him.

"Are you up for the berries?"

"Much did you make the day, then?"

"Where's your sword, eh?"

"Aye—and where's your kilt, Willie?"

"Going to give us *Macbeth*, Willie?"

"Should've brought your sword and kilt and gave us the Sword Dance!"

"Aye, there's plenty pipers and melodeon-players in the town!"

"Ach, his sword and kilt'll be in the pawnshop!"

"He wants a change from spoilt oranges and tomatoes, that's how he's up at the berries!"

"Give us the *Rattling Boy*, Willie!"

"Have you not brought the wife up for a holiday, Willie!"

"Aye, where's Jean, Willie? Are you up here with another woman?"

"Look, can you not see the man's up here on business? All right, how much, Willie?"

Eventually, three of the youths bought copies. Another jocularly explained that he would have liked to, had he been able to afford the twopence, but "It's a while to shutting-time yet; come on then lads!" and off they straggled to a pub across the road.

After many rebuffs he managed to sell another three copies; that made a shilling—

"So with the shilling I had earned from my poems I bought some grocery goods, and prepared my supper—tea, of course, and bread and butter. . . ."

Outside someone was shouting, almost screaming curses. He went to the window. A tinker unsteadily picking himself up from the gutter outside a pub, then almost falling again as he retrieved his worn bagpipes. *Was* it? Aye indeed it was, the tinker of the encounter on Deeside; but God pity him, in what terribly different circumstances from the pure air coming from God's mountains . . .!

"You set of bastards, *bastards*; every bastarding one of you!" swaying at the pub door. "You dirty set of bastards, every one of you in there!"

A muscular aproned barman flung the door open and shook a finger at him. "You've been warned now; mind I'm telling you——"

The tinker made a reluctant lurching retreat up the brae. Then when the barman went back inside, "You dirty bastards, you as well! I'm not a moocher; I spent all my money in your lousy, bloody shop; miserable bloody bastard!"

McGonagall sighed, and—

"Then I had my feet washed, and went to bed, and slept as sound as if I'd been dead. In the morning I arose about seven o'clock, and prepared my breakfast—tea again, and bread and butter. Then after my breakfast I washed my hands and face, and started for Dundee at a rapid pace, and thought it no disgrace. Still the weather kept good, and the sun shone bright and clear, which did my spirits cheer, and weary and footsore I trudged along, singing a verse of a hymn, not a song, as follows:

> *Our poverty and trials here*
> *Will only make us richer there*
> *When we arrive at home, etc., etc.*

"When at the ten milestone from Dundee I sat down and rested for a while, and partook of a piece of bread and butter. I toiled on manfully, and arrived in Dundee about eight o'clock at night, unexpectedly to my friends and acquaintances. So this, my dear friends, ends my famous journey to Balmoral. Next morning I had a newspaper reporter wanting the particulars regarding my journey to Balmoral, and in the simplicity of my heart I gave him all the information regarding it, and when it was published in the papers it CAUSED A GREAT SENSATION."

27

Oh! think of the struggles of the poor poet to make a living.

CHAPTER THREE

PERHAPS it would be best to explain the *Sir* William *Topaz* McGonagall, *Knight of the White Elephant, Burmah,* before going any further.

This was a students' hoax, a tittering-up-sleeve schoolboy kind of jape perpetuated on him through a letter complete with impressive seals in the year 1894 when he was living at Perth. The letter, purported to be written by C. Macdonald, K.O.W.E.B., Poet Laureate of Burmah at the Court of King Theebaw, Andaman Islands.

Two paragraphs from the letter—

"His Majesty also expressed it as his opinion, and the opinion of his grandfathers as far back as the flood, that such talented works as those of their holy fraternity of poets were, had always been, and for ever would be, above all earthly praise, their value being inestimable. He further stated that he failed to conceive how Roseberry could have been so blind as not to have offered to such a man as yourself the paltry and mean stipend attached to the Poet Laureate of Great Britain and Ireland. It is indescribable to him that any man of ordinary rummel gumption could possibly offer remuneration to such a gift of the Gods as yours."

And—

"King Theebaw will not injure your sensitive feelings by offering you any filthy lucre as payment for what you may compose in his honour after receiving the insignia of the Holy Order. . . ."

Yet McGonagall never gave any sign that he suspected the letter to be anything less than genuine.

But in the summer of 1878, on his return from Balmoral, he did not have even a bogus title to console him; and certainly few people seemed willing to risk offending his sensitive feelings by pressing filthy lucre upon him—so few, in fact, that just a matter of weeks before he set off to see the Queen the following appeared in a Dundee newspaper dated 4th June 1878:

The Great McGonagall in Financial Difficulties.

On Tuesday in the Dundee Sheriff Small Debt Court—before Sheriff Cheyne—William McGonagall, Paton's Lane, Dundee, who styles himself Poet to Her Majesty, was sued by David Stewart, grocer, Perth Road, Dundee, for the sum of £6. 3s. 6d. as an account for grocery goods supplied to the poet's family during the last six or eight months. From the state of the passbook it appeared that the poet had been gradually falling into arrears with his grocer. . . .

When the case was called the "great Poet" appeared in the witness box . . . cleared his throat, and with a magnificent tragic air, thus addressed the Sheriff—"Well, sir, I am a handloom weaver, and the charge against me here is debt, and poverty is the cause of my being unable to pay. I am willing to pay if I am allowed time to do so."

The Sheriff: "Why have you been getting all these goods since the New Year and not paying for them?"

The Poet: "The cause is scarcity of work, my Lord."

Mr Paul: "I believe, my Lord, he has given more of his time to other things—poetry and the drama—than to weaving." (Laughter.) "I believe that has something to do with his difficulties."

The Poet: "I would pay willingly if time were given me."

The Sheriff: "What are your wages?"

The Poet: "My Lord, I have no wages. Some weeks I might earn 7s. or 10s. or 15s., but it's not very regular."

Mr Paul: "How much can you give a week?"

The Poet: "In my present circumstances I could not give more than 1s. a week."

The Sheriff: "That would take 120 weeks to pay off the debt." (Laughter.) "You will have to pay 3s. a week."

The Poet then left the court.

Was David Stewart of Perth Road the grocer to whom McGonagall is reputed to have replied, when asked when he thought he would be able to pay, that he was a Poet, not a Prophet? Since he seemed to be entirely lacking a sense of humour *could* he have said this?

It is believed he probably did. Only to him it was *not* a witticism, but a plain statement of fact; like the humour to be found in his writings, unintentional.

However, here he was back at Paton's Lane. Far from returning in triumph he was actually poorer than when he set out—in fact he was penniless; and had not only been rebuffed at the Castle gates but threatened with arrest. The expedition had also featured a couple of sleepless nights, and meals that were few and far between And but for the sale of a paltry half-dozen twopenny editions of poems he would have been faced with the final twenty miles back to Dundee on an empty belly—not forgetting sore and blistered feet.

Well, he was a weaver to trade, and Dundee was a weavers' town. Seek work at the weaving again? After all there was nothing to stop him writing and performing as much as he wanted in his spare time. True, the din of looms from 6 a.m. to 6 p.m. was hardly conducive to the nurturing of poetic fancy; wages were low, conditions were stoorily unhealthy and mechanically hazardous. Nor could continuing employment be reckoned on due to fluctuations in the jute trade—a situation not helped by the exporting to India of jute-processing machinery which had been going on for some years. Yet, the alternative he had chosen was proving anything but an easy way of life; the minimal support of wife and family demanding an almost perpetual stumping of the town's streets peddling his doggerel and attempting to arrange "entertainments"—arrangements which when they weren't aborted, too often came to "fruition" in the most disastrous punning-sense of the word. Agreed, this can be the dogged way of genius, and if he had no other attribute of it (apart from flowing locks and eccentric dress) McGonagall certainly was handsomely endowed with the capacity to try-try-again even in the teeth of the most vociferous public discouragement frequently ending in physical assault.

But go back to the weaving?

"Look, you'll get started no bother. I tell you—the gaffer—we and the gaffer, we're thick. It was him was telling me about the big order they're getting; mind," putting his finger beside his nose for the umpteenth time, "I'm not supposed to let on; s'posed to keep it to myself, see. 'Know *you* won't let it go any further, Tom'—calls me Tom, always Tom; Tom this, Tom that. . . . He *says*, the gaffer, says Tom, a big order, a big one; but for God's sake don't let on; there's plenty round the gates every morning as it is hoping for a start.' Say the word, just say the word—come up with me at six on Monday morning, there you are! Come up with me, eh Mrs McGonagall? Tell you what—I'll chap you up—I'll come over and chap you, eh?

You tell him, Mrs McGonagall!"

"Oh, I can't tell him, he'll have to do what he thinks best himself."

Tom was a neighbour, and had a good drink on him; well, it was Saturday night. Tom and his wife had been visiting Jean when McGonagall arrived home, and there were beer bottles on the scrubbed wooden table and beer in cups, from one of which Jean, Mrs McGonagall, had been drinking. "It's the holidays; it's the holidays, Willie!" the other two had defended her on his unexpected return.

"And *he's* been away enjoying *himself*, hasn't he, Jean?" from Tom's wife. "You're left here with the bairns while he goes his holidays, eh? See men, eh, Jean. Did you get a lass up in the Highlands, did you? The truth, now, Willie, eh, Jean? Never mind looking at Tom—he'd be away if he got the chance; he'd be off enjoying himself on his own! Men, Jean; he?"

He uttered no word of reproach. God knows, his wife had had plenty to put up with, particularly in the past year since he had dedicated himself entirely to the Muse. And when they saw there was to be no lecture on the evils of drink, they were eager enough to hear his adventures; and between gulps from a mug of tea his wife kept topping up from the big brown chipped-enamel teapot and mouthfuls of bread spread with dripping given to her by a doctor's wife she was doing a temporary cleaning job for while her usual char was in Balmerino on holiday, he gave them it all with a wealth of dramatic mime; the terrifying storm in wildest Glenshee; the kindness of the peasantry; the stag and the tinker; the abruptness of the constable at the gate—with no trace of rancour; the scenes at Blairgowrie; his lifting spirits as he neared home once more.

And, as he had made no complaint against the imbibing of alcohol in his house neither, nor did they upbraid him in even the most oblique way over the gross central failure of his mission nor tax him about his misguidedness in ever thinking of embarking on it.

Of course, Tom's enthusiasm over him seeking weaving work beside him in a way was a very roundabout motion of censure; but he meant well, and, God help him, had no inkling of what it was like to be a poet and have a calling; a calling that would not be denied.

He said neither yes or no to Tom's proposition; and the man had drink on him anyway.

31

While Tom was stressing and re-stressing his friendship with the gaffer, McGonagall suddenly remembered—

"The bairns——?"

"Ben in bed this while."

He quietly opened the door of the only other room, which contained only two iron double-beds raised about six inches on wooden blocks, giving clearance for the battered tin trunk under one and below the other the black chest, and galvanised bath in which accumulated items for wash-day. In one bed the flushed faces of a boy and girl, the girl Mary about six, one arm thrown above her tangled tresses, the other over the form of the younger curly-haired boy, Jamie.

In the other bed, twelve-year-old Charlie slept in sole possession until his older brother would come in—

"Where's Jock?"

"Out with his pals."

"Time he was in; you never can tell what kind of——"

"Och, but he's seventeen, and working; and I've well warned him to keep out of the company of keelies——"

"Aye, it's Saturday night; the young ones need their bit of freedom——" from Tom's wife. "The laddie'll be all right; Jock has his head screwed on the right way. Here, he fairly thinks the world of you, Willie; thinks there's nobody like his dad. I'll warrant he'd loved to have been away with you to the Highlands, Willie," from Tom.

"Oh, he's aye on at his father to let him give a turn at one of his entertainments, but he'll not take him."

"Plenty of time yet; but I will, I will, some night—some occasion when it seems things will go well. . . . Ah, but then it always seems as if things are going to go well beforehand. . . ."

"Is he showing any signs of making up poetry, Willie?"

"He's a rare whistler, though!" with a laugh from the mother.

"*He* used to be a rare yodeller, weren't you, Tom?"

"Ah—before we were married; that was before we were wed— U—ah—*li* . . . ah-LI . . . Oh, my God, give us a mouthful of beer. Hah; lot's of things you can do *before* you're married. . . ."

"Dad! Da-ad!"

McGonagall had left the room door open; it was Charlie's voice.

'Jamie, here's dad home, Jamie."

"Shhhhh!" in concert from the grown-ups who all moved to the room door.

"Dad!"

"You should be asleep, son, if you're going down to see the whalers coming in tomorrow."

It's an early rise for a bairn, too. So it is, the soul."

"Dad, you bring anything from your holidays?"

"Now that's enough, Charlie; your father'll tell you all about it tomorrow. Now be quiet, and go back to sleep before you waken the others. Your father's tired, you'll see him tomorrow."

"Good-night now, son.""Time we were away to bed," from Tom and his wife. The room door was closed on the yawning boy.

"Tell you what, Willie; tell you what; see what—see how you feel tomorrow. If you like you'll be over the effects of your journey for Monday morning, you can tell me tomorrow if you want to come in on Monday. You'll get a start; a friend of mine. . . ."

"Come on, come on then, you and your gaffer—but I'll remind him of this tomorrow, Willie. Good-night to you both, then, And don't you be staggering crossing the street, showing me up!"

"Not me; I'm all right; all right, then, Willie? See you tomorrow. Good-night." With a precautionary hand extended to either side Tom set off through the narrow close to the street, his wife rubbing her arms and clucking impatiently at his heels.

"See me and the gaffer?" floated back.

"All right—we're fed up hearing about you and your gaffer; *I'm* the gaffer tonight; quick march to bed."

"Tha's right—more like a bloody sergeant-major. . . ."

"Tom's an awful man," as Jean closed the outside door. "There's plenty tea in the teapot." He passed the mug to her and went over to the dresser—little more than an ill-painted dark-brown longish box with double doors and two drawers above them; one of the glass drawer knobs was missing.

The dresser was in keeping with the rest of the room, the four wooden chairs with the seats worn bare of varnish, the bleached backless chair used to support the galvanised bath on wash-days, the wooden fireside chair with the legs shortened to make it a "nursing chair" more comfortable for suckling, an ancient high winged armchair with buttons missing from the back and a wad of newspapers sticking out from under the dingy cushion; more papers on the sagging sofa and a pile of folded clothes. The armchairs stood one each side of the blackleaded and polished steel range with the brass ashpan and steel fender. A crowded magazine rack hung by the winged chair. On the mantelpiece a pendulum clock with glass door and Roman numerals, behind it a sheaf of letters showed. . . a brass tea-caddy, a pair of surly-looking china pekinese, a pair of heavy brass candlesticks; a large box of matches beside the gas-bracket. Over the dresser two shelves, one above the other; the lower one holding three different sized jugs with matching deer patterns, the remnants of a willow-pattern tea-set including tea-pot with chipped spout and a large serving dish propped upright. The upper shelf carried a brass jelly-pan, copper kettle, some kind of white metal large chafing-dish cover. Few of the items on the shelves were ever used; they were intended to be ornaments, an essential part of the decor of the time. The edges of both shelves had pinned to them strips of scalloped crochet-work. Lace curtains looped back with strips of velvet at the recessed window, thin cotton blinds on the lower half of the window; below the window the black sink and brass tap, and the wooden coal bunker. A double bed filled the recess opposite.

The heavily-flowered wallpaper cost no more than threepence a roll; the floorcovering was a floral waxcloth with a threadbare rug at the fireplace. There were two photographs of McGonagall on the dresser, a smaller one of little Mary and Jamie, a blurred one of the eldest one, Willie, now at sea. On the walls; above the sink a small mirror with shelf and hairbrush with comb stuck in it; above the mantelpiece a three-quarter length enlargement of McGonagall; above the couch a framed drawing of McGonagall, and a much smaller one of the oldest daughter Margaret and her husband.

Between range and window was the press, or built-in cupboard, the door of which never closed fully because of the slops pail that stood in the bottom, the shelves above being used for provisions. Nails on the inside of the press door supported a vegetable-grater, the heavy wooden "beetle" or potato-masher, a cloth bag in which accumulated pieces of material for patching clothes. Between press and range hung the bellows. A brass rod ran the length of the mantelpiece underneath; on this were airing children's underclothing and stockings.

McGonagall pulled open a drawer, muttering, "Work; aye, work!"

His wife turned with the mug of tea; "Willie, do you really think that Tom can——"

"Eh? Tom? Oh, that I don't know; I wasn't thinking of him; I have writing to do," taking pen and paper from the drawer, then carefully the bottle of Moncrieff's Ink. "Aye, work; poet's work!"

He chose the cleanest corner of the table, and carefully spread out on it a newspaper from below the cushion before setting out his impedimenta and seating himself. He took from his pocket the few lines he had written before the storm overtook him in Glenshee . . .

"Dad, Dad, did you bring us anything home?"

"Aye, something better nor painted ball or skipping rope; a thing of infinitely more value; a poem, or at least the beginnings of one."

He took a deep draught of the tea, stewed and stringent with tannin, and set to work rapidly; it was all in his mind ready to be summoned forth; only one thing gave him more fulfilment than this; appearing before an audience; and the greatest excellence was to recite to a gathering your own latest creation. . . . He had it finished within the hour, just before Jock came in—*The Spittal o' Glenshee*—

Which is the most dismal to see—
With its bleak, rocky mountains,
And clear, crystal fountains,
With their misty foam;
And thousands of sheep there together do roam,
Browsing on the barren pasture, blasted-like to see,
Stunted in heather, and scarcely a tree;
And black-looking cairns of stones, as monuments to show,
Where people have been found that were lost in the snow—
Which is cheerless to behold—
And as the traveller gazes thereon it makes his blood run cold,
And almost makes him weep,
For a human voice is seldom heard there,
Save the shepherd crying to his sheep.

The chain of mountains there is most frightful to see,
Along each side of the Spittal o' Glenshee;
But the Castleton o' Braemar is most beautiful to see,
With its handsome whitewashed houses, and romantic scenery,
And bleak-looking mountains, capped with snow,
Where the deer and roe do ramble to and fro,
Near by the dark river Dee,
Which is most beautiful to see.

And Balmoral Castle is magnificent to be seen,
Highland home of the Empress of India, Great Britain's Queen.
With its beautiful pine forests, near by the river Dee.
Where the rabbits and hares do sport in mirthful glee,
And the deer and the roe together do play
All the live long summer day,
In sweet harmony together,
While munching the blooming heather,
With their hearts full of glee,
In the green woods of Balmoral, near by the river Dee.

He thumped the table with satisfaction and rose to his feet with the manuscript in his hand. He was pacing round the table absorbedly declaiming the stanzas under his breath when Jock came in.

"Hello, Dad, you're home. How did you get on? Did you see the Queen? What did she say to you?"

"*In the green woods of Balmoral near by the River Dee* . . . Eh? Ah; listen to this, Jock boy. . . . But where's your mother?"

"*There* she is, Dad!"

Legs crossed at the ankles, arms folded, head sunk onto the faded striped blouse which rose and fell rhythmically, in a chair by the fireside Mrs McGonagall quietly slept.

She straightened up yawning and pushing hairpins back into her hair when Jock laughingly shook her shoulder.

"Now!" cautioned McGonagall, raising a hand. "Hear this, now——"

"Ah— ha—aye—aye. . . . *Jock*! What's happened to you? You've been in a fight! Your nose!"

"Started again, has it?" He went to the mirror at the window and dabbed at his nose with a face-cloth.

"What's wrong with him? Jock; what happened?"

"Nothing; bit of a scuffle, that's all."

"Bit of a scuffle? And look at the time, by the way. Suppose I had not arrived back yet, what about your poor mother sitting worrying. You should know better and have more consideration——"

"Well, if you want to know, it was considering *you* nearly caused the fight. This bloke shouted after me, 'Doo-al McGonagall!' and when I went after him he said I was like my father, Daftworks; so I hit him in one eye, and he just managed to scriff my nose; and I hit him in the other eye; then our pals pulled us away; he'll have a pair of blackers tomorrow; could beat him anytime he wants—we used to fight at school."

"Who was he?"

"You don't know him, mother."

"Was it that big keelie of Mag M'Gregor's? There's aye some story about him——"

"Listen, Jock, how many times have I——"

Jock sniffed, and with an enigmatic smile put a hand into his coat pocket to slowly withdraw a brown parcel.

With a cry of surprised delight, his mother pounced as he laid it on the table, to rapidly unwrap—"Sausages! There must be over a pound there! And look at all the ham!"

With a triumphant slap, Jock set down another parcel taken from his other pocket—

"*And* all this, mother!"

"Oh, that's great, Jock! Look, Willie, aren't they bonnie chops? You'll get a good breakfast tomorrow—and all this mince; I'll put it on to half-do now; this weather. . . ."

"A shilling the lot, Dad. If you wait till they're packing up at the Greenmarket the butchers are practically throwing the stuff at you."

"Aye, you see if it didna keep till Monday it would be a complete loss to them. . . . But Willie, would you like a chop now? You only had a piece and dripping."

"Could I get a couple of sausages, mother?"

"An unexpected bounty! You're a good boy, Jock; but try to keep out of trouble; it isn't worth it. . . . Sausages, I think."

And as they sat with final mugs of the bitter black tea, he wiped his mouth and hands carefully and gave them a resounding rendering of the new verses as twelve midnight trembled from the spring-chime of the clock on the mantelpiece—

> ". . . *In sweet harmony together,*
> *While munching the blooming heather,*
> *With their hearts full of glee,*
> *In the green woods of Balmoral,*
> *near by the River Dee."*

*   *   *   *   *   *   *   *

The Sheriff: "*What are your wages?*"

The Poet: "*My Lord, I have no wages. Some weeks I might earn* 7s. *or* 10s. *or* 15s., *but it's not very regular. . . .*"

What would such paltry sums buy in the Dundee of 1878?

A few prices of that time:—

8,960 lbs. Prime Bacon to be cleared out at 3¼d. per lb.

737 doz. Hen's Eggs, 9d. and 10d. a dozen.

The Pork Store, 50 Wellgate.

7 lbs. rice, 1/-. American cheese, 5½d. a lb. Finest old Highland whisky, 16/- per gallon. Roast beef, roast mutton, 8d. to 10d. a lb. Roast lamb, finest fed veal, 8d. to 1/- per lb. Twist tobacco, 3½d. an oz. 3 lb. box of figs, 11½d. Tinned fruit: Apples per gallon tin, 10½d. Bass, 2/2 per doz. (pints). Superior Claret, 15s. per doz. Cake, from 4d. per lb. Raisins, 4d. per lb. Winter Claret, 7/6 per doz. pts. 7 lb. plums, 1/-. 7 lb. cooking apples, 1/-. Invalid Port, 27s. per doz. quarts. Tea from 1/- per lb.

The Old Steeple Dining Hall. Here you could sit down to porridge for 1d., milk another 1d. Coffee, 1d. Tea, 1½d. An egg, 1½d. Service of bread and butter, ½d. upwards per person according to appetite and purse. Ginger Beer and Soda Water, 2d. per bottle. They offered a four-course meal for 7d.—

Soup, 1d. ¼ lb. steak, 4d. Potatoes, 1d. Rice, 1d.

Sales offered—Skirts from 11½d. 6 pairs striped cotton hose, 1/11½d. Stays, 1/4½. Ladies' black hats, 4½d. White straw, 6½d. Elastic-sided boots, 2/11. High-legged lacing, from 6/-. Boys' kilt and knicker suits from 4/11-25s. Gent.'s trousers from 5/6. Braces, 6d. Boots from 7/6. Shoes from 5/6. Tweed suits from 35/-. White

Reverend George Gilfillan, who befriended McGonagall in his early years, and who was the subject of his first stanzas. The eleventh of twelve children of Rev. Samuel Gilfillan, he was a spellbinding orator and author of many books. He died suddenly in August 1878 at the age of 65, his last sermon having been on the theme of sudden death.

dress shirts from 2/6. Kirkcaldy striped shirts, 2/11. Cotton drawers, 11½d.

PARAPHERNALIA 1/- STORE, OVERGATE.

Skirts, Flock Pillows, Tweed Caps, Baskets, Door Mats, Pails, Chemises, Drawers, Canvas Jackets, Dulcimers, Vases, Mirrors, Purses, 2 Knives and Forks, 6 Teaspoons. Any for 1/-.

Elsewhere—Silk scarves, 4½d. Cloth jackets, 7/6. Scotch blankets, 8s.-12s. a pair.

A two-roomed house could be easily obtained at a rent of around £6 per year (less than 3/- per week). And for 1d. in the *People's Journal* you could read the continuing story of Grissel Jaffray, entitled "The Witch o' Dundee," and in the *Weekly News* McGonagall's latest.

CHAPTER FOUR

THE *Weekly News* regularly printed his effusions. And how many poets—good poets, bad poets, indifferent poets, never mind non-poets who merely thought they were poets, have had their very first lines published within a day or two of the first submission ? Suppose his first effort, quietly dropped into the newspaper's letter-box had returned to drop into *his* a few days later, and, let us say with a tactful but discouraging comment—would he have been discouraged? Had he gone ahead and written more, all to be returned, how long before he gave up ?

It seems likely he would have carried on. There is considerable evidence of his ability to persevere in face of massive discouragement long before he discovered himself—

". . . to be a poet, which was in the year 1877. During the Dundee holiday week in the bright and balmy month of June, when trees and flowers were in full bloom, while lonely and sad in my room, I sat thinking about the thousands of people who were away by rail and steamboat, perhaps to the land of Burns, or poor ill-treated Tanna-hill, or to gaze upon the Trossachs in Rob Roy's country, or else-where wherever their minds led them. Well, while pondering so, I seemed to feel as it were a strange kind of feeling stealing over me, and remained so for about five minutes. A flame, as Lord Byron has said, seemed to kindle up my entire frame, along with a strange desire to write poetry; and I felt so happy, so happy that I was inclined to dance, then I began to pace backwards and forwards in the room, trying to shake off all thoughts of writing poetry; but the more I tried, the more strong the sensation became. It was so strong, I imagined that a pen was in my right hand, and a voice crying 'Write! Write!' So I said to myself, ruminating, let me see; what shall I write ? then all at once a bright idea struck me to write about my best friend the late Reverend George Gilfillan; in my opinion I could not have chosen a better subject, therefore I immediately

40

found paper, pen, and ink, and set myself down to immortalize the great preacher, poet and orator. These are the lines I penned, which I dropped into the box of the *Weekly News* office surreptitiously, which appeared in that paper as follows:—

"*W. McG. of Dundee, who modestly seeks to hide his light under a bushel, has surreptitiously dropped into our letter-box an address to the Rev. George Gilfillan. Here is a sample of this worthy's powers of versification:—*

> *Rev. George Gilfillan of Dundee,*
> *There is none can you excel;*
> *You have boldly rejected the Confession of Faith,*
> *And defended your cause right well.*
>
> *The first time I heard him speak,*
> *'Twas in the Kinnaird Hall,*
> *Lecturing on the Garibaldi movement,*
> *As loud as he could bawl.*
>
> *He is a liberal gentleman*
> *To the poor while in distress,*
> *And for his kindness unto them*
> *The Lord will surely bless.*
>
> *My blessing on his noble form,*
> *And on his lofty head,*
> *May all good angels guard him while living,*
> *And hereafter when he's dead.*

It was, of course, a time of much amateur versifying, a great deal of which got into print in the dailies, weeklies, and monthlies. And slim volumes abounded often with a soulful portrait of the author, sometimes propping up with one hand a head weary with thought in a pose that nowadays would be taken for a Siedlitz commercial.

In a magazine article a few years back a writer suggested that "Might it not have been that, reading through some of the endless dreary volumes of pretentious local bards, so much in vogue at the time, he suddenly decided here was something he could do better ?"

preceding this with "It is curious that he should have had to wait *forty-seven years to discover he was a poet."

Yet it seems to me there is a haunting, genuine *something* in McGonagall's artless description of the descent—or rather *ascent*; he is reputed to have stated on more than one occasion that poems were heralded by a sensation which began in his feet—of the Muse. I would say that he experienced *some* kind of unusually exalted state, the power of which he misinterpreted woefully.

Again, it might be said that it was something he had read somewhere . . . He wasn't one who would *deliberately* plagiarise. Could he have recalled someone else's experience in his own words ? Whatever it was, hormone or glandular disturbance, neural disorder, brief mental aberration, it certainly triggered off a far from meagre response; the Library Omnibus of his works lists 215 pieces, many running to several pages, and a play; not bad for a late developer.

It is all the more surprising that he waited so long before beginning to write when we learn that he was deeply interested in poetry and drama from very early in life, and only the best at that—Shakespeare no less. . . .

"The books that I liked best to read were Shakespeare's penny plays, more especially Macbeth, Richard III, Hamlet and Othello; and I gave myself no rest until I obtained complete mastery over the above four characters." This study, along with the improving of his handwriting, was done in the evenings; often no doubt by the light of candle or lamp, after fourteen hours at the weaving in Ex-Provost Reid's factory in Scouringburn; a district of grim, grey mills, over-crowded tenement-warrens, second-hand shops, hard men, harder women. He could not have found it easy to begin with, for all the schooling he had ever had was a mere eighteen months before the age of seven. He MUST have loved Shakespeare. Poverty curtailed his schooldays (according to the "Brief Autobiography" in "Poetic Gems"), for schooling had to be paid for then, and with a young family to keep his parents couldn't afford to leave him at school when the weaving trade fell on slack times. This was in Glasgow, where the father had work in the cotton trade for two years, following three years working in Paisley; before this two or three years in Edinburgh until work became scarce there.

* In fact he was over fifty when he started writing.

42

Cowgate, from Grassmarket, Edinburgh, in 1825, when McGonagall was born. His immigrant parents were part of a large Irish colony of whom two resurrectionists and murderers were to become notorious—the Burke and Hare partnership.

In the "Brief Autobiography," McGonagall states he was born in Edinburgh in 1830, fifth child (three girls, two boys) of poor, God-fearing, sober parents* who had come to the capital from Ireland hoping for a bit more meat to go with their potatoes.

William would still be quite a young child when the family left for Glasgow, and would know nothing of literary Edinburgh; the celebrities meeting in clubs and coffeeshops, salons and taverns; Christopher North, Carlyle, Hogg; Scott reigning, a shelf of best-sellers to his credit, two years before he was to die at Abbotsford and ten years before the foundation stone of the celebrated monument was laid.

The McGonagalls were part of a large body of Irish immigrants who made a considerable contribution to the more than doubling of Edinburgh's population in the first thirty years of the nineteenth century. Many settled in the Cowgate, having exchanged the green fields, open sky and placid beasts of the countryside for gloomy mills and gloomier tiers of crumbling, cramped apartments, bugs, vermin; not to mention the beasts of the city.

Not the best time and place to be born . . . nor to die, for that matter. . . .

In the squalid streets, the unsavoury back-courts, the children sang:—

> *Burke and Hare*
> *Fell down the stair*
> *With a body in a box*
> *Going to Dr. Knox.*

And it was common practice to threaten children with being taken away by Burke and Hare if they didn't behave.

The two notorious Irishmen began by digging up bodies which they delivered in barrels, tea-chests, on horse-drawn carts, on hand-carts, even porter's back, to Dr. Knox for anatomical research at an average of ten pounds a time. They were far from being the only operators in this field, many medical students among others raiding the graveyards. Friends and relations guarded the newly-interred;

---

* Charles and Margaret (*nee* Maxwell). Other children followed; William had at least one younger brother, Joseph, who at 28 married Margaret Galloway, daughter of a coalman, in Dundee 1867.

grotesque iron cages were fitted over graves; fights between the resurrectionists and those on guard were not uncommon. Burke and Hare got round the increasing uncertainties of their macabre calling by turning to murder. The old and forgotten, the destitute and alone, the raddled bawds of the shadowed alleys began to disappear. Fears rose as darkness fell; rumours flitted like ghosts from close to garret, tenement to tenement.

"It's yourself, Mrs McGonagall; isn't it dark early tonight?"

"I'm just away to the wee shop for a bit o' cheese for his tea. I forgot this morning when I was out—and you daren't send the childer after dark——"

"I'll come with you—and we'll be company back up the close and that dark stair—sure you'd easy break your neck on it——"

"Or have it broke for you, Mrs M'Ghee. Is there no trace of that poor soul Jamie, yet?"

"Na, devil the sight; ah, he's a goner, there's nothing surer! God help him, and he wouldn't harm the hair of anyone's head!"

"Sure the youngest childer would put their fists up at him and him a man and running away. God rest his soul; and he was that glad of a crust of bread or a sup of broth."

"Wasn't he sleeping on our garret stair for a week before he went missing——"

"Ah God help him. Mind you, although they called him Daft Jamie he was as wise as us in some ways——"

"Aye, when somebody gave him a coat near new, and then asked how he didn't wear it; and says he 'if I'm too well put-on nobody'll give me anything.' "

"And his wee riddles—God, how many times did he ask me that one—I have it by heart:—

Though I black and dirty am,
And black as black can be;
There's many a lady that will come,
And by the hand take me."

"And you daren't let on you knew the answer, he'd be that offended——"

"Wasn't it myself cut him short, God forgive me, just the other week . . . 'the kettle, the kettle, Jamie,' says I. Ah but he was hurt!

'You never knew!' he shouts; 'You never—for somebody told you, that's how!'"

The murder of Daft Jamie aroused great public anger when it came to light. He was a well-known, well-liked harmless simpleton of the streets, just twenty years old when smothered by Burke and Hare. One thing contributing to the evidence was a baker seeing on a nephew of Burke's a pair of trousers he had given to Daft Jamie.

Hare turned Queen's Evidence. William Burke was publicly hanged in the Lawnmarket at eight a.m. on 28th January 1830 before an estimated crowd of between 25,000 and 30,000, all overlooking windows having been bought up some time beforehand for from 5/- to 25/-. He ascended the scaffold to shouts of "Choke him!" "No mercy, hangie!" "Bring out Hare!" "Hang Knox!" "You'll see Daft Jamie in a minute, Burke!"

His hanging body twitched to gleeful yells, and when he was cut down at near nine a.m. the execution assistants scrambled for bits of the rope and shavings from the coffin. It had been ordered that his body be delivered to Dr. Alexander Monro, Professor of Anatomy in the University of Edinburgh, for dissection; macabre justice indeed.

Students rioted to see the corpse, and eventually were admitted 50 at a time. Meantime the general public were clamouring for admission; and they were allowed in on the Friday. From 10 a.m. to dusk at the rate of sixty per minute an estimated 25,000 filed through.

"They say there *was* one or two women there after all, Mrs McGonagall, although M'Ghee says he never saw any; 'but you'd be that drunk to pluck up your courage,' says I to him, 'it's a wonder you saw the corpse itself!' "

"Arrah—what kind of brazen strumpets would go near a thing like that, Mrs M'Ghee; and him lying there without a stitch at all, and the murderous eyes glaring back at every one that looked down at him!"

"Aye, naked he was entirely, M'Ghee told me; laid out straight on a black marble slab, a fine figure of a man, with the mark of the rope easy seen on his neck, and a scar right round the top of his head with the dried blood on it where they's sawed the lid of his skull off to show the students the brains of a murderer. 'Is it a wink

45

of sleep you'll get this night ?' I asked M'Ghee, 'thinking of the purple face staring back at you——' God knows, Mrs McGonagall, if I'll shut an eye myself with the way he's been describing the sight of every last bit of Burke's corpse!"

Looking back from his poethood to the city of his birth, with his taste for tragedy, melodrama and sermonising, I wonder that McGonagall didn't attempt a major epic on Burke and Hare; the names were on everybody's lips for many years after. Apart from often hearing about them from his parents, brothers, sisters, a reading man such as himself would every now and then come upon one more serialisation of the unholy duo. He may have done, of course; the epic may be lost.

(Incidentally, not only bits of the rope, shavings of the coffin were taken as souvenirs of Burke. An assistant of the Professor of Anatomy obtained for a friend two pieces of Burke's skin—one from the neck, which still showed the mark of the rope after it had been tanned brown and turned into a tobacco pouch; and a piece off the forearm, tanned white, on which the recipient had printed a picture of Burke and his wife.)

McGonagall left two accounts of his childhood. In "A Summary History of the Poet McGonagall" from "Last Poetic Gems" he tells us:—

"Poet McGonagall was born In the Month of March 1825.* His parents were Irish. and his Father left Ireland, shortly after His marriage and came to Scotland. And got settled down in Ayrshire In a place called Maybole as a Cotton Weaver, and lived there for about ten years until the Cotton Weaving began to fail there, and Then he was induced to leave it owing to the very small demand. There was for Cotton Weaving In that part of Scotland. Then he and his family left Maybole, and came to Edinburgh Where he got settled down again to work Cotton Fabrics which there was a greater

*McGonagall's age: In "A Summary History of Poet McGonagall" he writes he was born in March, 1825. In "Brief Autobiography" he gives 1830 as the year of his birth. On his death certificate his wife Jean (who could not read or write) gives his age in that year, 1902, as 62. Their marriage certificate states they were married in Dundee, 11th July, 1846. This last is bound to be correct, so he must have been considerably older than 62 when he died—and in fact in 1891 he said he was 62 (when applying for a Civil List pension). Reports of his death all assume he was quite an old man verging on 80. So 1825 seems likeliest birth-date.

demand for, than in Maybole. and by this time they family consisted of two Sons, And three daughters. William, The Poet, was the youngest, and was born in Edinburgh. And the rest of the family was born in Maybole And Dundee. his Father lived in Edinburgh for more than eight years, untill the Cotton Weaving began to fail, then his Father and they family left Edinburgh And travelled to the Orkney Isles, And to a house for they family to live in the Island of Southronaldsay. And his father bought the living as a Pedlar, and supported the family by selling hardware, among they Peasantry In the Orkney Isles, and returning home every night to his family, when circumstances would permit him. Charles the eldest son was herding Cows to a farmer in the Island of Southronaldsay, and his eldest sister Nancy, was in the service of a Farmer in the same locality, and William, the Poet, and Thomas, the second eldest brother, was sent to School to be teached by Mr James Forbes, the parish Schoolmaster, Who was a very Strict Dominie indeed, of which our readers shall hear of as a proof of his strictness, a rather curious incident . . ."

This was when William dropped the dominie's pet tortoise. When the master saw this he beat him black and blue until—

". . . some of the older Scholars cried out to him to Stop! beating William. and when William went home to dinner, and told his kind father all about it as it had happened his father flew into a rage and said he would be revenged upon him for beating William so unmerciful, and accordingly he went to a Magistrate, with William, and related the Case to him as it had happened. and when the Magistrate examined Williams face and seen the marks, the Dominie had left thereon he ask'd Williams father if he was willing to put him from ever being a Schoolmaster in the parish again, but Williams Father would not consent to hear of that owing to the Kindness he had shown towards his Son, Thomas, and he simply ask'd the Magistrate to give him a line, to certify, to Mr Forbes, that he could put him from ever being a Schoolmaster in that parish again if he would just say the word. so Williams Father went with him to the Dominie, and showed him the line he had got. . . ."

The Dominie promised never to do the like again. Relishing his revenge, William did as he pleased thereafter until his father often had to beat him for truancy. Thus, in this account, he explains his lack of education. No mention of school in Glasgow; in fact no mention of Glasgow.

After about three years on the island the family came to Dundee.

This differs strangely from the first version of his boyhood—and not just the birth-date being five years earlier. Exploiting the Dominie's discomfiture by staying off school, the apparent enjoyment of revenge—these do not square with the eagerness for education nor the characteristic of forgiveness so marked in later life as to the point of softness.

But to continue with this account . . . The family came to Dundee—"and settled down in it and those of the family that were able to work were sent to the Mills and some of his Sons wrought at the handloom in the Factory along with himself, that was Thomas, and Charles, and William wrought in the Mill for a few years. and then his Father took him from the Mill, and learned him the handloom himself and he has followed that occupation up to the present when he Can get it to do. he had always had a great liking for Theatrical representation and has made several appearances upon the Stage . . ."—and at this point this account comes into register with his other versions.

The Stage

A letter referring to what was probably his earliest appearance thereon; from the *People's Journal* 22nd June 1872.

After describing a theatrical booth of twenty-five years earlier (making it 1845) on the site now occupied by the Albert Institute Public Library and Museum complex, the writer goes on—"Among the male members was one who often attracted attention. He had such a grim and ghastly look about him that I was impressed with the idea that he at least looked upon acting as a rather grave and important occupation. He had likewise such an air of sorrow and melancholy about him that one could not help thinking there was some cankering care or secret sorrow gnawing away his peace of mind. And yet, at times, if you watched him narrowly, you could observe that when any leading members of the company got hissed for not playing their parts too well, a Mephistofelian gleam of pleasure would flit across his countenance, which would afterwards change into a settled and self-conceited expression, as much as to say 'If I only had the opportunity of playing those parts, *I* would soon show you *how* they should be acted!' "

In these early days the young would-be actor (depending on which birth-date you believe he was about fifteen or about twenty) seemed to occupy the lowly but high-sounding general-factotumship of stage-manager, shifting chairs, props; attending to the candles, getting a walking-on part when there was no one else to call on. But this was to change with a vengeance; for his first real part on the stage was a part indeed; Macbeth, no less!

This was in Giles' Lindsay Street quarry theatre—built of brick, McGonagall reminds us—no penny gaff shanty of canvas and rickety wood. The debut was achieved, he tells us, by giving "Mr Giles a pound in cash before the performance, which I considered rather hard, but as there was no help for it, I made known Mr Giles terms to my shopmates, who were handloom weavers in Seafield Works, Taylor's Lane . . . they made up the pound by subscription." Two of his shopmates took the pound down, and when they brought back a written agreement from Giles "my shopmates cheered again and again, and the rapping of the lays I will never forget as long as I live."

Now, in the interests of objectivity, we go back to the letter in the *Journal*—"The gent to whom he first applied, although a showman, was also a man of the world. He made enquiries at the work where our friend was employed, and he found that the people there would only be too delighted with the treat of seeing (McGonagall) strutting the real boards. As the work was a pretty large one, the man saw at once it would be a good speculation for him. . . . The eventful evening having at length arrived which was to place (his feet) on the lowest steps of the ladder of fame, his fellow workers made great efforts to give him a bumper house. There being three performances in one evening each house was crammed, many going in all three, while most went in twice. Our friend having no stage wardrobe of his own, was under the necessity of borrowing an article or two of dress from some members of the company. Whether it was, however, that these gentlemen had not much of a wardrobe themselves or unwilling to lend their best to a new beginner, when (he) made his appearance he was more like a Highland beggar than the 'Great Thane.' Nothing daunted, however, and feeling confident that his own inherent abilities would soon overcome these trifling matters, he went at it with might and main, and certainly wrought hard to show the audience how Shakespeare ought to be delineated. . . ."

At least one member of the audience, an old Irish fellow-worker, seems to have been carried away by the reality of McGonagall's performance in the last act, for at the fight "he could contain himself no longer, but jumping to his feet, he shouted in vehement tones, 'Pitch into him, Willie, into him!' But alas! when he saw him fall under the weapon of Macduff he could not conceal his contempt, but, making for the door, he turned, and with a look at the fallen (McGonagall) that bespoke how serious and indignant he was on the matter, said 'Och man, I always thought that the dirt was in ye.' "

"The evening's entertainment having consisted in the performance of Macbeth three times, our friend's voice, not being very carefully husbanded by him, soon gave way under the strain . . . until he became so hoarse that he could scarcely be heard by those in close proximity to the stage. Not having received any refreshment during the whole evening, he at length applied to the manager for some, when a gill of whisky and a bottle of ale were brought to him. Just as these were set down, however, he had to make his appearance on the stage, and on his return, on looking for his refreshments, he found that, like the witches in his favourite tragedy they had vanished. No doubt the members of the company had taken the opportunity of his absence to drink his health."

But hoarse, unrefreshed or not, McGonagall was well pleased with the evening, as his account shows—"that ever memorable night, which can never be forgot by me or my shopmates, and even entire strangers included. At the end of each performance I was called before the curtain, and received plaudit after plaudit of applause in recognition of my able impersonation of Macbeth.

"What a sight it was to see such a mass of people struggling to gain admission! hundreds failing to do so, and in the struggle numbers were trampled underfoot, one man having lost one of his shoes in a scrimmage; others were carried bodily into the theatre along with the press. So much then for the true account of my first appearance on any stage."

The Irishman who urged McGonagall to have a go would have

been much happier at his *next appearance* as Macbeth, this time at the Theatre Royal, recounted in the same letter in the *Journal* by "Old Stager."

After describing how the derision of his fellow-actors made it more like a farce than a tragedy, there came the combat scene, when McGonagall as Macbeth refused to die when run through by Macduff; "he maintained his feet and flourished his weapon about the ears of his adversary in such a way that there was for some time an apparent probability of a real tragedy." Macduff, continually telling him to go down "became at length so incensed that he gave him a smart rap over the fingers with the flat of his sword." McGonagall dropped his weapon, but dodged and pranced as if to wrestle. Macduff threw the sword aside, seized Macbeth and "brought the sublime tragedy . . . to a close in a rather undignified way by taking the feet from under the principal character.*

McGonagall described this, or a similar, or maybe a telescoping of incidents in "The Autobiography of Sir William Topaz McGonagall' as taking place in the Grocer's Hall—better known as *Music Hall*, a large square building at the foot of Castle Street, the Theatre Royal being further up. Both buildings still stand; a bust of Shakespeare high above the street marking what was the Theatre Royal; the Music Hall building for long housing a firm of printers, printers of this book and various collected editions of McGonagall's works.

While McGonagall was rolling them in the aisles another young man with stage ambitions was getting his first breaks at the Theatre Royal, having progressed there from the old Yeaman Shore Theatre. He soon progressed even further—to Drury Lane and £150 a week, changing his name from Tom Powrie (born 1824) to Tyrone Power. (What, if any, connection there is with today's film star I have not been able to find out).

Near the old Yeaman Shore Theatre, on the west side of South Union Street, stood a theatre with a name that would seem to

* McGonagall's aversion to "dying" is in marked contrast to the attitude of a later actor-manager of a "penny gaff"—John Young, celebrated for his realistic "deid man's fa' " complete with gory bursting of concealed bladder of animals' blood. This used to bring such applause that John would get to his feet, hold up his hands and declaim, "For the pleasure of the audience John Young dies again!" and thereupon repeat the routine. Such was his enthusiasm that on at least one recorded instance he crashed off the stage altogether, climbing back up for the encore with "I cannot rest in my grave!"

guarantee a star's dressing-room for McGonagall—the Royal Shakespearean Pantheon. Alas! It had not been a year built when on the night of Queen Victoria's Coronation Day, June 28th, 1838, celebrating youths set fire to an old tarry coble too near it, setting alight the wax figures decorating the outside and burning the Pantheon down. It was later rebuilt to house a circus.

A pity . . . *At the Royal Shakespearean Pantheon: The Great McGonagall in Macbeth* . . . It sounds right.

"During the Dundee Holiday Week . . . I sat thinking about the thousands of people who were away by rail and steamboat . . . to gaze upon the Trossachs in Rob Roy's country, or elsewhere wherever their minds led them. . . ."

Trips advertised for the week commencing Monday, 24th June 1878:

Caledonian Railway: Tour of the Trossachs 9/-. Edinburgh 3/9. Glasgow 6/3. Loch Lomond 7/3. Perth 2/-. Arbroath 2/6. (All return).

North British Railway offered similar excursions. The Highland Railway, Inverness return 7/-.

And there was "The Powerful Sea-going Steamer *May*" which would take you to the Isle of May and North Berwick, allowing two hours ashore at both, for 2/-. Montrose return 1/6. Arbroath 1/-. Leith 2/6. Also the ferry service to Newport and Tayport.

Cooke's Royal Circus in the Nethergate advertised a holiday programme of "legitimate circus entertainment of the best class" which could be enjoyed for 2/- Boxes, Pit 1/-, Gallery 6d.; Children half-price.

CHAPTER FIVE

McGONAGALL'S love of the role of *Macbeth* brings up the speculation about Shakespeare having visited Dundee. . . . In 1601, in answer to a request from James VI, Elizabeth sent from England a company of players to the Edinburgh Court. The Lawrence Fletcher company was the first from London to embark on a tour of Scotland. Shakespeare is believed to have been with them. It is known that they played not only in Edinburgh, but also in Aberdeen, and it does seem feasible they would stop at Dundee between these somewhat distant places. Only a few years later *Macbeth* was written, and some theatrical historians think there is a good case for supposing that Shakespeare got his local colour while in the area. Did McGonagall ever discuss this ?

The earliest reference to anything like a play in Dundee is in 1553, when shows were more of instructive tableaux, lessons put across to an illiterate audience; so-called morality plays. These were watched from the slopes of the Witches' Knowe, high ground between West Port and the beginning of Blackness Road. But the acting profession fell into disrepute before long, the clergy hitting them hard—

It is agreed upon by sober pagans themselves that play-actors are the most profligate wretches and vilest vermin that Hell ever vomited out, that they are the filth and garbage of the earth, the scum and stain of human nature, the pests and plague of society, the debauchers of men's minds and morals, unclean beasts, idolatrous papists or atheists and the most horrid and abandoned villains that ever the sun shone upon! as one pamphlet put it.

And on one occasion the fishing community of Broughty Ferry complained to the Town Council that the presence of certain actors had caused all the fish to leave the river!

But in 1743 the occasion of a visit from an Edinburgh company was made something of a holiday, and, in full regalia, officials and

53

Masons marched to the venue of the entertainment accompanied by a band of "hautboys and other instruments."

Yet, in 1784, when the Edinburgh Theatre Company proposed a visit to Dundee—

The Council and Trades, being informed that Mr Jackson, Manager of the Edinburgh Theatre, and his Company intend to perform plays in this Burgh, they are of opinion that exhibiting plays here is not authorised, but in direct opposition to the laws of the country and prejudicial in many respects to the interests of Society. So *that* particular band of players had to stroll elsewhere.

Of course in the long run the show had to go on in Dundee as well as in the more culturally-enlightened towns. Eventually there appears to have been no objection to the town having a permanent theatre.

This was preceded by a letter in the *Dundee Magazine* of December 1799:—

"Two histrionic detachments have lately been attempting to enter this town, but have yet not been able to find a room to enact in. One of the managers proposed to rent the ground floor of the Steeple. The greenroom, he thinks, would be improper in the vestry, but one could be fitted up in the flat above, and they could whisper readily through the rope hole of the bell."

However, more suitable premises were found, and on the 23rd July 1800 the *original* Theatre Royal opened by a Mr Moss and Mr Bell in Yeaman Shore in a converted granary, the ghostly aroma of fermentation reputedly adding to the atmosphere; the first offering being *The Merchant of Venice* with Moss as Shylock. Kean, John Kemble, Henry Johnston, and the Great Dowton were to play there —varied with such fare as Sexti the Tight-rope Walker and the prize-fighters Belcher and Mendoza.

The part of the water-front where the theatre was situated had an evil reputation as the hide-out of thieves and cut-throats, and as it could only be gained from High Street by dark alleys and narrow wynds this may have had something to do with its eventual abandonment, being out of operation for many years before it was taken over by the Dundee and Perth Railway Company in 1846 as a site for the West Station.

Theatre Royal, Castle Street, as it was in McGonagall's lifetime, and where he and many celebrities appeared. The building is still in use as a store, and may be identified by the bust of Shakespeare in a niche high up

The young McGonagall no doubt mourned the demolishing of what had been a theatre; but it was a Tealing farmer, strangely anticipating him, who left this picture of it in its hey-day:—

> *In my ain coarse and hamely lays,*
> *I sing the Royal Theatre's praise,*
> *That's now established in Dundee,*
> *And is the best that I e'er did see,*

and the last verse, while almost a vernacular parodying of what was to be McGonagall's style, also might be describing the reaction of the house to one of his appearances:—

> *Those in the gallery, back and fore,*
> *Get up at times wi' sic' a roar,*
> *As sometimes seems to stop the play,*
> *Which is a bad ill-mannered way.*
> *Sometimes they near ding ither doon.*
> *To sum up in my ain way,*
> *They manage brawly every play,*
> *But as I dinna monny see,*
> *The very warst weel pleases me!*

The new Theatre Royal, where McGonagall was to experience some of his earliest "triumphs" opened in Castle Street on 27th June 1810—with a benefit concert by the band of the Forfarshire Local Militia!

It was an upstairs hall, which inspired another poet, Thomas Hood, to write in 1915:—

> *Their buildings—as though they'd been scanty of ground*
> *Are crammed into corners that cannot be found.*
> *Or as though ill-built or contrived they had been*
> *That the town were ashamed they should ever be seen.*
> *And their rooted dislike and aversion to waste*
> *Is suffered sometimes to encroach on their taste*
> *For beneath a Theatre or Chapel they'll pop*
> *A saleroom, a warehouse or mean little shop.*

With only a few seats in the galleries and standing elsewhere, the hall could pack in 1,200, at prices from 6d. to 2/-.

Although it opened inauspiciously with a band concert, in its span of seventy-five years it featured most of the big names of the era; including the Siddons and the Kembles—as well as a waxworks; and McGonagall.

But the "penny gaffs"—housed in various small halls and in a variety of flimsy canvas and wood structures erected on sundry pieces of waste ground, common land, etc., would offer more frequent opportunities to McGonagall. The building of the Albert Institute in 1856 meant sweeping away a conglomeration of shanties from the site, for long a fair ground, among them the one where stage-struck youthful William did the chores and occasionally walked on—likely enough the one a man called Wee Scott ran under the impressive name of the Royal Victoria Theatre. Giles' Theatre in Lindsay Street quarry—his first real debut—and M'Givern's in Seagate where he also appeared were both "penny gaffs" where the clientele would prefer a rumbustious melodramatic rendering of Shakespeare rather than sensitive interpretations featuring subtleties and delicate nuances of performance. In such places, also, for cheapness, and because it delighted the crowd to have someone to ridicule, local *worthies*—in the sense of being eccentric in a deficient kind of way—would often be persuaded to come and be mocked, into which category McGonagall didn't seem to know he had been alotted.

But the gaff showmen were merely trying to give the customers the sort of entertainment they wanted—although keen enough to try out a novelty; the first films were shown on the penny gaffs. And names of some of the old showmen are still mentioned even today—*John Young, Fizzy Gow, M'Indoe.* . . .

Until his cataclysmic illumination during that holiday week of 1877 McGonagall's days would be spent at the loom, when he could get the work, and in the evenings going over *Hamlet, Othello, Macbeth* and *Richard III*, as well as taking the occasional look at Swinburne, Burns, and Tennyson—a poet he was to come to feel a certain rivalry and even jealousy towards, eventually embodying strongly-suspected streaks of superiority. Marriage to Edinburgh-born Jean King (11th July, 1846) and the coming of a family would certainly not bring him *more* freedom to indulge his increasing ambitions; but being McGonagall, such matters would not be allowed to interfere very much either.

The showmen would usually be prepared to give him an occasional break, especially when he put up money beforehand; and there would be various concerts and functions in which he would be invited to participate to give the company the releasing reassurance of a mickey-taking belly-laugh.

In his "pre-poet" period, when he was William McGonagall, plain tragedian and part-time weaver, there is no record of him trying to rent halls in order to get to his public. The shrewd financial course, so surprisingly often adopted by virtuosi presumed to be unworldly, of hiring the premises and pocketing the receipts, may have occurred to him, but does not seem to have been put to the test until after the summer of 1877 when his cards were now printed *William McGonagall, Poet & Tragedian.*

Before that he had to rely on such reputation as he had, and such friends who were willing to club together to make up a pound guarantee for the manager of some high-sounding fire-trap. Oh, and he had testimonials—

"We willingly certify that the bearer, Mr William McGonagall, has considerable ability in recitation. We have heard him recite some passages from Shakespeare with great force; and are of the opinion that he is quite competent to read or recite passages from the poets and orators in villages and country towns with pleasure and profit to his audience. We also believe him to be a respectable man."

No sly snigger here; and signed by responsible, respectable men—

29th March 1864.   *Islay Burns, Minister of St. Peter's F. Church.*
                       John Alex. Banks, M.A. Edin., Headmaster, Propy. School, Dundee.
                       William Knight, Assistant, Free St. John's Church, Dundee (now Prof., St. Andrews University).

And as straightforward—

Dundee, 30th May 1865.

"I certify that William McGonagall has for some time been known to me. I have heard him speak, he has a strong proclivity for the elocutionary department, a strong voice, and great enthusiasm. He has had a great deal of experience, too, having addressed audiences, and acted parts here and elsewhere."   *George Gilfillan.*

His first volume was certainly the slimmest of the slim. Reviewed in the Dundee *Evening Telegraph* May 6th, 1878—

"The volume which lies before me as I write is modestly personfied in the matter of size. It consists of four pages and is sold at twopence. This is exactly a halfpenny a page; but every purchaser will have the worth of his money in the title page alone, so the other three pages to to make up a capital bargain. The title page states that the book contains 'Poems and Songs by William McGonagall, Poet to Her Majesty'; and further contains the gratifying announcement that 'Mr McGonagall holds in his possession an Acknowledgment from the Empress of India dated 16th day of October *anno Domini* eight hundred and seventy-seven and signed by General Sir Thomas Biddulph.' This statement is gratifying because it shows that Her Majesty has time, even in the midst of the present increased anxieties of her regal state, to recognise literary worth. If the traditional butt of Malmsey has not yet reached Mr McGonagall it may be due to the fact that vested rights must be respected, and while Temperance lives, it would be invidious to abate in favour of another one jot of the privileges of the Laureate. Time will change all that, however, and now when McGonagall is definitely fixed upon as the successor to Tennyson, McGonagall can afford to wait."

As we know, he waited a long time. True, the Queen had refused to substantiate his claims, but his poetic career was still in its infancy. Meantime he made up for lost time.

And every new piece meant an addition to his repertoire, as well as another source of extra coppers when he could manage to pay for a printing of pamphlets. Unpoetically, he must often have been pre-occupied with the intensely important juggling and judging of when or not to re-invest what proportion of his trivial earnings with a view to earning more. He was, it should be noted, quite realistic about money; perhaps in his grinding circumstances he could hardly be otherwise . . . "being rather at a loss how to get a little of that filthy lucre, as some people term it. But, my dear readers, I never considered it to be either filthy or bad. Money is most certainly the most useful commodity in society that I know of. It is certainly good when not abused; but, if abused, the fault rests with the abuser—the money is good nevertheless. For my own part I have always found it to be one of my best friends."

This building, in which McGonagall appeared when it was known as the Grocers' Hall, was later known as the City Assembly Rooms, and for long has been the premises of the printers of this book—who once printed McGonagall's broadsheets, often free of charge.

It is generally thought that he worked at the loom no more after that blinding realisation of his vocation in the summer of 1877. Now he pursued the filthy lucre in tireless peddling in the streets, penetrating into such shops, offices, places of work as he was suffered with his verse-panphlets, and twopenny edition; pursued it in persuading clubs and societies to have him entertain at their functions; in persuading the penny gaffs to give him return dates.

There was another way he could get to an audience. In those days, when two or three gathered together it was either at a street corner or in a pub. And the gatherings in pubs were obviously where the money was. So the arch-templar McGonagall was compelled at times to ingratiate himself with the detested publicans, not for a drink but in the hope of raising the price of a meal. He was forced to do this many times, yet, give him his due, he never withdrew one inch from his obdurate stand against the licensed trade.

Equally, publicans generally seem to have known him as an enemy; to be allowed at an odd time on the premises when customers expected this, but to be watched carefully, and to be discredited as fully and humiliatingly as possible as soon as opportunity offered.

According to McGonagall the stage had a good moral influence—

> *Good people of high and low degree,*
> *I pray ye all be advised by me,*
> *And don't believe what the clergy doth say,*
> *That by going to the theatre you will be led astray.*

No, in the theatre we see vice punished and virtue rewarded,
The villain either hanged or shot, and his career retarded;
Therefore the theatre is useful in every way,
And has no inducement to lead the people astray.

> *Because therein we see the end of the bad man,*
> *Which must appal the audience, deny it who can—*
> *Which will help to retard them from going astray,*
> *While witnessing in a theatre a moral play.*

The theatre ought to be encouraged in every respect,
Because example is better than precept. . . .

(Lines in Defence of the Stage).

His anti-drinking crusading, however, was unending, and was even blatantly carried into the enemy's camp. Despite this fervour, however, he seems to have been unable to keep it out of his own home in the long run . . .

"*Domestic Troubles of a Poet.*

In the Dundee Police Court on Monday, before Bailie Perrie, Mary McGonagall, millworker, Paton's Lane, was charged with committing a breach of the peace in Paton's Lane, by swearing at and using violent language to Mrs McGregor, wife of a ship's steward, on Saturday night. She pleaded guilty. Her father, the 'poet' McGonafall, appeared on her behalf.

The Bailie enquired if Mary had anything to say; Mary made no reply.

Mr Dewar: 'Perhaps her father has something to say?'

The Bailie: 'Is this the daughter of the poet?'

'Yes, sir,' promptly returned the poet, assuming one of his most imposing attitudes.

The Bench: 'Have you anything you would like to say, then?'

The poet, in lofty, measured tones, thus delivered himself—'I have nothing further to say, except that she is a well-disposed daughter, only her mother gives her drink at times, that is the cause of the breach of the peace. In my opinion there will never be peace in society until strong drink is abolished from the land.'

Bailie Perrie: 'Oh, that will do!' (Laughter.) 'Five shillings or five days in prison.'

The poet bowed and retired as his daughter was shown downstairs to the cells."

(From an undated cutting. Could well have been in 1894 when he was reported to be having domestic trouble).

Bridge of the Silvery Tay,
Which stands unequalled to be seen
Near by Dundee and the Magdalen Green . . .

CHAPTER SIX

"THE second poem I composed was my famous Tay Bridge poem and where I composed it was sitting on a wooden seat, at the end of the Magdalen Green, in view of the beautiful structure. and as I gazed thereon I felt inspired to write in praise of such a wonderful Construction. and after I had Completed the poem, I read it over Carefully I felt quite delighted, and quite sure it would please, when it pleased your humble Servant."*

". . . the *Railway Bridge of the Silvery Tay*, which caused a great sensation in Dundee and far away. In fact, gentle readers, it was the only poem that made me famous universally. The reading of the poem abroad caused the Emperor of Brazil to leave his home far away incognito and view the bridge as he passed along *en route* to Inverness."

If this was his next assignation with the Muse after the Address to Gilfillan, it must have been composed some time before the 6th September 1877, the date on MSS of *Requisition to the Queen*. The bridge was not opened to traffic until June 3rd the following year.

He lived in Paton's Lane during the years of the bridge's construction, a thoroughfare which rises practically right from the end of the bridge; he would see it take shape with the growing up of some of his children. . . . There would be a trafficking of workers on the project up and down past his window; in time the people of the district would be less liable to be awakened by the tramp of navvy boots early in the mornings, less liable to be kept awake at night when cranes screeched, girders clanged, rivets were rammed home. The pubs round about would roar with trade on pay-nights, bringing crowded streets, brawls and camp-following women to a previously quiet part of the town.

There is no specific record that McGonagall tried to take advantage of the great potential audience on his doorstep by offering to enter-

* The Autiobiography of Sir William Topaz McGonagall in "More Poetic Gems."

61

tain in some of the bars—although he might very well have done, and been rebuffed as something that would merely hold up the sale of drink. On the other hand, some of the *Reminiscences* ("Poetic Gems") may well very likely deal with Perth Road pubs. . . .

The Railway Bridge had edged noisily over the Tay from the foot of Paton's Lane, gradually establishing an escape route from the grey townscape of mills and tenements, stacks dwarfing church spires, over to the green braes of another county, Fife. Its making filled the days and nights of the district with sound; its makers filled the district's bars. . . .

"Hello, Willie, hello! You know this man, Michael?"

"Heard of him; haven't you told me yourself about him many a time; pleased to meet you Mr——"

"Willie; *Willie*—thar right, Willie? Where have you been the day then; when are you thinking of going back to see the Queen, eh? Come on in and have one—all right; we're ALL going home for our tea when we've had a couple. . . . You can have a lemonade then; would you not have a drink with a neighbour on pay-night? Come on—Michael wants to hear you giving a recitation; heard so much about you—all the lads have; come on now. . . . Here, I'll warrant you'll get a good collection—I'll put the hat round myself."

"Well, if you thought I'd get a hearing. . . . I've never had any dealings with that particular publican——"

"Ah, he's a grand fellow, isn't he, Michael? He'll thank us for bringing in a bit of entertainment, you'll see if he doesn't; come away now, Willie—I knew you would. . . ."

The evening was young enough for no one to be drunk enough to want to interrupt or join in off-key; there was still enough money in pockets to make for a tolerant give-him-a-chance atmosphere. And many neighbours were there, in their local, and sympathetically inclined and expansive to the less-better-off. Others there were who had seen him, heard *of* him, had never heard him. So into the room into which they had managed to squeeze their way from the jammed sawdust after a not-displeased nod from the publican in answer to their prodding of McGonagall and shouting, "All right if he gives a turn?" "Let him entertain the company, boss?"

The pub was packed with men with various degrees of dirt on faces, hands and clothes; greasy engineers and plumbers and their greasier, blacker, semi-skilled helpers; painters, war-striped and clownishly daubed with red lead; riveters in scorched jackets shouting at each other as if still at their clangorous trade; barrel-chested labourers, patient oxen at work, now with the yoke off vociferous and and opiniated about everything from the crawling natures of gaffers to the design of the bridge. The more work-stained were as caricatures of minstrels, eyes flashing, mouths washed large with swilling beer, against black faces; the palest were fiery redskins.

In comparison, McGonagall might have been described as pale tinker or kipper colour, for of course he spent much time outdoors, a grotesque hare seeking to lay throughout the town generous trails of his doggerel-pamphlets and succeeding only in a sparse scattering most of the time.

Among the varieties of headgear present, from caps known in the vernacular as *hooker-doon* and *doo-lichter* to what might be described as ex-garbage trilby, none came near resembling his clerical-aesthetic wide-brim. Nor did any of the hair styles, from scalped to grossly-neglected, approach his deliberately-grown long black locks. And since it was a tavern seldom visited by actors, travelling quack doctors, barkers, or the more eccentric buskers, his was the only frock-coat. . . .

By talk and gesture the customers had seemed to be trying to materialise the bridge itself on the already overcrowded premises, but now gaps appeared in the talk, a new speculation began to be bandied—

"A what? A *poet*? Looks like one anyway——"

"He's going to do a bit of a play or something——"

"Mind what you say—maybe he's a relation——"

"Hasn't a fiddle anyway."

Add your own lacing of profane ejaculations, obscene observations; the company knew and used them all. Only one or two guffaws.

The intangible presence of the bridge faded to a shadow in the background. "The best of order, please!" "The singer's on his feet!" shouted the escorts.

McGonagall made a courtly bow. He raised his hands; his black eyes sparkled as he cleared his throat. . . .

They were a good audience; he was glad he had agreed. They gave him a good hearing, and cheered when he came to his Tay Bridge piece which he had saved for the big item . . .

> *Who have succeeded in erecting the Railway*
> *Bridge of the Silvery Tay,*
> *Which stands unequalled to be seen*
> *Near by Dundee and the Magdalen Green.*

. . . ending in cries of approval and stamping of feet.

As he bowed acknowledgment, his friend took a collection, and he was gratified to glimpse the frequent twinkle of silver. Perhaps now they were ready for something longer; something from Shakespeare; should he give them——

He raised his eyes, and saw the publican's face back of the crowd that had turned from the bar to the door of the room. It had the look he had seen before on publicans' faces when he had performed on their premises. He knew about this look, and what caused it. He was being too successful in holding the attention of the customers; the process of getting beer and spirits over the counter and coin and banknotes back had fallen off to a degree displeasing to the publican. And he embarked on "The Rattling Boy from Dublin" in the memory that on more than one occasion it had seemed to be the precipitant of sundry steps publicans had taken—

> *I'm a rattling boy from Dublin town,*
> *I courted a girl called Biddy Brown,*
> *Her eyes they were as black as sloes,*
> *She had black hair and an aqualine nose.*

> *Whack fa de da, fal de darelido,*
> *Whack fal de da, fal de darelay,*
> *Whack fal de da, fal de darelido,*
> *Whack fal de da, fal de darelay . . .*

—once a publican had thrown peas at him.

> *Says I, Biddy, this will never do,*
> *For tonight you've proved to me untrue . . .*

. . . for the only music the publicans had any ear for was the chinking of money into the till.

> *Whack fal de da, fal de darelido,*
> *Whack fal de da, fal de darelay . . .*

. . . and the publican who had thrown peas at him while he was entertaining and holding everyone's rapt attention—it wasn't even his pub; he was on a visit, just!

Says I, to the devil with your glass,
You have taken from me my darling lass . . .

. . . much worse befell him on another occasion in another pub. He had sung "The Rattling Boy" and five shillings had been collected —and the company was that pleased it was proposed he sing it again, and they would contribute again—ah, but the publican couldn't see any more money being diverted from him; so he declared the entertainment at an end.

Whack fal de da, fal de darelido . . .

. . . but another time another place could be considered even worse; certainly more humiliating; when he was hit full in the face by a wet towel thrown by a waiter, of course on instructions from his master the publican.

So do not make a hullaballoo,
For I will bid farewell to you.

. . . and the time his stick went missing. Hidden by the landlady, who correctly guessed he would leave on missing it. Again, the company were being too attentive to him and neglecting the drink. The same landlady on another occasion simply marched into the room nd ordered him to "hook it!"

. . . botheration to you and Biddy Brown—
For I'm the rattling boy from Dublin Town . . .

. . . and yet again (from *Reminiscences*)—

". . . being in very poor circumstances, I thought I would call at a public-house where I was a little acquainted with the landlord, and ask him if he would allow me to give an entertainment in one of his rooms, and I would feel obliged to him if he would be so kind. Well, however, he consented with a little flattery . . . the entertainment was to come off that night, and to commence at eight o'clock. So, my friends, I travelled around the city—God knows, tired, hungry, and footsore—inviting the people to come and hear me give my entertainment; and, of course, a great number of rich men and poor men came to hear me, and the room was filled by seven o'clock. But, remember, my dear friends, when I wanted to begin, the publican would not allow me until he had extracted almost every penny from the pockets of the company. And when he told me to begin, I remember I felt very reluctant to do so, for I knew I would get but a small recompense for my entertainment. And it just turned out to be as I expected. My dear friends, I only received eighteenpence for my entertainment from, I dare say, about sixty of a company. I ask of you, my dear readers, how much did the publican realise from the company that night by selling drink? In my opinion, the least he would have realised would be eighteen shillings or a pound. But depend upon it, they will never take the advantage of me again."

> *Whack fal de da, fal de darelido,*
> *Whack fal de da, fal de darelay.*

The company had joined in at the second chorus, and the song ended with a rousing shout of approval and cries for an encore. The publican had gone from the door; but before McGonagall could launch into something else a waiter appeared and handed him a note. On an intuitive impulse McGonagall handed it to his friend, telling him before he had opened the envelope that he knew it was a hoax, to make him leave—he was competing too well with the till. The letter invited him to proceed immediately by cab to Gray's Hall where a ball was being held that night, and where the company was eager to hear him perform. Remuneration was promised. A hoax, obviously; yet; on the outside chance—

". . . I left the public-house directly, but I was not so foolish as to hire a cab to take me to Gray's Hall. No, my friends, I walked all the way, and called at the hall, and shewed the letter to a man that was watching the hall door, and requested him to read it, and to show it to the master of the ball ceremonies . . . he soon returned with the letter, telling me it was a hoax, which I expected. My dear friends, this lets you see so far, as well as me, that these publicans that wont permit singing or reciting in their houses are the ones that are selfish or cunning. They know right well that while anyone is singing a song in the company, or reciting, it arrests the attention of the audience from off the drink. That is the reason, my dear friends, for the publicans not allowing moral entertainments to be carried on in their houses, which I wish to impress on your minds. It is not for the sake of making a noise in their houses, as many of them say by way of an excuse. No! believe me, they know that pleasing entertainment arrests the attention . . . off the drink for the time being, and that is the chief reason for them not permitting it, and, from my own experience, I know it to be the case."

The publican had got him out, the doorman at Gray's Hall wouldn't let him in, but he'd made about five shillings, which at the same time would have amounted to much more if he had been allowed to continue.

He turned down a street away from Perth Road. He didn't feel like going into any of the other pubs, or shops that were still open, to try and sell a broadsheet or two. He would return home by the river; he'd made enough to make sure of Jean being able to get in the week-end messages. The rent? Well, it could always wait another week if need be.

In the pub he had left he was discussed for the short while it took for the bridge to re-establish itself. Trade briskened into a swelling tide of drinks; the publican's manner becoming noticeably more buoyant as the flood of orders increased. The history of the building of the bridge—history, to the extent that it was now sufficiently near completion for there to be plans to run the first engine right across it in a couple of months or so—was relived; the navvying, the mud and rock and blasting; the masonry and bricklaying; the making of the roads to the landfalls; the height of the girders, the dangers and the accidents; the big wages and the bitter winters; the tearing winds far worse than anyone ever remembered on top of the Law, the hill whose skirts the town encroached more on every year.

The work had been going on since 1871, now as completion came in sight the great army of workers had been reduced by successive pay-offs, but still enough were left to fill many pubs and bring approving geniality to publicans' features as they pushed through the swing doors.

On this particular evening the bridge was generating more noise in the pub which McGonagall had left than it was in actuality where he now sat on a bench in the Magdalen Green, a public recreation ground overlooking the end of the bridge. Lights had begun to wink on the structure; every now and then a series of muffled bangs floated over the river; the screech of metal dragging over metal; an occasional puff of steam arose, momentarily brilliant against the lowering sun.

67

This was where he had sat not long ago writing about the bridge. There was every sign the piece would achieve a great success. Look how well it had been received by the company that night—and they knew about the bridge! He had planned to offer copies for sale; an opportunity lost through the publican's conniving. . . .

An idea! He would go down among the bridge workers, say at a dinner-time with a fairish bundle; which meant keeping some of this money to get more printed. . . . Jean would understand; anyway, week-ends were good for selling other poems. . . .

Watching the sky redden against the pillars wading in a line over to Fife, he had a feeling of great satisfaction and optimism.

He declaimed sonorously to the few gulls that wheeled and circled continuously into the updraught that rose from the embankment wall, shooting up with a marvellous abandonment to be borne swiftly downwind before a few powerful flaps brought them into circuit again. He saw only the bridge; or was it only his lines on it he was aware of? Or did he see, unsuspectingly, more than he knew he saw?

Beautiful Railway Bridge of the Silvery Tay!
With your numerous arches and pillars in so grand array,
And your central girders, which seem to the eye
To be almost towering to the sky.
The greatest wonder of the day,
And a great beautification to the River Tay,
Most beautiful to be seen,
Near by Dundee and the Magdalen Green.

Beautiful Railway Bridge of the Silvery Tay!
That has caused the Emperor of Brazil to leave
His home far away, incognito *in his dress,*
And view thee ere he passed along en route *to Inverness.*

Beautiful Railway Bridge of the Silvery Tay!
The longest of the present day
That has crossed ever o'er a tidal river stream,
Most gigantic to be seen,
Near by Dundee and the Magdalen Green.

Beautiful Railway Bridge of the Silvery Tay!
Which will cause great rejoicing on the opening day,
And hundreds of people will come from far away,
Also the Queen, most gorgeous to be seen,
Near by Dundee and the Magdalen Green.

Beautiful Railway Bridge of the Silvery Tay!
And prosperity to Provost Cox, who has given
Thirty thousand pounds and upwards away
In helping to erect the Bridge of the Tay,
Most handsome to be seen,
Near by Dundee and the Magdalen Green.

Beautiful Railway Bridge of the Silvery Tay!
I hope that God will protect all passengers
By night and by day,
And that no accident will befall them while crossing
The Bridge of the Silvery Tay,
For that would be most awful to be seen
Near by Dundee and the Magdalen Green.

Beautiful Railway Bridge of the Silvery Tay!
And prosperity to Messrs Bouche and Grothe,
The famous engineers of the present day,
Who have succeeded in erecting the Railway
Bridge of the Silvery Tay,
Which stands unequalled to be seen
Near by Dundee and the Magdalen Green.*

Back in the pub, as always near closing time, tongues loosened, the great engineering creation became somewhat tarnished of image.

Slurred voices more than hinted at sharp practices, even dangerous subterfuges, much less than minimum specified standards being worked to, faults that were in fact worsened by below-standard replacements, shoddy substitutes, even blatant *faking* . . . heads shook sorrowfully over beeswax. . . . Who would credit *beeswax*

---

* In later years he claimed to have had a premonition a few days before the bridge fell.

being in liberal use as a camouflage for structural deficiencies? Many of the men knew, and only mentioned it in their cups. The publican had heard of it many and many a time; but it wasn't *his* business.

Had McGonagall paid any attention to rumours he had over-heard?

He certainly didn't come out with anything directly, either before or after, so far as is known.

But now a cold wind had sprung up over the river, as it was always liable to do. McGonagall got to his feet and set off the short distance home. Looking back at the bridge from the foot of his street he promised himself an early trip over it as soon as the service started; combined with a tour of Fife; shouldn't take much to hire a hall in little towns and villages there; new territory to him; take plenty of copies with him. . . . Ah, yes; much lay ahead!

His step was jaunty as he walked up Paton's Lane singing to himself the chorus of *The Rattling Boy*.

CHAPTER SEVEN

THE Tay Railway Bridge opened for general traffic on 3rd June, 1878, but it was over a year later that McGonagall crossed it for the first time.

But before he did there was a quick look at "the sticks"—an offering of himself and his talents to the villages of Strathmore.

The Dundee Holiday Week had upon him what seemed to be becoming a habitually stimulating effect; 1877 "Write! Write!"; 1878 To see the Queen; 1879 Tour of the Provinces. . . .

In the words of a newspaper report which appeared on his return, McGonagall had "again distinguished himself by performing another Quixotical adventure."

Setting off on a Saturday in mid-June he walked some fourteen miles to the village of Coupar Angus, where he arrived late in the afternoon, drenched and penniless—

"Undaunted by the weather and his empty pockets, the 'Poet' set about making inquiries to obtain the use of a hall wherein to display his histrionic talents to the benighted villagers. Whether it so happened that all the public halls in Coupar Angus were pre-engaged . . . or whether the hard-hearted, hard-fisted proprietors refused to let their premises without a material guarantee for payment is not very clear, but the result was that all Mr McGonagall's efforts to secure a place proved an utter failure."

So on he plodded, doggedly, through flood and mud a good few more miles to the village of Burrelton—

"Here he was, benighted in a strange place, miles away from home and friends, weary, hungry, cold and wet, and not a penny in his pocket to obtain food or shelter. In the midst of his perplexities, however, a Good Samaritan took him in, warmed, fed and lodged him for the night. A country woman who admired his effusions in the *Weekly News* took pity on the forlorn stranger and entertained him most hospitably until Monday morning dawned bright and fair,

71

and brought fresh hopes of success to the poet's despondent heart."

The newspaper's "Burrelton Correspondent" now takes up the tale—

"On Monday we were honoured by no less a personage than Mr. William McGonagall, Poet Laureate of Dundee, etc., etc. For some time past it would appear that Mr. McGonagall has had more than suspicions that Dundee was not altogether the most suitable place for an exhibition of his genius, and the growing tightness of his finances duly affirmed the correctness of his suspicions. But it seems that the last straw that broke the back of his patience was laid on when Her Majesty passed through Dundee on Friday. As we were informed by this neglected son of genius, he modestly remained in absence all the while the royal train stopped in the station, lest it should be represented that he wished to throw himself a second time under the notice of royalty."

(*I* think he was still worried about the threats of the constable he encountered at Balmoral Castle gates!)

"Of course, Mr McGonagall added, had Her Majesty sent a deputation asking for an interview, as a willing and obedient servant he would have felt bound to comply. But, alas! the royal summons did not come, and Mr McGonagall, wearied hoping against hope, rushed to set out in quest of fresh fields and pastures new."

The village of Burrelton had no hall, but Robbie Fenwick's smiddy was put at his disposal; but, alas! (again) "The people just came to make game of me, and they gave me nothing." And horseplay resulting in a broken window completely aborted the project in any case.

"With a heavy heart and a light purse the 'Poet' took the road next morning for Perth, where he arrived tired and at an early hour in the forenoon. He had not been long in the Fair City before he recognised and buttonholed a party of excursionists from Dundee to whom he poured forth the story of his hardships and adventures. 'And now,' he said, 'here I am without a farthing in the world, and I know not what to do. I was indebted for my breakfast this morning to a gentlemen who had seen me play Othello in the Dundee Music Hall. It is time, I think, that I should be recognised; and, indeed, it cannot come too soon, considering my own condition and the circumstances of my family. But,' he added in a more hopeful strain, 'my time will come yet; I will never despair. Bouch* has got knighted, I am glad to see.' 'Oh, you'll be knighted too some day,' replied his sympathisers.

" 'I wish I could get some remuneration for the labour of my brain,' replied the 'Poet' humbly. A literary gentleman of the city happened to pass at that moment, was introduced by the sympathisers to the poor poet. 'I never saw you before, Mr McGonagall,' remarked the citizen, staring dubiously at the figure before him. 'Well, you have the honour of seeing me now,' was the lofty reply, extending his hand patronisingly to the stranger; who took it, stared for a minute in the poet's face, smiled—and walked away. A small *douceur* having been tipped the poet by his Dundee friends, they also bade him good-bye, and left him to retire to Dundee, a sadder but not a wiser man."

A month later he was in the news again, this time no further than the suburb Lochee; although at that time it was regarded as a separate village (and many of the older Lochee folk today still think of it as such).

ENTERTAINMENT BY
MR McGONAGALL IN LOCHEE

"For the past week or so, flaming posters have been exhibited in various prominent parts of the village, announcing that a Grand Entertainment would be given by William McGonagall, 'Poet to Her Majesty.' Long before the commencement of the entertainment groups of men of all ages and conditions, many of them from Dundee, gathered in the vicinity of the hall, mostly all evincing by their manner intense amusement, and the whetted appetite of the street indicated that something extraordinary was on the *tapis*.

"The hall was filled by a large audience, the majority of whom were young men and lads, all evidently in a thorough mood for fun.

"Punctual to the hour the distinguished bard appeared on the platform, and stood for a considerable time there in dignified solitariness. There was a tremendous hubbub in the getting of a chairman, the din being literally deafening. Mr A. B. Donald, bookseller, was proposed again and again, and with evident reluctance at

* Engineer-designer of the first Tay Railway Bridge.

73

last consented; his ascent to the platform being hailed with deafening plaudits.

"The chairman asked a patient hearing for the performer. Mr McGonagall then appeared on a small stage which had been improvised in front of the platform, and amidst the cheers and laughter of the audience, made his bow to them."

He opened with "The Rattling Boy" after explaining it had to be done in *character*; thus he wore his hat and brandished an umbrella (beginning to get fed up of drenchings?).

The audience participated wholeheartedly, roaring out the choruses and thumping mightily in time with their feet.

Then came the recitations, received in a manner "most uproarious, altogether past description. Every now and then, and particularly when the performer was uttering some choice bit and giving it the 'sweetness long drawn out' the audience would burst out with the chorus of *John Brown's Body* in a manner that completely 'shut up' the gifted artiste. Notwithstanding all the irreverence on the part of the audience, the bard remained perfectly calm, and seemingly not in the least disturbed by the riotous proceedings around him; and whenever the noise ceased he resumed where he had left off with the greatest nonchalance.

"Matters came to a thorough climax when the chairman intimated that Mr McGonagall was to give a selection from *Hamlet*. This was received with howls of laughter, several voices shouting for well-known invididuals in the hall to perform the part of the ghost.

"Mr McGonagall, however, had not proceeded far with his recitation when a number of the audience who were seated near the platform rose from their seats and ascending the improvised stage they forcibly seized hold of the 'Poet to Her Majesty' and, notwithstanding his frantic struggles, carried him shoulder high to the street.

"A scene, seldom if ever paralleled in the history of the village, then ensued.

"A tremendous crowd thronged the street, almost all of whom seemed to be in a very frenzy of amusement. Mr McGonagall had ultimately, owing to the great crowd, to take shelter in a shop nearby. The excitement, although not so intense, continued to prevail for a considerable time afterwards. The general impression of the audience seemed to be that they never in their lives were so thoroughly entertained as they were by the celebrated McGonagall. A complimentary poem on him was read during the course of the evening."

After these newspapermen's stories of scenes from the life of a parochial laureate, it is interesting to compare (from the *People's Journal* 11th October 1879)—

POET McGONAGALL'S TOUR THROUGH FIFE
(Narrated by Himself)

SETS OUT
Poor William McGonagall left Dundee on Monday afternoon September 20th at four o'clock on board the *Star o' the Tay*, and landed at Newburgh in high hopes of getting a lodging for the night; but unfortunately for him all the lodging-houses were full with men belonging to Wombwell's Menagerie; therefore William had to travel on to Abernethy, a distance of three miles, and got lodging there, which he paid fivepence for, and when Tuesday morning came he arose about eight o'clock and made his breakfast and ate it heartily. Then he inquired of the landlady, Did she think he could get a hall in the village to give an entertainment in? and she told him she considered it would be very foolish for the poet to try to give an entertainment there.

JOURNEY TO KINROSS
William took the landlady's advice and left Abernethy and travelled to Kinross, a distance of twelve miles and more perhaps where he obtained lodgings for the night for which he paid fivepence for. He then went in search of a hall to give his matchless entertainment in and he very easily succeeded in getting the Temperance Hall, which was to cost him one shilling only for the night, or perhaps nothing if he failed in drawing a large audience, and which, to the poet, no doubt, seemed to be very generous indeed—and the entertainment was to be held in it on Wednesday evening, and to commence at eight o'clock, and the admission was to be 2d. each for adults; and 1d. each for children—which was to be announced by the village bellman, which he would charge the poet 1/- for doing so.

Then when William had got arrangements made for Wednesday evening's entertainment in the Templars' Hall, he returned to his lodgings and had his dinner.

MAGNIFICENT POEM ON LOCH LEVEN

After he had got his dinner he went out to have a view of Loch-leven and the surrounding beauties of Kinross, and as the poet viewed the beautiful scenery around the Loch, he felt so enraptured he composed the following lines:—

Beautiful Loch Leven, near by Kinross,
For a good day's fishing the angler is seldom at a loss,
For the loch it abounds with pike and trout,
Which can be had for the catching without any doubt;
And the scenery around it is most beautiful to be seen,
Especially the Castle, wherein was imprisoned Scotland's
 ill-starred Queen.

Then there's the lofty Lomond Hills on the eastern side,
And the loch is long, very deep, very wide;
Then on the southern side there's Benarty's rugged hills,
And from the tops can be seen the village of Kinross with
 its spinning mills.

The big house of Kinross is very handsome to be seen,
With its beautiful grounds around it, and lime trees so green,
And 'tis a magnificent sight to see, on a fine summer afternoon
The bees extracting honey from the leaves when in full bloom.

There the tourist can enjoy himself and while away the hours,
Underneath the lime trees shady bowers,
And listen to the humming of the busy bees,
While they are busy gathering honey from the lime trees.

Then there's the old burying ground near by Kinross,
And the dead that lie there turned into dusty dross,
And the gravestones are all in a state of decay,
And the wall around it is mouldering away.

76

After the poet had composed the foregoing lines he returned again to the village of Kinross, highly elated, and by this time it was five o'clock in the afternoon; so William made his supper ready, and partook of it with a hearty appetite—after viewing the beautiful scenery of Lochleven—and went to bed at an early hour, and slept very sound all night.

A FAITHLESS BELLMAN

When Wednesday morning came again, the poet arose and donned his clothes and had his breakfast. Then he sallied forth in search of the bellman; but the bellman could not be got. He had gone to the village of Milnathort and had promised to his wife to be back at four, and at the same time telling her it would be time enough to announce to the village of Kinross the poet's entertainment. Therefore William felt a little discontented; so he left the bellman's wife, telling her he would call again. So William called again and again, until seven at night, and the bellman didn't come. Therefor the poet's entertainment proved abortive all through the bellman of Kinross.

ADVANCES TO COWDENBEATH AND INTERVIEWS A POET

William resolved to leave Kinross on Thursday and go on to the village of Cowdenbeath and try and give an entertainment there, if he could get a hall, so when Thursday morning came and William had breakfasted, he took the road for Cowdenbeath, eight miles from Kinross, and arrived in it about twelve o'clock high noon of the day with one shilling in his pocket and a little dispirited, of course, owing to the failure of his entertainment in the village of Kinross.

However, an idea struck the poet that he would try and find out the poet of Cowdenbeath, and perhaps he could find him a hall or some small room to give his entertainment in. William soon found the poet, however, and William introduced himself to him as poet McGonagall all the way from Dundee, at the same time asking him if he could get a hall for him or a small room to give his entertainment in and he would feel obliged to him, but the poet, he said, he was rather doubtful about it.

The poet treated William very kindly by giving him a good dinner and also gave William some of his satirical effusions, which William thanked him for. Then when William had got his dinner the poet, Charles Baxter, for that is his name, told William to come along with him and he would try and get a hall for him in the village; and when he asked the keeper of the hall, Mr Gardiner, what he would charge for one night of the hall, he told him the lowest he could make it would be ten and sixpence, at which William replied he wouldn't get the half of that from him because he had not got it, at which Mr Gardiner replied that there was no harm done; so the poet of Cowdenbeath was very sorry because he could not get the hall for William; besides, he told William he considered it would be a failure, allowing he had got the hall, owing to the poverty of the coalmining districts.

So William bade the poet good-bye and thanked him for his kindness, and went and secured lodging for the night, resolving to try the village of Lochgelly on Saturday—it being the pay night—if he could get a hall in it.

AT LOCHGELLY—ANOTHER FAILURE

When Saturday morning came, William got up, and when he had got some breakfast he took the road for Lochgelly, resolving to make application to the Worthy Chief Templar in the village, thinking he would assist him in getting a hall. So when William arrived in Lochgelly it was about eleven o'clock in the morning. He made for the Worthy Chief Templar and soon found him, Mr M'Connell of the I.O.G. Templars, which Mr McGonagall is a member of. However, Mr M'Connell received Mr McGonagall in a very courteous manner. After he told him he was Poet McGonagall from Dundee, and how he was a Good Templar, then he wrote out a note and gave it to William, and told him to give it to John Greenhill, No. 30 South Street, and he thought when the proprietor read the note he would have no objection to give William the hall. So William found John Greenhill and gave him the note. So John Greenhill went with William to the proprietor of the hall and got it for him. So William began to tell the villagers about his entertainment in the Co-operative Hall of Lochgelly, which would commence at seven o'clock and the admission would be one penny each.

However, it turned out to be a failure, for only two boys came, so William returned the boys their pence again and locked the hall rather downhearted, owing to the second failure he had met with. Then when Mr M'Connell heard of the failure of William's had met with he gave him a sixpence, also Alexander Skene and David Anderson, also James Greenhill, which helped to keep poor William McGonagall living until Monday.

ATTACKS DUNFERMLINE—A COLD RECEPTION

When Monday came poor William left Cowdenbeath and went to Dunfermline, thinking he would do better there, but, alas! no success in Dunfermline. He first made application to the Secretary of an I.O.G. Templars, thinking he would assist him, but he firmly refused, telling Mr McGonagall it was not compulsory. Then Mr McGonagall asked him if he would be so kind as to tell him where the Worthy Chief belonging to some other Lodge lived, and he done so with great reluctance. He told Mr McGonagall to go to St. Catherine's Wynd and he would find a Mr George Wright there who was a Worthy Chief, but whom Mr McGonagall could not see until six at night. He considered that would be the most convenient time to speak to him.

AN APPRECIATIVE AUDIENCE AT LAST

Mr McGonagall left the city of Dunfermline and travelled to the little village of Crossford, about a mile and a half from Dunfermline, and there he succeeded in a Smithy for to give his entertainment, and the admission thereto was only one penny each. So William made no delay in announcing it to the villagers. However when the time came to open there were a few boys came and asked William if it was near time to begin, so William told them to come inside for he would soon begin. So by seven o'clock William had but a very small audience to entertain. He instructed the master of the Smithy to take the money at the door while he was delighting his little audience with his matchless entertainment.

By the time William got finished with his entertainment he had received two and tenpence by it, and he returned his most sincere thanks to God and his little audience for their kind support, for which McGonagall received a hearty vote of thanks. Then McGonagall bade them all good-night, and left the smithy amidst the deafening plaudits of his audience and travelled to Dunfermline and got lodgings for the night.

ANOTHER DISCOURAGEMENT—UNKIND TREATMENT

When Tuesday morning came he took his breakfast and started for the road again in the direction of Limekiln to get a hall there but in that he failed. By the time he returned to Dunfermline it was six o'clock, so he called upon the Worthy Chief Templar who received him in a very unchristian manner, by telling him he could not assist him, and besides telling William his poetry was very bad; so William told him it was so very bad that Her Majesty had thanked him for what he had condemned, and left him, telling him at the same time he was an enemy and he would report him.

THOUGH CAST DOWN STILL HOPEFUL

Mr McGonagall left Dunfermline on Thursday the second of October, and crossed the Tay Bridge, for the first time, by rail, on Friday afternoon, and is now in Dundee, and in good health, hoping his admirers will rally round and give him a hearty welcome home again to "Bonnie Dundee."

It seems they did not rally round all that much.

And crossing the railway bridge for the first time was also to prove the last time. Macabrely enough, McGonagall's verses were to long outlive the structure that inspired them. . . .

But, to his admirers. . . . He does not seem to have afforded them very many opportunities for admiring.

December the fifth, 1879—

"McGonagall the great has once more emerged from his obscurity. Last night he appeared before an admiring, though rather a small audience in Blair's Hall, Overgate, when a real poetical and dramatic treat was enjoyed. The poet attended at the hall door in person to welcome his friends and take the coppers."

Standing on a rough deal table he gave them *The Rattling Boy*. Following this a recitation in which he lost his place in a sheaf of papers. "I must put on my spectacles," causing laughter that was echoed by youngsters outside. There were cries of "Upside down!" "Missed a verse!" etc. An attempt at a reading from Hogg brought "Too long!" "Give us a song!" "Let's have a dance!" "Give him a bottle of tuppeny!"

He carried on until drowned by a chorus of "Tra la la."

His sentimental "Forget-me-not" got a better hearing; but then a man mounted the platform to deliver—

> *McGonagall the Great,*
> *Most beautiful to be seen,*
> *Who has written that glorious work*
> *"The Magdalen Green."*
> *Let us toast him with honour,*
> *For his fame's spread abroad,*
> *But I'm afraid he's a goner*
> *If he does not go to bed!*

to great applause and laughter.

McGonagall then delivered the Tay Bridge poem with his usual gusto; then at the chairman's request a newly published poem about the Rev. D. Macrae. After reading this piece the poet "intimated that copies could be had at the low charge of one penny. At his announcement the audience crowded round . . . but no one seemed to be disposed to purchase a copy of his latest work.

A gentleman mounted a chair and delivered a very eloquent address in which he expressed the opinion that Mr McGonagall ought to come oftener before the public. He said it was evident he was a great genius, and he ought not to hide his light under a bushel. He concluded his address with the following appropriate couplet—

> *He had something to say about Mr Macrae,*
> *But he should take my advice and go away.*

"Several ardent spirits then seized the Poet with the intention of carrying him through the town shoulder high, but the Poet pleaded that he was not very well, and in pity he was allowed to retire to the anteroom, when the audience reluctantly dispersed."

He walked home, counting the profit, considering the reception various items had received—*at least the Tay Bridge poem, as always, had gone down well,* as he gazed across at its lights reflected in the black water.

It was only a matter of days before the bridge itself was down.

I hope that God will protect all passengers
By night and by day . . .

CHAPTER EIGHT

The "Poet of the Tay Bridge" did not receive one of the eight by
five inches cards—as big as one of his broadsheets, inviting him
to the opening ceremony on the 31st May 1878.

There were 1,500 passengers in the train, drawn by the green
"Lochee" engine, welcomed at the wonderfully-appointed Tay
Bridge Station by Dundee's Provost Robertson. Millmaster James
Cox, Chairman of the Tay Bridge Undertaking, declared the bridge
open.

On this gala day the bells of the Old Steeple rang; and the band
of the 1st Forfarshire Volunteers led the procession to the Albert
Picture Gallery Hall where the luncheon was held. There was a
crowd estimated at 15,000 outside. . . .

"Hey—what are *you* doing *outside* among all us common folk?
Did you lose your ticket, McGonagall—I mean Sir Willie?"

"Och YOU don't need an invitation card—make way for Poet
McGonagall. . . . What are you hanging back for? Away you go in;
you'll get a damn good drink——"

"Ah, but he's an abstainer; aren't you?"

"THAT'S what it is, then! That's how you weren't invited,
McGonagall——"

"Aye—the bigwigs didn't want showing up when you stood up to
lecture them on the evils of booze!"

"They were afeared you'd keep them from enjoying themselves!"

"Never mind, Willie—a poet's a poet for a' that, eh? What?
Should've kept my mouth shut! All right, I'll buy your poetry—
what's a penny on a day like this. . . . Come on, Jim, you stump up
as well; we appreciate you even if the gentry doesn't. . . ."

"Thank you, gentlemen. Any more? You, sir? A penny only for
the famous Tay Bridge poem."

"I'll take one—but do you know the competition you've got? There's at least half-a-dozen folk—bairns as well—hawking verses about the bridge."

"Not *my* verses; I peddle my own."

"Sure, they're not your bairns? I hear you've got a houseful."

"Certainly not. I do my own selling. . . . Any more? The original *Railway Bridge of the Silvery Tay*; only one penny. . . ."

The day was young, and fine; now that the elect had passed in to lunch there was nothing for the crowd to do except go home, or just hang about; no entertainment laid on for *them*, only what they could make for themselves.

"Hey—there's McGonagall; c'mon and give us a turn, poet!"

"Well, if we buy your poetry will you give us a song?"

And now someone *had* started to sing; McGonagall was forgotten. The crowd turned, pushed its way past, craned necks to see the busker who could not see them—the tall man, head thrown back, sightless eyes up to the bright sky, his rapt expression and the sincerity in his voice bringing out of the sentimental old ballad more than the forgotten composer probably knew he had put into it. Blind Hughie was always sure of an audience; people surged towards him. McGonagall, jostled, staggered, dropped a few broadsheets, was nearly knocked down altogether trying to retrieve them; clutching what remained, withdrawn from the crowd, yet forced to go with it, but going with it as a swimmer wisely goes with a current to gradually edge his way out of it.

On the edge of the multitude he started on a wide detour; a drunken melodeon player bursting into a reedy, uneven jig of slurred flourishes just as he thought he'd reached a quiet section.

Since there was no one focal point now, the crowd broke up into groups around many focal points; more buskers were heard; a fiddle wavered out a slow air, a woman's voice rose.

Groups of friends conversed; young males sought the attention of young females with varying degrees of ribaldry. McGonagall stalked round through the thin outskirts of the crowd.

Hawkers shouted, waving booklets commemorating the bridge, offering lithographs—and, McGonagall turning sharply at this— even rival broadsheet poems of celebration.

He was just thinking of offering his verses again where there were no buskers or hawkers, when—

"Hello, hello—the Great McGonagall, lads!"

A large group of grinning youths surrounded him, one of several with bottles of beer thrusting a bottle towards him with, "Have a swig; it's a day for celebrating—for *everybody* to celebrate——"

"Aye—like hogmanay; even the miserable bloody teetotalers—g'on—don't insult the company——"

"When are you coming back to Lochee, McGonagall? We'll soon have the trams."

"Wait till the man's had a drink——"

"Then you can give us a song, eh, Willie?"

"Give us a song, poet!"

"Let him wet his whistle first!"

No use trying to reason with them. He tried to edge out of their midst without success.

"What's this you've got? Are you giving away pound notes, McGonagall?"

"Aye—all the money he makes at them entertainments he gives. Going to give us the price of a drink, eh! Ach, look—they're just his rotten poetry," making a clumsy swipe and nearly scattering the broadsheets which McGonagall now clutched tightly to his chest in alarm, making the crowd shout with laughter, which stopped dead when—

"Leave the poor soul alone—he's not harming you, is he? Well, leave him, d'you hear? Get to hell, the lot of you—away home and get your mothers to wipe your noses, bloody bairns trying to be men on a couple of bottles of tuppeny!"

The youths vanished, such was the reputation of the Iron Horse, a notorious amazon who did the work of two men in the mill, and was liable to clear a space around her in any crowd anywhere when in her cups.

In thanks McGonagall proferred a broadsheet.

"It's poetry, isn't it? I know the way the lines are, although I can't read. Ah, but somebody'll read it to me; God bless you!"

"And God bless *you*, madam," as she lurched off, swinging a tartan shawl round her mighty shoulders.

The crowd round the Albert Institute—if you ignored the ragged, and the noisy, and the occasional wink of sun on tilted bottle; the men in their good suits and the women in their summer finery in conversational knots, resembled the lingering of a vast congregation after some extraordinary church occasion. But, they had been nowhere, had attended no function or congress except as the unpaid extras—a flattering living background for the "head lads' " proud procession. Here and there you would have heard cynical observations to the effect that, having got their feet under the table inside, some of the notabilities would remain until they were entirely under the table. And it would likely be some time before any of them came out again, unsteadily or otherwise; but the crowd, which was now a loose grouping of small crowds, lingered, some encouraging the buskers, others conversing, and other groups breaking up and drifting away.

McGonagall gazed around. Soon, a statue to Burns was to be erected. . . . Not so long ago, it seemed, the place had been a fairground of booths where he had had his first experiences behind the footlights as a laddie in his few hours of leisure from the handloom. Now, he was a poet; and if he was not of the elect invited today, at least no rival poet was either. And there was plenty of time; his time would come. Things hadn't gone that well with Burns during his lifetime; and if Dundee honoured an Ayrshire bard with a fine monument, then without a doubt *his* turn would come. . .

Whooping barefoot urchins in chase tore past, spinning him round. He set off home; perhaps he would visit Mr Lamb first, he might have a few magazines for him. . . Maybe not; the restaurant in Reform Street would be busy today. He'd walk out by the Magdalen Green, there would be plenty strolling out that way, prospective customers for his broadsheets.

Passing the large group round Blind Hughie who had just finished another song, he heard the chink of coin, the blind minstrel's expression of thanks.

Well, so far he had not descended to busking, although no doubt it would be profitable. But if a poet had no dignity he had no true vocation; such was no better than a *mountebank*. . . . And a mountebank he was not and never would be, as he was to be forced to point out to the constable at the gates of Balmoral Castle in a few weeks time.

"Hot Pies!"

The vendor had a voice that some folk claimed to have heard in Newport, across the river, on a still day.

It was down by the river, on the Esplanade, that they met.

"The breeze off the water gives folk an appetite; sold a lot outside the station when the crowds were there——"

"Plenty of people round the Institute yet."

"I'll make my way up that way. God, this thing sweats you this weather!"

He rested the little box-oven on the low wall by the river and took his arms out of the straps.

"Did you do much trade yourself, McGonagall?" They were familiar figures to each other through Pie Jock getting his wares from a baker in the Perth Road not far from Paton's Lane.

"I managed to sell a few copies of my poems."

"Does it pay you? I mean, after you pay the printer? This is a good thing; not so much in this weather, except like when there's crowds out for the day. Mind, I like a pie myself anytime, could go them anytime; many a time had a cold one for breakfast; aye—in fact I think I'll have one now while things are quiet."

The rich aroma wafting out of the opened door of the little oven made McGonagall close his eyes momentarily. He had had nothing since a slice of bread and a cup of tea that morning.

"Are you not wanting one? Look—there's a broken couple there— a whole one and them two, tuppence; there's a bargain!"

The heady savour could not be resisted, although pies were an extravagance. He gave Jock the coppers, wrapped the sound pie and one of the damaged ones—only bits of the crusts were broken— in a newspaper he had picked up earlier, and sat on the low wall wolfing the other, looking up the river to the long thin line of the bridge.

"Och, I was going to wait till I landed at Maggie's, you know, the lass, in Devil's Wynd,* for she'll make tea—but I can always have another." He peered into the oven in preparation to packing up again; "Another broken one; I'll have to watch better what I'm doing putting them in. . . . Here; a halfpenny?"

* Hean's Lane.

In the end the pie-man accepted a copy of the Tay Bridge poem, although neither he nor Maggie could read, but agreeing that "Right enough; funny creatures, women; I believe she *will* value it."

The pie went into the newspaper with the others. The vendor swung his oven on to his back. Wiping their mouths on the backs of their hands they parted with a wave and a nod.

With his parcel of bargain luxury-food, and what was for him a good feed inside him, McGonagall strode along the riverside with a renewed optimism in his powers, in the future.

What a pity that this great occasion on this bonnie day had not been graced by the attendance of Her Majesty! Perhaps he might even have been able to get some of his poems presented to her; different entirely from receiving them through the post, which apparently she was not allowed to keep—if indeed they ever got the length of her!

But surely, had she come, she would have wanted to meet the Poet of the Tay Bridge; have wanted to hear the Poet himself declaim his immortal stanzas?

As he strode along he forgot the discomfort of hat, weight and heat of flapping frock-coat on this warm day, for there came to him an idea so blindingly *simple*. . . . His pace quickened with his pulse; yes; he could and *would*! Her Majesty would not refuse to see a poor loyal poet who had walked all the way from Dundee to Balmoral Castle! And then—afterwards; who would not recognise his genius then?

The sun sparkled with a new intensity from the broad rippling river; the idea was so wonderfully *simple*. . . .

"*Hot pies!*" followed him, faintly, on the breeze, as Simon, called McGonagall, went with a certain arrogance on his way.

* * * * * * * *

After the failure to communicate at Balmoral, the Queen had in the long run come to see the bridge, a year after unwittingly blighting—no, *postponing*—his hopes of a laureateship.

The year of her visit, 1879, was certainly not for the workers of Dundee a year of progress; was in fact in ill contrast with the triumphant symbol of man's ever-increasing mastery of his environment spanning the tides and currents to link two counties in defiance of the elements.

A cold winter persisted late into the year. Navigation between Dundee and Perth was impossible in January owing to the Tay being frozen.

In February, millworkers went on strike in protest against a 5% cut in wages and increase in hours, but had accepted and returned to work. (Not long after the foundry workers accepted a cut of 5% and increase of working week from 51 to 54 hours to "bring them into line with hours worked all over England.")

There was much unemployment, and indeed destitution. A Relief Committee distributing provisions and coal had to continue until the end of March; there was a severe snow-storm in the middle of this month.

A lecture was given in the Kinnaird Hall which was lit for the first time by electric light. Electric lighting was also being tested in Cox's Mill; had been tried in the Picture Gallery of the Albert Institute but was found to be too fitful and glaring; but it was in constant use now in Gourlay's Shipyard, the system being regarded as unequalled for outside use where cost was not the prime consideration.

A Mr Frank Henderson was selected to write the Life of Rev. Geo. Gilfillan, McGonagall's late great friend and benefactor, whose discarded mantles he had long been wearing.

In April a start was made on the foundations for the statue of Robert Burns to be erected in Albert Square. . . . McGonagall could wait.

Winter lingered. . . . On the first of May it was reported that there was no May dew, but rime was plentiful.

£12,000 was raised for a Sailors' Home.

A committee of ladies planned to open Coffee Palaces of an elegant character in densely-populated areas to "counter the attractions of the Whiskey Palaces." Rev. David Macrae was appointed successor to Gilfillan at School Wynd U.F. Church. A trial planting of six trees each side of the carriageway was made at Esplanade.

On the tenth of May the whaleship "Ravenscraig" limped back to port leaking badly and with the dead body of the captain on board.

On the twelfth the Newport Railway was opened for traffic, and McGonagall wrote—

> Success to the Newport Railway,
> Along the braes of the Silvery Tay,
> And to Dundee straightway,
> Across the Railway Bridge o' the Silvery Tay. . . .
>
> . . . the thrifty housewives of Newport
> To Dundee will often resort,
> Which will be to them profit and sport
> By bringing cheap tea, bread, and jam,
> And also some of Lipton's ham. . . .

At *Lipton's Irish Market* ham was offered at 6d. per lb., bacon from 3d. per lb.

On the twentieth the centre girders of the Tay Bridge were lighted with twenty-six gas lamps.

Mechanics' hours at Cox's Camperdown Works increased from 51-56 hours.

Arrangements were in hand to teach swimming to school children.

On Friday, 20th June, at exactly 6 p.m., the Royal Train drew into Tay Bridge Station. The centre of the town was decorated with flags, the bells of the Old Steeple had been ringing from 5 p.m.

During the seven minutes the train remained in the station, an address on vellum was read and presented by Provost Brownlee, and the Queen was presented to the bridge-designer Thomas Bouch and his assistant John Stirling, and ex-Provost James Cox, mill-master. As already stated in the previous chapter, the Poet of the Bridge of the Silvery Tay stayed at home.

The Royal Train left over the bridge two minutes late, crowds lining the vantage points. Six longboats of boys from the *Mars* Training Ship permanently anchored in the Tay saluted with oars the train passing high above, and the pleasure steamer *May* sailed along to a fluttering of handkerchiefs.

A gun boomed out from the *Mars*, and at the other end of the bridge 140 more boys from it lined the route, including a band; the train did not stop here. (Earlier in the month, engine and special coach had come down from Deeside to make a test run and back over the bridge).

McGonagall stayed at home, half-hoping it seems from later reports that he would have been summoned to the Royal Presence.

It is doubtful if he consoled himself with a visit to the Theatre Royal that evening, which advertised in honour of the Queen's brief dallying "a Grand Fashionable Night Under Distinguished Patronage," the programme being *Stolen Kisses* followed by the *comedietta A Perilous Pic-nic*. Nor was he likely to be lured by—

V R

Tonight

in

Honour of Her Majesty's Visit to Dundee,
Performance will commence with the National Anthem.

Newsome's

Hippodrome and Circus, Dundee.

Eschewing the *New Bathing Coaches Working Daily at Broughty Ferry* and daily trips on the *Star o' Gowrie* to Perth, 1/- for the whole week, he set off on the Saturday morning to Coupar Angus and round about as described previously, thus missing the Tay Yacht Club's Annual Regatta.

*   *   *   *   *   *   *   *

In July, in consequence of the late season, the Newport Horticultural Society's Show was postponed from the 19th to the 9th August; and McGonagall was borne shoulder-high from the Weaver's Hall in Lochee with such enthusiasm that he felt the necessity to seek sanctuary in a shop.

At the end of August the pedestal for the Burns statue was set in position in the Albert Square. In September a fifteen-year-old boy died from poisoning through swallowing a piece of tobacco he had been chewing; and McGonagall toured Fife, crossing the railway bridge for the first time on his return.

*   *   *   *   *   *   *   *

In November the Rev. David Macrae began his ministry with an address on his predecessor, Rev. Geo. Gilfillan; municipal elections were held in Dundee; a skating pond was constructed in Magdalen Green. At the start of December it was decided to offer Mr Gladstone the freedom of the burgh; he declined the invitation to visit the town. . . . There were heavy falls of snow and skating on Stobsmuir Ponds; and M'Gonagall gave an entertainment in Blair's Hall

91

in the Overgate, including a new poem to the Rev. David Macrae. On the 24th December trams began running between Dundee and Lochee.

On the afternoon of the 28th a passenger train left Burntisland at 5.20 p.m. for Dundee in a howling gale. . . .

It had been a day of high winds that tore slates off to send them flying like lethal discuses, slapped lums into the streets and gardens, tore a turret off steepled St. Peter's Church across the Perth Road from Paton's Lane. A huge panel of wood (fascia board?), thirty feet long, crashed into Reform Street from the hotel of McGonagall's friend and patron, Alec Lamb. . . .

Near 7 p.m. a man sat in his home in the west end of Dundee telling his children Bible stories, when the crashing of lum cans from a house opposite brought the whole family to its feet. The man crossed to the window of his living-room and looked out. . . .

From *The Dundee Advertiser*—

". . . just then a blaze of moonlight lit up the broad expanse of the Tay down below, and the long, white sinuous line of the Tay Bridge came with a ghastly glimmer into view. . . . Great masses of clouds were scouring across the expanse of the heavens, at times totally obscuring the light of the full moon. . . . When the engine entered the tunnel the cloisters of the great girders, my little girl exactly described the effect of the lights as seen through the lattice work when she exclaimed, 'Look, papa, isn't that like lightning?' . . . a comet-like burst of fiery sparks sprang out as if forcibly ejected into the darkness from the engine. In a long visible trail the streak of fire was seen till quenched in the stormy waters below. . . ."

The narrator went out to investigate—

". . . descending the slope of the Magdalen Green I had to crouch down to prevent being bodily blown away."

A massive signal post was bent like a willow-wand. Sand and pebbles were blown in a stinging hail from the Esplanade.

The water pouring out on high from the broken water pipe to Newport was "lashed into a misty spray in the ghastly gap . . . in the iron highway."

Within a matter of hours two mailbags were washed up at Broughty Ferry; the first body, that of a lady's maid, appeared off Newport, across the river, next morning at 9 a.m.

Along with reports of the catastrophe there appeared in the papers North British Railway's necessarily altered timetables for the area, and—

Interesting Sketches
connected with the
Tay Bridge Disaster
will appear in
"ILLUSTRATED LONDON NEWS"
on Saturday next, January 3rd.
Price 6d.; post free 6½d.

and—

THE TAY BRIDGE DISASTER.
A Double Page Extra Supplement
showing
THE TAY BRIDGE
before and after the recent sad
calamity, and any other views
that may be obtainable will be
issued with
THE GRAPHIC
Next Saturday, January 3rd.

McGonagall had written—

Beautiful Railway Bridge of the Silvery Tay!
I hope that God will protect all passengers
By night and by day.
And that no accident will befall them while crossing
The Bridge of the Silvery Tay,
For that would be most awful to be seen
Near by Dundee and the Magdalen Green.

Yet, although the bridge was practically on his doorstep, his later lines on the disaster do not seem to be an on-the-spot account; for instance (from *The Tay Bridge Disaster*)—

It must have been an awful sight,
To witness in the dusky moonlight,
While the Storm Fiend did laugh, and angry did bray,
Along the Railway Bridge of the Silv'ry Tay.
Oh! ill-fated Bridge of the Silvery Tay, etc.

93

Surely, having written so much about catastrophes of the past, he would have been drawn to the dreadful one at the foot of the street as soon as he learned of it? Is there a faint possibility that the man who relished gore so much in the roles he sought to play in the theatre, who dwelt in his writings on bloody carnage, shipwrecks, multiple incinerations, funerals, had no stomach for the real thing? Did he avoid the scene, afraid that the bobbing corpses he might see would haunt him for long after?

The Tay Bridge Disaster is certainly not composed as a first-hand account; nor is it even by his standards one of his better efforts. It reads as if it was something *he* had read about.

He has been described as being not a poet, but a *reporter*, because of the way his effusions are studded with facts, figures, dates. Well, the Tay Bridge calamity could not have offered more scope to talent of this nature; a tremendous opportunity which it seems he did not care to, or perhaps could not, take.

It seems that nearly all the clothes he wore were second-hand; perhaps he had, through some psychological peculiarity, to get most of his ideas at second-hand as well.

. . . I'd have ye resort
To Newport on the braes o' the Tay for sport.

CHAPTER NINE

"HELLO, Jean; is your man keeping all right? I was just saying to Ned I haven't seen Mr McGonagall this while—'maybe away on his travels again,' says Ned . . .'tween you and me, Jean, I felt like saying I wished HE'D away for a while——"

"Aye, Annie—as long's you still got his pay!"

"Oh God, aye; that I *do* want, the price of everything. Still, we have the trams on the Perth Road now; makes an awful difference coming from the town with a load of messages. Pays you to go in with what you save——"

"You know this—I haven't been on the trams yet!"

"Och, *Jean*! I'll have to come over for you some time I'm going in to town. But your man will maybe be taking you in to the theatre some night before that . . . he's—interested in the stage, isn't he?"

"I've times thought he was interested in nothing else——"

"Oh, but I was asking how he was——"

"Really, not too well—he gets that bronchitis; you know, the chest. I used to blame the pubs——"

"I always thought he wasn't a drinking man—och, you mean he's been *working* in one?"

"No; well, you wouldn't cry it *working*—entertaining. I blame that—the *reek* in the pubs; get on anybody's chest. But he hasn't been doing anything like that for months now."

"Well, you can't work if you're not right—and the weather; you'd think it would be a bit warmer in April—well, I hope he's soon able to work—*entertain*, Jean. Well, I'll have to away and make up Ned's piece; he's on the back shift. Still, its maybe long hours and awkward shifts on the railway, but it's steady. . . ."

"Aye, you don't know how lucky you are, Annie. Och, but we manage; Jock's working, and I think we'll soon be able to get Mary away from school—oh, and I'm hoping to get a job in the laundry at the Asylum."

"God Jean, I couldn't work *there*! Would you not be afraid some of them would get out of control or something? It's a pity McGonagall wouldn't get something to do. . . . He'll have plenty of time for his poetry just now, then. Ned was just saying it's a wonder he hasn't had a bit in the paper about the Tay Bridge Disaster——"

"Whether he ever will make up verses about that I could not tell you, Annie. But I do know that he's going over to Fife next week; the hall's all arranged and everything——"

"Well, I must tell Ned to tell all his pals—there's a lot comes over on the boat to work on the railway—to look out for McGonagall and go and hear him——"

"Oh, but there's going to be bills printed and put up in different places——"

"Well, good luck, tell him; but I'll have to run and make the working man's piece; mind and come up some time. . . ."

April 24th, 1880: *from a newspaper report*—

The scene is Newport Free Church Schoolroom, where there are about 70 youths with penny whistles and crawmills "each discoursing popular airs on their own account, and relieving the stillness of expectancy . . . the poet appeared on the platform heralded by a torrent of applause. He bowed his acknowledgment, and immediately struck an attitude, and with an air of comic tragedy he recited something, if we might judge by the movement of his mouth, for little could be heard above the music of the whistles and the tumult of enraptured voices. When finished with his oration he retired to his 'dark room,' and in answer to the continued uproar he reappeared on the platform and bowed to the audience for their encore.

"A few minutes more and he appeared as the *Rattling Boy from Dublin Town*, with his shillelagh over his shoulder, and hung on the end of it what was supposed to be a pack, but what looked like a window-blind extemporised for the occasion. During the exciting portion of the 'boy's' story the pack got loosened, and sliding gently down the 'shillelagh,' covered the Poet's back like a mantle. But the great 'draw' of the evening lay in his own 'Bannockburn.' Slowly he emerged from 'the wings,' and in a thoughtful mood stepped on the platform. Immediately his left leg flew forward in advance of all other limbs, as if it smelt the battle afar, and was eager for the fray. Then suddenly his right hand was raised in the attitude of a pump handle, his mouth was formed into a circle as round as a cannon's mouth, and with the ardour of a warrior who fights for glory, he plunged into a description of that terrible day in June when Bannockburn was lost and won.

Sir Robert the Bruce at Bannockburn
Beat the English in every wheel and turn,
And made them fly in great dismay
From the field without delay . . .

By daybreak the whole of the English army came into view
Consisting of archers and horsemen bold and true;
The main body was led on by King Edward himself,
An avaricious man, and fond of pelf . . .

Then the Scots charged them with sword in hand,
And made them fly from off their land;
And King Edward was amazed at the sight,
And he got wounded in the fight;
And he cried, Oh, heaven! England's lost, and I'm undone,
Alas! alas! where shall I run?
Then he turned his horse, and road on afar,
And never halted till he reached Dunbar. . . .

"We were somewhat disappointed with the personal appearance of the Poet. There was no evidence of a face 'sicklied o'er with the pale cast of thought'; no dreamy lineaments, no sad expressive eyes, and no domed forehead. His 'crowning glory' consisted of jet-black hair, with two locks projecting slightly in front of his ears, and the remainder thrown behind, and terminating at the back of the head like the curls of a drake's tail. Adieu, McGonagall."

Annie's railwayman husband put down the paper and reached for his pipe off the mantelpiece, "So there you are, then; a bit noisy, certainly, but nobody threw anything at least."

"It says it was his *first* visit to Fife—but, of course, he'd be wanting to forget about the last time; but it was all over the paper at the time, wandering from this wee place to that; little more than begging his way; he's be hoping that was forgotten——"

"Ah, but be fair, Annie—his first *official* visit, it says, you see."

"Well, and what does he mean by that?"

"Mmhhmm . . . aye; must mean that this occasion was all arranged with a hall booked beforehand and the like—bills stuck up advertising the thing, and such, like I read out at the start——"

"Aye—the bills inviting the gentry, you said. God, what would gentry want with the likes of him and his daft carrying-on? Mind you, he has no little idea of himself, the same McGonagall."

"Well, it wouldn't do if we were all alike; he's harmless anyway."

"Cute, you mean—no getting up in the middle of the night or coming home through the night from work for *him*——"

"There's not that much work to *be* got, through the night or not."

"He has never tried; *and* a big family. Of course, folk take pity for the bairns' sakes—many's the frocks and jerseys and breeks she gets from the church folk and others—and still gets into debt. *I'd* make him look for work—or leave him to bring the family up himself!"

"Och, he's doing his best in *his way*, and they seem to suit each other."

"She's as bad as him, if you ask me; there must be a kind of want about the both of them——"

"Well, they say like attracts like. . . . What's on the piece the night? Ah—that's the thing! Cold fried ham!"

"Aye—the McGonagall's won't see much ham, cold or otherwise!"

"Only that he's often been cried a *ham* actor, eh? Ha, ha, ha. . . ."

In fact McGonagall had done well enough out of the Newport entertainment for Mrs McGonagall to make a purchase of a quantity of the cheaper bacon. It was mostly fat, thinly streaked with meat, and of a degree of saltiness guaranteed to have most men watching the clock for opening time at the nearest ale-house.

But "Tasty, very tasty, indeed," said William, nodding in agreement with his wife's observation and patiently chewing and chewing the rind. As for drouth, they all drank a deal more tea that tea-time than usual; but there was plenty of that too—and an egg for the head of the house. The two youngsters got a bit of bread dipped in the yolk. William mopped the grease and egg off his plate with satisfaction; he had not yet began to go off eggs. . . .

"Aye," said Jean, pouring hot water from the kettle into the teapot and the remainder into the chipped enamel basin at the sink for the dishes, "if you could do as well every week we'd soon be on our feet."

"*A tide in the affairs of men* . . . this might well be the start of the flood."

Seeing him examine the fresh pages of newspapers on the table, she set his fears at rest with "The new paper's behind the cushion on the big chair."

The fire in the range was so good he had to draw his chair back a bit—they'd laid in a couple of bags of coal from the coal-merchant across the street as well. Pleasant to sit with the paper to savour again, with a comfortable feeling at the back of the mind that Jean had enough for a couple of weeks' rent in her purse. . . .

She shouted after the children to keep clean the almost-new pinafore and jacket bought for coppers from a nearby second-hand shop, then set a mug with the last of the teapot in it on the hob beside his chair . . . where he was reading over yet again—

". . . the nobility, clergy, and gentry of Newport were asked through the medium of posters to assemble in the Free Church School to signalise the occasion of the first professional visit to the 'kingdom' of the 'Queen's Poet' McGonagall. The Poet was announced to recite from Shakespeare's, his own and other great poets' works. . . ." *An exaggerated bit about noisiness then; young people carried away with enthusiasm, no more. . . . Ah, yes——*

"Desiring to rub shoulders with a 'poet' in the flesh, your correspondent, through the kindness of one of the Poet's managers, received the honour of an audience with 'son of song.' " (*Jock had been pleased with the title of manager!*)

". . . we were ushered through a door in a panelled partition, into a room off the hall, where the Poet was in waiting, ready for the commands of the prompter. As we entered, there stood the bard, his left hand leaning on a table, and his right pressing against his side like the handle of a Greek vase. When we were announced his hand was stretched forth in the most genial and condescending manner, which put us quite at our ease. . . .

99

" 'Do you find poetry to pay? for it is often said that poets are always poor and generally die in a garret'; and we instanced the case of poor Burns, whose last moments were embittered by the craving of a 'wretched haberdasher' for some paltry five pounds.

"With an ominous shake of the head which spoke volumes, he replied, 'Ah, yes, like Burns I, too, have been often craved.'

" 'What is the first part of your evening's performance?'

" 'Oh, the tent scene from *Richard the Third* comes first. I'll play that well.'

"I then expressed a preference for a recitation from his own works rather than from those of Shakespeare.

" 'Oh, yes,' was the reply, 'I always find that those who come to hear me do that. You see I am much more versatile than Shakespeare. The only man I ever knew who could come up to me in versatility was Edmund Kean; *he* could tell a story, he could sing a comic song, and declaim a tragedy.'

" 'Did you never think of writing a tragedy with yourself as hero?'

" 'No, but I have the tragic feeling within me.'

"We inquired how long he was engaged on his wonderful poem *The Bridge of the Silvery Tay.*

"He was unable to say how long he had dreamed over this great poem, but as it was no ordinary production, he knew it took him a long time.

"The Dundee newspapers give your public appearances considerable prominence.

" 'Oh, yes, they are very kind in that way, and I am proud to learn that there are two members of the Edinburgh press here to-night to write notices of my appearance in Newport. This night in Newport is the greatest step in my life.' "

"I was speaking to Annie the other day—she was asking about you; I didn't tell her much; she was looking for news; I didn't tell her you'd been away a few days last month; always an awful nosy woman, could never keep anything to——"

While she had been talking she was picking up children's clothes, straightening the room. Picking up his fallen newspaper she noticed he was asleep. Quietly she took his wide hat from the bed-post in the bed recess and hung it over his coat on the coat-hook back of the door . . . *just as he was sweeping it off with a courtly bow in the presence of Her Majesty, Queen of Great Britain, Empress of India.*

The few days away she had not mentioned to Annie had been an unprofitable excursion of McGonagall's to the west.

Starting with a twenty miles walk to Perth he managed to get permission to perform in a pub for a couple of nights but left the town with only a couple of shillings in his pocket. He had chosen a bad time to tour Perthshire; elections were being held, and every hall, schoolhouse, even smithy was in use. In Greenloaning he tried in vain to persuade the smith to let him have the premises for an evening, offering to clean out the cinders, etc., himself.

Tired, sore feet, hungry, he arrived in Stirling with sixpence in his pocket. . . . A cup of coffee and a penny roll, tuppence; and fourpence for a bed and that was it.

Without breaking his fast next morning he set off to Stirling Castle and managed to get a word with the Quartermaster; a kindly man who allowed him the use of the reading-room for an evening entertainment; and although this attracted only twenty of an audience, at least he got his breakfast, dinner and supper at the barracks; and then next day started on the long tramp back to Dundee. As a report which appeared some months later said of this and other desperate failures to establish himself as a star—

"Few men, unless they were endowed with nerves of brass, could have borne up so long and patiently in the face of rebuffs, slights and ridicule as McGonagall has done. If no one believes in his genius he is strongly convinced of it himself, and in full confidence of earning public favours he never once shrank abashed before a jeering audience. Persistence overcomes all difficulties. . . ."

And then had followed the success of Newport. At last the way seemed to be opening up for him.

In his dream he naturally took for granted the Queen's rapt interest, followed by her surprise that he had never been brought to her attention before. Her Gracious smile was encouraging him to think that some royal recompense for his past frustrations would be announced any second, when he awoke to his wife's angry shouts— not at McGonagall—

"Didn't I warn the both of you? Didn't I? Didn't I? What did I say before you went out? What did I tell the pair of you?"

101

"He made me——"

"Did not! She's a liar! It was her pushed me!"

"I NEVER! He made me; I was *falling*——"

"And she had to pull *me* in with her——"

"You're both going to bed this minute; your father'll——"

A sickening stench was getting stronger every second. "What's wrong in God's name? Are they hurt? What happened? What have you been doing for heaven's sake?"

"She pulled me——" "It was him, dad——" "Fell in the midden; come on—get them off; every stitch; quick!" as they hurriedly stripped off their stinking garments and tried to wipe their eyes at the same time.

"You'll have to take more heed of what your mother says. Look at you now, and the pair of you so nice going out. I'll get the bath out . . . there; what else will I do now?"

"You won't be able to help much. I'll wash these things as soon as I get them to bed, and that'll be NOW, are you both listening?"

"Would I be as well as to get out of your way then?"

"You would."

So he put on his frock-coat and wide-brimmed hat, and escaped the atrocious smell and the snivelling and threats. Outside, he decided to walk *down* the way, and along by the river and the broken bridge. He had not been down that way for a long time.

He remembered Jock coming home a few Saturday nights ago to tell them of the old man selling whelks in the market-place—"and there was this big bloke, a big drunken ploughman, says the whelks should be flung back into the river—and the old man after them; for everybody knew that whelks fed on dead bodies, and that the corpses they were fishing out the Tay were covered with them! Then another even bigger man said that was an old wives' tale—he was a whaler and he's seen *plenty* drowned people and never a whelk on them. . . . Anyway, *I* never bought any, dad!"

There had been much in the papers of Mr Law of the Institute of Civil Engineers' report in the Board of Trade Inquiry into the disaster, and the designer Bouch, raised to Sir Thomas no more than a year ago, was not coming out of the thing at all well. God help him too.

TAY BRIDGE FROM SOUTH (AFTER ACCIDENT) 1863 VX

The first Tay Railway Bridge, opened in 1878, the summer McGonagall walked to Balmoral—and back. The centre of the bridge was blown down in a gale on 28th December 1879, with the loss of lives of seventy passengers and crew on a train crossing at the time. Twenty-nine bodies were never recovered.

More than half the bodies had been recovered; the old men and the young men; grannies, mothers, maidens; bairns . . . the wee soul like his own Jamie, with his penny pencil . . . and the young man with the book of verse, Longfellow; a young man that might well have heard of the Poet of the Bridge of the Silvery Tay, and might well have hoped to hear him recite. Ah, God, God, it was a terrible catastrophe, not counting the men that had come to depend on the bridge one way and another for employment.

In the first few months after the tragedy there had always been crowds at the scene, whatever the weather; a few no doubt relations of the victims, but most just morbid sightseers, waiting for the divers or the boats with their grappling irons to bring up the pitiful cadavers or half-hoping for the even more fearsome pang of the silent suffering of a bleached face with black eyeless sockets.

There were not that many boats below the breached colossus. Work was going on from one of them according to the *chugging* echoing over the still water; still enough you would think to reveal all that lay even far, far below. There were a goodish number of people around, most of them keeping on the move, for loitering was not encouraged now, and constables kept up a patrol—even after dark with lanterns—to guard such relics of the dead which might be washed up and made off with; for it had been happening.

McGonagall stood for a while on the other side of the road, recalling his composing of his lines on the bridge. Now, many folk would be wondering why he had not already composed verses on the Disaster; he would be expected to; even as an *un*official laureate it befell him as his *duty*.

He would, he would. He would not shirk his duty. There would be an even more celebrated poem by McGonagall on the Fall of the Bridge of the Silvery Tay; but it was not time yet. All right to write of *distant* catastrophes as soon as you heard of them, but this—*this* required a little decent waiting; to seize immediately on a fellow-townsman's grief, no; he felt too much sympathy with them to do that.

But it *was* his duty, and in due course he would discharge that duty fittingly.

Meanwhile, the engine had been recovered and was beached at Tayport. (It was later repaired at Cowlairs, to have another forty-five

103

years of life, nicknamed The Diver by its crews) and there was no doubts about another bridge being built. . . .

A new bridge; and that would be another call upon his powers.

His lines on the old one had brought him a measure of fame; and he would not flinch from commemorating its fall. The new one; the phoenix . . . phoenix-like his verse would have to soar from the destroying of his first poem of celebration—and, aye, not without its warning note it would be pointed out!—to gain a new niche for McGonagall!

It would be a while before the Silvery Tay was spanned once more, and likely enough then the Queen coming to declare it open, And by that time, things going on with McGonagall the way they had been going lately; who knows but by *that* time——?

A refreshing breeze came off the river. He breathed deeply to get the last of the midden-stink out of his lungs. Gulls cried out and honked as if in irritable argument with the rhythmic chugging coming over the slow undulations of the mauve secrecy of the river—*as McGonagall marched ahead to a vista of royal red carpeting and with only the sound of the National Anthem in his ears.*

For I am going to London far away,
But when I will return again I cannot say.

CHAPTER TEN

IN mid-April the body of one of the Tay Bridge victims was
washed up on the shores of distant Caithness. A few days later
another appeared not very far at all from the scene of the disaster,
near the *Mars* Training Ship in the Tay. The remaining twenty-nine
of the seventy-five bodies were never recovered. In May the Court of
Enquiry sat for the last time and its Report was presented to
Parliament in June, condemning the construction and maintenance,
blaming Sir Thomas Bouch; against whom no action was to be taken,
it being thought he had suffered enough.

But as the star of the designer of the bridge waned, it seemed that
the star of the Poet of the Bridge was in the ascendant. On the fifth
of June 1880 there appeared under the heading—

"THE BARDS OF AVON AND THE TAY BRIDGE
Honour and Glory to McGonagall

"The scene of his triumph was the Argyle Hall, that classic spot
where 'Fizzy Gow' of immortal memory strutted his brief hour on
rickety planks. There McGonagall the Great held a grand levee on
Tuesday evening last. His friends rallied round him to a man on that
occasion, and gladdened his heart with a silver collection kindly
taken up with the hat in the interval between the first and second
parts of the programme. The audience, though composed wholly of
the sterner sex, was very select, intelligent, and appreciative. It was
whispered in certain circles that the Provost, Magistrates and Town
Councillors in a body, intended honouring the levee with their august
presence, but from some unexplained cause they failed to put in an
appearance. Doubtless these civic functionaries would be more at
home in deciding the respective merits of concrete and paving
blocks than on the poetry of McGonagall and Shakespeare. At
eight the chairman took his seat accompanied by a numerous and
influential body of supporters, and shortly after the Poet, arrayed in
Highland costume, made his appearance.

"As the gallant, all plaided and plumed in Rob Roy tartan, with a massive sword dangling by his side, stepped gravely on the platform and bowed his acknowledgment, the audience greeted him with lusty cheers renewed again and again. The chairman, a wag of the first water, introduced the hero of the evening by reading a long speech in which he ingeniously pointed out the intrinsic merits of McGonagall's 'poetry' over that of Burns and even Shakespeare. He said that they had met that night to decide the much-vexed question whether William Shakespeare, the Bard of Avon, or William McGonagall, the Bard of the Silvery Tay, ought to bear the palm. They were to be favoured with selections from the works of both these great men, and then the audience would decide the question by their vote. He concluded by calling on McGonagall to acquit himself like a man, and begin the proceedings by singing his matchless song, 'Forget Me Not.'

"McGonagall began operations by gravely adjusting a pair of 'specs' on his poetical nose. A kilted chieftain, armed with broadsword and dirk, and glittering with shining buckles, looked rather droll in a pair of 'specs,' but though the audience laughed McGonagall rattled on with his ditty. These 'specs,' we were afterwards informed, had been presented to him, as was his massive shoulder buckle which sparkled *like silver* in the gaslight. The buckle bore an inscription to the effect that it had been presented by 'A few friends.'

"The evening's entertainment was quite characteristic. 'Bruce at Bannockburn' was rendered with a vigour and force truly unique. When he reached the point in the narrative where the Scots charged the English, he drew his long broadsword and cut and slashed the empty air with the flashing blade like a thrasher on a barn floor, which made the chairman and the platform audience quickly evacuate the place of honour.

"A poem on the Newport Railway was much appreciated, especially where the poet gave vent to the aspect that he hoped its expenses would very soon pay..

"Amongst other novelties was a poem on the City of Perth, which informed all whom it may concern that the said city was situated on the beautiful Tay, and was one of the fairest cities of the present day. This piece, he remarked, was composed during a thunderstorm. He was then on a tour and was resting himself on the North Inch

Dion Boucicault (1822-1890), celebrated dramatist, who was impersonated in a hoax played on McGonagall in Stratton's Restaurant, Reform Street, Dundee, in June 1880.

admiring the beautiful scenery and the buttercups. A wag remarked that he believed McGonagall would have admired a butter biscuit better!

"At the conclusion of the entertainment, the chairman called on the audience to decide on the respective merits of the Bard of Avon and the Poet of the Tay Bridge by a show of hands. Not an arm was raised in defence of Shakespeare, but the vote in favour of McGonagall was carried by acclamation. The 'Poet' thanked the audience for the compliment and retired amidst roars of laughter and derisive cheers."

The year 1880 was not to be entirely roses all the way, however—

"McGonagall, William, the poet, had a cruel hoax played upon him, of which the *Weekly News* of June 12th gives an amusing account."

From the *Weekly News* of that date—

"CRUEL HOAX ON McGONAGALL: Shabby Treatment of the 'Poet.'

"*Hope deferred maketh the heart sick*, and a sick heart is followed with an aching head and all the other ills the flesh is heir to. If this be true, no man in Christendom, not to mention Dundee and Broughty Ferry, has suffered more from both head and heartache than our worthy townsman, McGonagall. Many a time and oft he has soared up beyond the moon on the wings of faith and hope only to come down again in double quick time. . . ."

A letter had arrived with the magic heading *Theatre Royal* where one of the celebrated Dion Boucicault's (actor, playwright; author of *Colleen Bawn*, etc.) companies was appearing—and the letter was from Boucicault referring to the favourable impressions he had gained of McGonagall from accounts of his entertainments in the newspapers.

"Furthermore," said McGonagall to his wife, adjusting his spectacles, "I am invited to lunch with Boucicault at Stratton's Restaurant——"

"That flash place in Reform Street?"

"The same, no less; to discuss terms, etc., for a starring role in one of his touring companies!"

"*When*, Willie?"

107

"Well, that has yet to be decided. I shall tell him I am at his disposal entirely, of course. You will be all right—and this time I'll be away earning considerable fees. Yes! I knew——"

"When is the lunch, as you cry it?"

"Today, today. Boucicault is obviously not a man to waste time."

"You'll have to put on Jock's clean shirt then; and I'll have to brush your hat and coat. . . ."

"There's plenty of time; the appointment isn't until twelve noon. Well, this looks like the end of our financial difficulties, then."

"Will you have to take the letter with you? Could you leave it—then I could show it to the grocer, and he'd maybe let us have a few more messages?"

"Well, we won't have to worry about *him* very long, now. I can't leave the letter, but I'll bring it back—I shall want to keep it anyway, of course."

"I wonder if I told the grocer about it—what's the gentleman's name again?"

"Boucicault, Dion Boucicault—everybody has heard of him. Better to wait until I come back with the letter—better still! I'll probably be offered an advance! Of course—there's costumes to think about and travelling expenses and one thing and another! Rest assured, while I am enjoying a good lunch you and the children won't be forgotten. He's bound to offer me something in advance—and if not, I will *ask* for it."

"Would you not be afraid of spoiling the thing, Willie?"

"*Spoiling*? After all, *he* is approaching *me*—*he* is seeking the favours. . . . Depend upon it, we will eat well tonight—and from now on! I'll be back as soon as I can, with an advance—a sizeable one."

The newspaper report continues—

"Prompt to the hour the poet called at the restaurant and enquired for Mr Boucicault. The attendant stared at the poet; but a 'friend' of the poet who just at that precise moment chanced to drop in, came to the rescue and offered to take him to the gentleman, who, he said, was patiently awaiting him in the smoke-room. . . .

". . . upstairs, he was led into the presence of a middle-aged man with a fine dark beard streaked with silver . . . who shook hands and expressed pleasure in the privilege of meeting one whose fame had spread over the whole habitable globe. . . .

"McGonagall was requested to take a seat, and 'Dion' went straight to the business in hand . . . if they could come to an arrangement for the poet to star in a tour of the provinces it would tend to their mutual benefit.

"The poet would be most happy.

" 'What are your terms?' promptly enquired 'Dion.'

"This was to the point, and meant business. The poet scratched his pow and thought for a moment. It would not do to sell his talent for an old song. A guinea a night might do in Dundee, but travelling is expensive. Taking all things into consideration, the poet finally came to the conclusion that two pounds a night was a modest salary to begin with.

" 'Oh, you are very reasonable,' replied 'Dion'; 'of course, we don't want to kill you right off. I am going to propose that you shall appear only four nights in the week and more if necessary.'

"Here the poet suggested he be paid twenty pounds a week, receive the first week's salary in advance, and give him five pounds expenses.

"To this arrangement 'Dion' at once agreed. But when McGonagall insisted that the engagement be written out and mutually signed . . . he jumped to his feet and went to the other end of the room and left the poet staring in astonishment at his eccentric patron.

"After some mutual friends 'chance' to drop in, it is decided that McGonagall should demonstrate his abilities; and with a red handkerchief tied round his waist and his trusty cudgel for a sword he launched into 'Bannockburn,' giving a performance that 'Dion' said would bring down the house in London.

" 'Forget Me Not' and 'Address to the Moon' were subsequently called for, until at last the poet sat on a chair, completely exhausted.

"Someone suggested that refreshments should be provided for the poet; and after some discussion as to what he would take, a glass of beer and a sandwich was called in. The poet looked askance at the scanty bill of fare, but as half a sandwich and a glass of bitter was better than no dinner, he restrained his feelings and partook of the bread and beer. Then 'Dion' and the company withdrew one by one . . . a faint suspicion now began to dawn on the poet's mind,

109

that the whole affair was not exactly up to 'dick' . . ."

He went round to the Theatre Royal that evening, and Mr Hodges the manager, pronounced the letter spurious. Boucicault was not in Dundee, never had been in Dundee. . . .

"We understand that the poet has put the matter in the hands of the authorities, who are busily engaged in investigating the circumstances, and we can assure the authors of this heartless hoax on a poor strugling genius, that they may yet be called upon to stand the poet a good dinner to compensate him for the one he was so shabbily cheated and deprived of."

In the *Autobiography of Sir William Topaz McGonagall* he writes at some length of the hoax. A few short extracts for comparison—

(After saying that he knew all the time 'Boucicault' was an imposter, he oddly enough agrees to give a sample performance) "Then he told one of the gentlemen to fetch in some refreshment for Mr. McGonagall, for he was more than delighted with my Bannockburn recital. Then a gentleman waiter came in with a little refreshment on a tea tray, simply

> *A penny sandwich and a tumbler of beer,*
> *Thinking it would my spirits cheer.*

And I remember I looked at it with a scornful eye before I took it, and I laid it down on a little round table beside me and screwed my courage to the stickingplace, and stared the imposter Boucicault in the face, and he felt rather uneasy, like he guessed I knew he wasn't the original . . . and before leaving he bade me good-bye, telling me he would see me again. Then I kept silent, and I stared the rest of my pretended friends out of countenance until they couldn't endure the penetrating glance of my poetic eye, so they arose and left me alone in my glory. Then I partook of the grand penny luncheon I had received for my recital of *Bannockburn,* and with indignation my heart did burn."

Then at the Theatre Royal, the manager, Mr Hodges, "asked me if I would let him make an extract from the letter and he would send it to Boucicault, so I said I would; so he made an extract, telling me he mentioned my poor circumstances in it, and he had no doubt but Mr Boucicault would do something for me by way of solation for my wounded feelings and for using his name in vain. He told me to come down to the theatre inside of three days, and he would have a letter from Boucicault by that time, he expected, so I thanked him for his kindness, and came away with my spirits light and gay.

"Well, I waited patiently till the three days were expired, then called at the Theatre Royal and saw Mr Hodges, the manager, and he received me very kindly, telling me he had received a letter from Mr Boucicault with a £5 cheque in it on the Bank of Scotland, so he handed me five sovereigns in gold along with Boucicault's letter."

Apparently McGonagall was advised of the arrival of the dramatist's letter through a letter from Mr. Hodges, the theatre manager, for, according to a newspaper report—

"The well-known poet gave an entertainment last evening (22nd June) in the Argyle Hall. During the proceedings the following letter was read amidst rapt applause—

Dear Sir,

On the publication of the particulars of the recent imposition upon you by some person representing himself as Mr Dion Boucicault I thought it my duty to bring the matter under the notice of the distinguished dramatist, author and actor. Some years ago, Mr Tom Taylor, the great playwright and present eminent editor of 'Punch,' declined to enter into controversy with a critic who had entirely misinterpreted the scene of one of his works, contenting himself that 'to answer a fool according to his folly' was but a mere waste of time. Mr Boucicault is indignant at the fraud practised in his name, but on your account only. In a communication I have received from him he says: "The hoax was a very cruel one. It was a heartless affair. I should be glad to give the Poet proof that actors are incapable of such unkindness. Tell him that all poets feel for one another, and that practical jokers are practical fools.' Mr Boucicault has entrusted me with the generous contribution of £5 as a solace for your feelings, and I shall be happy to hand the amount over on your calling tomorrow morning at the Theatre Royal. Those who imposed on you should at least double this. I may add that Mr M'Farland who was from home at the time of the occasion, expresses his deepest sympathy with you, in which, as you know, I join, and am

Yours truly,

J. M. Hodges,
Acting Manager, Theatre Royal.
Dundee, June 22nd, 1880.

111

£5! Five golden sovereigns!

"Oh, Willie, the joke fairly turned on them!"

"Aye. Now, you'll pay the grocer and the rent before another penny is spent."

"Do you not think you'd do better staying here just now anyway, while—while they seem to be on your side?"

"True enough, the affair seems to have brought a more sympathetic feeling towards me. But *now* is the time to storm the metropolis! And if I don't go now, when? The money will just slip away; and perhaps the sympathetic attitude won't last long enough for me to really establish myself. No; now is the time for London—and while I am fresh in Boucicault's thoughts; now is the time to go and offer my talent to him!"

"Right enough, Willie; you'd think he would give you a chance at least; that letter you read me could not have been more encouraging. But then it's maybe one thing while he's down there and you are up here."

"He'll welcome me. Apart from that London is full of theatrical opportunity. I'll go and see Boucicault first, of course; but there is Irving as well, you know. There are few opportunities here."

"Maybe—but look at the crowds that couldn't get in to see Irving that time he was here."

"That's just it, Jean—the London reputation. If *I* came back after a London success it would be the same! No, this is the time to take affairs at the flood!"

There was enough to pay the grocer and the rent and buy summer blouses for Mary and her mother and gutta-percha sandals for Jamie. . . .

A return passage to London on the boat was £1; and when he had made his intention known a surprising number of people had subscribed—small sums certainly—towards his expenses.

Then there was the farewell entertainment in Argyle Hall. . . . Packed with a noisy but good-natured audience. . . .

Weekly News, 26*th June*, 1880—

"Alas! alas! and has it come to this! McGonagall has bid farewell to Dundee, and tonight he embarks on the raging sea, to seek fortune and fame in 'London citie.' Reader, you need not stare so incredulously, it is a fact and no mistake. Wail and howl ye men of

112

Juteopolis, McGonagall who has so long gone about unrecognised amongst you has turned his back on your bonnie town and gone to London far away.

" 'Will ye no' come back again?' was the cry of many a sorrowing admirer, and the only answer we can give for their consolation is that recited by the Poet in his matchless farewell address, 'But when I will return again I cannot say.' Ponder deeply that line ye litteratii of Dundee, and you obdurate 'Smiths' of Perthshire, and consider whether you have done poetic justice to a poet worthy of the name. Have you not despised and rejected his rhymes, refused the free use of your 'smiddies' and offered him a sandwich instead of a dinner? But your sins have been visited on your own head; the Poet is gone though he is not yet dead. . . .

"The Poet has made up his mind to visit Metropolis on a starring campaign, either in Drury Lane, Covent Garden, or the taverns in Ratcliffe Highway, if he can find no better field for his 'talents.' The question will be asked, 'What induced him to embark on such a Quixotic undertaking?' The only answer that suggest itself is, because the Dundonians have failed to appreciate his talents; and as he has no intention of drowning his 'silvery' notes in the clatter of a jute carpeting loom, he determined to sell them in the highest market.

"Various circumstances conspired to hasten his departure from Dundee. For months and years he had borne with Spartan-like endurance—

The spurns which patient merit
From the unworthy takes,

but the last and unkindest cut of all was the cruel hoax played on him in Stratton's Restaurant the other day. That was the last straw. . . .

(His friends came to his aid) "with laudable liberality, a subscription was opened, and in a few days his passage money was made up, and his berth secured to London aboard the steamship *Britannia*.

(He consented to give) "a farewell *levee* in Argyle Hall, which came off with a great *eclat* on Tuesday night. Never before did those classic walls witness such a brilliant assemblage as that which gathered to listen to the last words of departing greatness. Long before the advertised time the body of the hall was completely filled, but so great was the influx of visitors that in the course of the evening the gallery doors had to be thrown open when the 'gods' rushed in like a torrent and filled the spheres above.

"Punctual to the hour the Poet, all plaided and plumed in his tartan array, appeared on the platform accompanied by his chairman, etc. . . . thunders of applause, waving of hats, stamping of feet whistling, cock-crowing, caterwauling and other demonstrations of delight, to all of which he gravely bowed his plumed head and smiled complacently.

"As usual, the Chairman introduced the Poet with a speech highly seasoned with compliments, and quotations from the works of McGonagall, and wound up with a valedictory address in rhyme which he modestly confessed was immeasurably inferior to the poorest efforts of the 'Poet of the Silvery Tay.'

"A long and varied programme was provided for the delectation of the guests. . . . Suffice to say that on this occasion he surpassed himself even if that were possible. 'Bruce of Bannockburn' was rendered with a lung power that would have made the fortune of a Forfar cadger, and we venture to say that if he had been in a 'tattie' field when he so valiantly drew his broadsword on the dastardly Southerners, he would have given a good account of the 'shaws.' The Chairman fled the platform in terror, and the audience in the reserved seats, who were in very close proximity to the stage, ducked their heads and shut their eyes as the glittering blade soughed over their heads; but luckily no one met with any harm beyond a slight scare. . . .

"One dull-brained fellow in the audience with no idea of the strength and force of true genius had the audicity to ask the Poet if he was 'on piece-work.'

(A new poem) "written last Sunday was read in public for the first time. . . . The internment of the late Rev. G. Gilfillan in the 'Burial of Sir John Moore' style . . . he entered, as he always does, into the minutest details of the scene. Amongst other choice bits of information, the piece set forth that '*On the Gilfillan internment day, Which took place at the Hill of Balgay, there was a very large array, upward of fifty cabs being in the procession I venture to say, and a strong body of police in grand array.*'

"All we can say is that McGonagall must be seen and heard before he can be appreciated. Tame, lame, and defective as his works appear in type, the sound and fury with which he thrusts them forth in the ears of his audience gives them a new and strange effect. No one can read McGonagall but McGonagall, or sing him either for that matter.

" 'Bannockburn' is worth all the money, and once heard will never be forgotten; and that ludicrous and sentimental rhapsody 'Forget Me Not' tickles the risible feelings to a painful degree. But the Poet is not straitened in his powers; without doffing the Highland garb or unslinging his broadsword, he fists the shillelagh and dashes off with the 'Rattling Boy of Dublin Town,' in which the audience takes up the chorus so lustily that they can hardly be prevailed upon to stop.

"In the course of the evening the following letter was read by the Chairman and received with great applause. . . ." (the letter from Hodges, the manager of Theatre Royal).

"At the close of the entertainment the Poet read the following farewell address which was specially prepared for the occasion—

Fellow Citizens of Dundee.
I now must bid farewell to ye.
For I am going to London far away.
But when I will return again I cannot say.

Farewell! Farewell! to the bonnie banks o' the Silvery Tay.
Also the beautiful Hill o' Balgay.
And the ill-fated Bridge o' the Silvery Tay.
Which I will remember when I am far away.

Farewell! to my friends and patrons all.
That rallied around me in the Music Hall.
And those that has rallied around me to-night,
I shall not forget when out of sight.

And if I ever return to Dundee again,
I hope it will be with the laurels of fame,
Plac'd on my brow by dame fortune that fickle Jade,
And to Court her favour I am not afraid.

Farewell! to every one in the Argyle Hall,
That has come to hear McGonagall,
Recite, and sing, his Songs to-night,
Which I hope will long be remember'd when I'm out of sight.

Adieu to all my enemies that want to mock me when passing by,
But I excuse them for their ignorance and leave them to the most
    high.
And, once again, my friends, and enemies, I bid ye all good-bye,
And when I am gone ye will for me heave a sigh:—

I return my thanks to my Chairman and my Committee,
For the kindness they have always shown me.
I hope the Lord! will protect them when I am far away,
And prosper them in all their undertakings by night and by day.

"In the reading of the above pathetic farewell the Poet threw into
it all his nervous energies, and every line was applauded to the echo.
The touching farewell he tendered to his Music Hall friends drew
forth a piteous howl from some of the 'gods' enthroned in the
gallery, and that brilliant allusion to the 'ill-fated Bridge of the
Silvery Tay' brought the back water to many an eye. But when he
reached the third stanza, the Poet rose to the dignity of the occasion.
With a bold stamp to his foot and a majestic wave of his arm, he
held the MSS. close to his spectacles, and shouted out with a sten-
torian voice the bold and dashing lines—

And if I ever return to Dundee again
I hope it will be with the laurels of fame

the effect was irresistible. The audience rose to their feet as one man
and cheered and yelled vociferously, waving their hats and stamping
their feet with enthusiasm. Again and again the cheers were renewed,
in the midst of which the Poet in vain attempted to proceed. At last
from sheer exhaustion the cheering subsided to a titter, when
McGonagall with renewed vigour read the couplet again.

"With reinvigorated lungs the audience cheered wilder and louder
than before. Again and again McGonagall read the couplet, and
again and again the cheering was rendered till the audience were
wearied of their exertions and lapsed into quietude. But the con-
cluding lines of the same stanza, which show the Poet is game to the

backbone and not afraid to court Miss Fortune, once more brought down the house. The final stanzas, though rather tame as compared with the centre of the piece, were on the whole well received. This concluded the entertainment, but did not cool the ardour of the Poet's friends.

"Pell-mell they rushed to the platform, and nearly overturned the Poet in their mad determination to render him the honour of a triumphal march home. The more rational of the pack, however, contented themselves with a farewell shake of the great man's hand. Those who were not fortunate enough to obtain a hold of his digits were consoled by the Chairman announcing that the Poet would be glad to see as many of his friends as could find it convenient to accompany him to the station steamer on Saturday afternoon. The announcement was received with three ringing cheers.

"We trust for the honour of Dundee that there will be a large turn-out on the occasion, and that though a Poet has gone from amongst us the world may see that his pluck is duly appreciated."

The above is an on-the-spot report, according to which McGonagall left for London on a Saturday on the steamship *Britannia*. But in "The Autobiography of Sir William Topaz McGonagall"—

"I remember it was in the month of June when trees and flowers were in full bloom, and on a Wednesday afternoon I embarked on board the steamer *London*." However, since this was written many years after the trip his memory may be excused.

"Gentlemen, if you please,
Stop throwing peas."

CHAPTER ELEVEN

THERE were holiday-week-and-farewell bottles of beer on the kitchen table in the McGonagall's front room of the but-and-ben in Paton's Lane.

McGonagall made no outright objection; they well knew his views on drink; anyway, they had company—Tom and his wife had come over to say farewell to their neighbour.

"It's a holiday he's after again, Jean!" Tom beamed, his round face red with summer sun and beer. "Here, Willie—have one glass—heavens knows when we'll see you again!"

He allowed Tom to pour half a cup of ale before he stopped him; this token sup on such an occasion to please friends could be overlooked. But he refused a drop from the half-bottle of whisky Tom now brought over from the dresser where he had set it on coming in; and he wasn't pressed. His wife, Jean, however, put up a transparently mock protest and took the dram, to hold the glass up and say "My!" archly to it.

"Good stuff,' said Tom, with a wink; "special; none of your shop whisky."

"Hey—you're forgetting your wife!" cried his wife in gay reproach.

"Ha—she doesn't need coaxing, Willie; don't have to force *her*, Jean!" His wife now held up a dram, cocking her head on one side to it as if affectionately regarding a child. The two women drank, quickly, and making shuddering faces after.

"Do you good," said Tom, filling cups with beer. "Make you sleep," with a wink to Jean that you could almost hear. "Well, you're getting grand weather by the look of it, Willie——"

"Would you not like to be going with him, Jean?" from Tom's wife.

"Na—they can keep London; Dundee's big enough for me! Too big; I've never seen the half of it yet for all the years I've lived in it!"

The Albert Institute; Public Library, Museum and Art Galleries complex where previously stood the wood and canvas "gaffs" where the young McGonagall first appeared in minor roles. Later, at the unveiling of the Burns Statue in 1884, he was turned away by the police.

"What about when your man sends for you, eh? You'll have to go down to your man, eh, Willie? Wait till you see the fine house he'll have ready for you in a little while—you'll not want to come back here. . . . Well, any way, Willie, the best of luck—eh?"

"I'd go in a minute," said Tom's wife, a sparkle in her eyes.

"We know, we know what YOU would do," from Tom, with another heavily confidential wink; "You'd appear without warning—aye, that's what she'd do, Jean; see what I was up to!"

"Well; what would you have to hide from your wife? Not jealous in case Willie gets nabbed by a London lass? Some bold hussies down there, they say, Jean!"

"What do you think he's going down for, eh? Eh, Willie?" nudging him with a beer bottle. "Ne'er mind, Willie," closing one eye and keeping it closed conspiratorially—"if I get wind that Jean plans to sneak in on you I'll send you a letter of warning—no—a telegram; send you a telegram, Willie!"

The drink that was turning Tom into a clumsy, semi-somnolent genial bear came out in the women in screeches of merriment. McGonagall was silent. There was nothing he could say here; they were not an audience for him—or even company; but he knew they meant well, and didn't show any disapproval . . . sipped at the bitter ale and waved his cup in a friendly manner to Tom.

"Now, you're sure, Willie?" as Tom thumped down a beer bottle and picked up the half-bottle of whisky; but didn't press him; turned to the women—

"Another wee drop, Jean—oh, I know *you'll* have another—here now, Jean; make you sleep."

The women looked at their held-up glasses with a fond interest again, drank quickly and shuddered. "Willie," said Tom, "*I'll* give *you* a song. . . ."

He stamped his foot clumsily twice, then with an emphatic swing of his right arm he threw his head up and—

"Bonnie Willie's now awa', awa' to—to London o'er the foam—"

"Come on!" his wife cried; "Time bonnie Tom was awa' to—to bed. Come on, now; let Jean and Willie get to their bed."

"Eh?" Tom stopped so suddenly and looked at them in such comic puzzlement that the women screeched with merriment again, clutching at each other's arms.

119

"Willie," he said, "You're not saying much; no offence, Willie, eh?"

"He can't get a word in for you; good-night then, Jean; good-night, Willie, we'll see you tomorrow before you go."

McGonagall lay awake long that night. Not worrying about the possible outcome of his expedition, but dwelling on what it might very well lead to—the rewards of *recognition*. And all stemming from the actions of those who sought to denigrate him. How strange how it had all worked out. The elaborate hoax that brought about Boucicault himself writing to him. A wonderful letter, that! He knew it by heart, and mouthed it to himself in the dark.

He had, of course, written to the playwright, advising him of his proposed visit to London, saying that he did not really expect *him* to give him the lunch he didn't get in Stratton's in Dundee. He had also written to Irving at the Lyceum. . . .

He lay recalling Irving's *Macbeth* and *Richard III* at the Theatre Royal three years before—and comparing his own readings of the roles. Certainly, Irving knew his Shakespeare, and was well worth queueing up to see, but he, McGonagall, had given the plays years of study, had the ability to bring out the depth. . . .

The Bells, played on his third and last night—now *that* was Irving; he'd grant him that—no one could touch Irving in that. . . . Boucicault, Irving—perhaps they could both offer him something; not unlikely . . . see what they offered . . . call on Boucicault first though . . . courtesy. . . .

He drifted into sleep; *and great red and gold curtains parted before him—revealing a vast sea of expectant faces.* . . . His wife rolled over onto her back and began to snore.

*   *   *   *   *   *   *   *

There was a fair crowd to see him off and "wish me success on my perilous enterprise, and to give me a hearty cheer my spirits for to cheer, and a merry shake of hands all round, which made the dockyard loudly resound. Then when the handshakings were o'er the steam whistle began to roar. Then the engine started, and the steamer left the shore, while she sailed smoothly o'er the waters of the Tay, and passengers' hearts felt light and gay. . . ."

After passing Broughty Ferry the passengers got up a concert, and McGonagall gave the company "Battle of El Tel-el-Kebir" and the "Rattling Boy" for an encore, for which he received "a small donation."

Without a doubt he would be extremely glad of even a small donation, for despite the five golden sovereigns, the subscribing from friends, etc., after he had paid for a week's lodgings in advance (fourpence per night in the White Horse Inn, Fetter Lane), he was left with one-and-ninepence. He was entirely dependent on something turning up—and fast. Capital; his talent, and a bag holding his few props which he took judicious care of—

"Well, as soon as I got ashore I held on by the Fish Market, and as I drew near very discordant sounds broke upon my ear; the babbling of the fishmongers was disagreeable to hear; and I had my properties with me in a black bag, and as I was passing along where there were about thirty men lounging near to the market-place they cried after me, 'Hi! Hi! Scottie, I'll carry your bag,' but I paid no heed to them, because I would never have seen it if I had allowed any one of them to have carried the bag."

He paid the landlord "and then I gave him my bag to lock up; then my mind felt quite at ease."

He wasted no time in trying to improve his circumstances; was immediately on his way to the Lyceum "and saw the janitor at the stage entrance, and I asked him if I could see Mr Irving, and he said snappishly I could not, and that Mr Irving wouldn't speak to the likes of me. Well, of course, I felt indignant, and I told him I considered myself to be as great a man as he is, and came away without delay. . . ."

His treatment at the Adelphi stage door when he sought to meet Dion Boucicault was even more disheartening, the card which he sent in being brought back to be torn before his eyes. All right; there were no lack of Music Halls in the teeming Metropolis, there must be many opportunities; and given even a start in the most lowly unpretentious, he would soon rise to stardom. But there was no opening at all for McGonagall; except—

"How did you get on today, Scottie?"

"Not a thing. I am forced to consider giving up hope of finding use for my talents in London."

"Like me, you need an audience."

"Very true."

"YOU can't find an audience, right?"

"That is right, without a doubt."

"*I* have an audience, every day, every night, any time. I never have to look far for an audience."

"Well, then, you are fortunate."

"There's plenty of them; enough for you as well."

"Oh?"

"Of course, *You* think you have to get *inside* the theatre to get any one to listen to you, and more important, *pay* for listening to you? That's where you are wrong. You don't have to be *inside*—you don't need to be able to get *inside* a theatre before you can perform—before you can give your entertainment. Audiences? There's dozens of them all over the place, just waiting for you—and me—to entertain them; the crowds *outside* the theatres, waiting for omnibuses, going in and out of shops. London is full of people going about the streets; some of them—enough of them, can spare a minute to listen, and give a copper for the privilege——"

"I have no doubt but that you manage to ——"

"I don't starve. What I'm trying to tell you is, there's room for two. For a good bit of the time I could do with help . . . even just someone to pick up the coins. With another performer. . . . Look——"

"Now wait. You are suggesting that——"

"That you join me. I can get my breath back now and then. Listen, one could be performing—me on the whistle or you singing, while the other one picks up the money—better still, goes round with the hat. One of us performs, the other is collecting; it would man more money with less bother. What about it, eh? An audience? There's millions out there just waiting for someone to give them a song or a tune. Are you game to give it a try, Scottie? I think we'd make a fortune!"

"In other words you are suggesting that I——"

"Come into partnership."

"Join you?"

"Well, you can sing; turn about performing and passing round the hat. Two's always better——"

"I am indebted to you for your thoughtfulness, but. . . . Well, I haver yet performed under such circumstances. No. If nothing turns

Sir Henry Irving. He appeared in Dundee several times during McGonagall's lifetime. In November 1894 in Edinburgh, Ellen Terry and he called on McGonagall who was also performing there.

up tomorrow I will just return home to Bonnie Dundee, where my friends will be delighted to once again welcome me. I could not perform on the streets with you; but I appreciate the good turn you are trying to do."

He embarked on Saturday and was back in Dundee on Wednesday, glad to see family and friends again, and bringing a poem with him; herewith a sample from "Jottings of London"—

> *As I stood upon London Bridge,*
> *And viewed the mighty throng*
> *Of thousands of people in cabs and buses*
> *Rapidly whirling along,*
> *And driving to and fro,*
> *Up one street and down another*
> *As quick as they could go.*
>
> *Then I was struck with the discordant sounds*
> *Of human voices there,*
> *Which seemed to me like wild geese*
> *Cackling in the air.*

He went to the Tabernacle to hear the greatest preacher he had ever heard, with the exception of Gilfillan—

> *Then as for Mr Spurgeon,*
> *He is a divine surgeon,*
> *Which no one can gainsay.*
> *I went to hear him preach on the Sabbath day,*
> *Which made my heart feel light and gay*
> *For to hear him preach and pray.*

July 20*th*, 1880:

McGONAGALL RETURNS FROM LONDON
Consolation and Presentation to the "Poet"

"The hall was crowded from ceiling to floor by a respectable and appreciative audience." (The Marine Hall, Marine Place, Hawkhill.)

The Chairman began by giving a graphic account of McGonagall's adventures in the big city—"The only offer he got was from a fellow lodger, a young man who earned an honest penny by playing a tin whistle in the streets. . . .

"In the course of the evening, the Chairman, in the name of the 'Ninth Ward Dramatic Club,' presented the Poet with the 'gold' medal of the Club as a token of their appreciation of his genius. . . .

"At the close a gentleman moved the following resolution: 'That this meeting appoints a deputation to wait on the Provost and Magistrates to memorialise their honours to take into consideration the propriety of conferring the freedom of the Burgh on Poet McGonnagall.' The resolution was seconded and carried unanimously.

"Another gentleman moved that a committee be appointed to raise subscriptions to present the Poet with a silver service. He also proposed that steps should be taken to memoralise Her Majesty to depose Tennyson from his office of Poet Laureate and instal McGonagall as perpetual Poet to the Queen. The gentleman concluded an eloquent speech by expressing the hope that when McGonagall had shaken off this mortal coil his sacred dust should be entombed in Poets' Corner in Westminster Abbey. All three resolutions were carried with acclamation and the meeting quietly dispersed."

A *respectable and appreciative audience*; or an audience which had really turned up to appreciate the mocking? Yet, for Dundee it *was* a comparatively well-behaved crowd; and if their behaviour made it only too clear they were welcoming back a favourite "worthy" rather than setting the laurel wreath about the noble brow of a peerless laureate, at least it *was* a welcome. . . furthermore, the hall was full, and no one had thrown anything. Oh, McGonagall was happy enough to be back; compared with other receptions in other places it was indeed like going down the primrose path to the sound of flutes.

* * * * * * * *

Eighteen hundred and eighty . . . looked like being a memorable year for McGonagall? True to a great extent so far. The tables turned on the hoaxers, financially; and if the trip to London had not led to fame and fortune, at any rate he *had* been to London, a journey which probably very few of his mockers would achieve in their lifetimes. Now he would build upon the kindlier tolerance audiences at home appeared to have towards him? Could he even perhaps begin to lose a little of his buffoon image?

Could he hell—at least not for very long. . . .

Not very many weeks later in the Thistle Hall—

"ROUGH RECEPTION OF THE POET. McGonagall is still alive and struggling on in his endeavour to win fame and fortune. He has succeeded in gaining a wide notoriety, the goal of his ambition financially is about as far distant as ever. A few will-o'-the-wisps have lured him on lately, but just as he had got the glittering baubles in his hand grasp they vanished like the baseless fabric of a dream and left not a copper behind. A document was handed to him one night in a public meeting which purported to be a communication from Her Majesty to confer on him the honour of knighthood accompanied with a bank cheque for £7. 'Sir William McGonagall' still sounds well, but alas, the latter turned out to be a forgery and the cheque a sham.

"Close on the heels of that came another letter from a certain Jack Sheppard who professed to be a great admirer of the poet's genius. Enclosed was a cheque on the City of Glasgow bank for £20, to be applied for the purpose of erecting a wooden theatre wherein the Poet could display his talents. The cheque was signed Dick Turpin & Co. We need not inform the general public that both the firm of Dick Turpin & Co. as well as the famous City Bank have stopped payments long ago.

"Deceived and hoaxed by pretended friends the poet turned aside sick and heartsore. Still he had one bright star of hope to cheer him on. He and his son. . . ."

His son Jock.

Jock had for long wanted to follow in his father's footsteps.

"Oh dear no—one's enough!" Jean would seek to dissuade him.

Maybe indeed to Jock's young mind it was merely a case of seeing his father enviably free from the need to answer the early morning call of the mill hooters, no more than an entirely sensible wish to be free.

Until recently McGonagall had refused to let him accompany him; there had been many, many occasions when he would have been sorry to have anybody's laddie on the platform with him. But of late, things having improved and seemingly to get better, he had let Jock come along; not to perform so far, although he had a fairish voice, at home anyway, and could whistle a bit; and was always talking about buying a melodeon if he made enough money (you could get one for six shillings). So far he had not attempted enter-

125

taining, had been along more to see what went on from the other side of the footlights, to help with changes of costume and things like that; a kind of junior manager, or rather stage manager—which was, after all, the way his father had started.

He certainly didn't take Jock along as a kind of bodyguard; yet in a way that was the role he was most suited to, with his harum-scarum independent nature. In the long run Jean came to believe that he probably would be better off with his father; and they would know where he was. . . .

The newspaper report continues—

"He and his son, who bids fair to fill his father's shoes, had arranged to give a grand entertainment in the Thistle Hall on Saturday evening last.

"Great things were expected to come out of this affair. Blue, green and yellow hand-bills *a la* Music Hall were widely circulated through the mills, factories, and other public places announcing that McGonagall, Vocalist, Poet & Tragedian, was to be supported by his son and a long list of professionals, male and female.

"Saturday night came, and the hall having been duly hired and paid for, the doors were opened to the public at the advertised time. Instead of his fellow-townsmen rallying round him in their thousands as he confidently expected, the whole audience scarcely numbered a hundred. There were a few ladies, but the majority were composed of young blades who seemed ready-prepared to make a 'night' of McGonagall.

"The roughs were determined to be jolly. Half-a-dozen youths who had invested 2d. each in tin trumpets took possession of the gallery and began to act as a voluntary orchestra. While the audience were mustering the trumpeters blew with might and main. The effect was deafening. It was nearly half-an-hour past the time when the audience were informed that the local talent would not go on unless the lessee, McGonagall, 'stumped up first,' and as poor Mac had no money and the doorkeeper had taken nothing to speak of, the professionals had to be dismissed.

"Deprived of his grand supporters the Poet began himself. The 'Rattling Boy' went rattling off accompanied by a roaring chorus and trumpet blasts of an unearthly character. 'Bannockburn' was fought

126

amidst the braying of trumpets and vociferous cheering, so loud and long that the Poet was effectually drowned.

"Next he made his appearance as Macbeth, in a new costume glittering with silvery spangles. The trumpets blew a louder blast, the boys gave a louder cheer, but it was plain to be seen McGonagall they would not hear. The platform was invaded, and the Poet, afraid of his spangles, bolted for the ante-room and prepared to disrobe. He had only got his toilet half-completed when the roughs burst into the green-room like a torrent, and in their flurry to see the Poet they upset buckets of water all over the properties and soaked them as thoroughly as if they had been put in the wash-tub.

"The Poet and his son lost their tempers, and the junior threatened to fight all-comers and sundry. At last, the hallkeeper turned off the gas on the platform and intimated that 'it was all over' with the Poet. The audience then began to disperse, and left the Poet to gather up his traps and wander home.

"We are afraid this has turned out a rather unfortunate spec. for poor McGonagall. Really, we would seriously advise him to abandon poetry and the drama, and turn his attention to some more lucrative occupation, as it is pretty evident the present generation are not prepared to appreciate his talents. Whether he will get justice at the hands of generations as yet unborn is a question we leave time to answer."

What had happened to the goodwill so evident on his return from London?

The phrase had not yet been coined; had it been, McGonagall was certainly of a sufficiently philosophical nature to have used it to Jock later . . ."*Well, that's show business!*"

That was in October. Did there follow then a period of analysis, self-reappraisal, a time to develop a new entertainment?

If there was such a period it was a shortish one. In November appeared the advertisement—

McGONAGALL IN EXCELSIS

Trades Hall, King's Road

Friday the 26th at 8.30 p.m.

127

"No other poet in the universe can extract laughter from the solemn pageantry of a funeral."—*Madagascar Murderer.*

"But he stood like a modest tobacconist's sign, with his tartan curtain around him."—*Delhi Times.*

Come Early and Bring Sixpence.

Nothing here to encourage him to think he would get much of a fair hearing on this occasion. But in a real trouper style—and if anyone ever earned the title of Super-Trouper it was McGonagall—in the finest tradition The Show Would Go On.

One suspects that then, as now, materialism was as much involved as idealism . . . *Bring Sixpence.* . . .

How did it go, then? A report appeared next day—

"The famous Poet of the Tay Bridge made another personal appearance last night which was more successful in a financial point of view than his last speculation in the Thistle Hall. The scene of the Poet's triumph was the Trades' Hall, King's Road, where about 200 ardent admirers assembled fully prepared to give him a warm reception. When we reached the door a few minutes late we found it besieged by a band of rough and roistering youths who were bent on having a share of the fun for nothing; but the money-taker had taken the precaution to bar the door on the inside and keep them out in the cold. It was therefore with some difficulty that we gained admittance; and when we were at last ushered into the crowded hall we found the audience laughing heartily at the Chairman's speech.

"The fun and frolic began in earnest, however, when the Poet rose at the call of the Chairman and began to read from a sheaf of foolscap his notorious poem on Gilfillan's funeral, which was followed by the 'Tay Bridge Disaster.' Both these pieces may be classed as 'sublimely ridiculous.' One of the audience inquired pertinently if this was 'a new disaster,' but the Chairman quietly informed him it was the old affair. The Poet was greeted at the close of these pieces with a volley and a shower of green peas. This last salute called forth an involuntary couplet from the gifted bard which deserves to be immortalised. Smarting under the shower of eatables he exclaimed—

Gentlemen, if you please,
Stop throwing peas!

128

"When 'Bannockburn' was announced, the 'gods' sounded the charge on a toy drum accompanied by a 'crawmill.' The cheering when the celebrated charge was made was perfectly deafening. The warrior Poet was encored, and had to fight the battle all over again.

"An interval of five minutes was allowed to give the Poet time to recover his breath during which his son appeared on the platform and mumbled some incoherent jargon in a weak, squeaky voice which was completely drowned by the shouts of laughter of the audience.

"A gentleman remarked that the foolishness of the father was more perfectly developed in the son—a remark which all present fervently endorsed.

"The 'Rattling Boy' concluded the entertainment, and the Poet rattled away at the rattling song amidst a rattling fire of green peas by the audience. At the close, the Chairman invited the Poet's friends to shake hands with him, when there was a general rush to the ante-room.

"The pressure of admiring spirits proved rather obnoxious to the Poet, who lost his temper, and to rid him of his tormentors he drew his broadsword and drove the mob into the hall like a flock of frightened sheep."

Poor Jock! Had he been alive today, with electronic apparatus to put him across, he would certainly be a leading show-biz personality. "Son of McGonagall," he couldn't miss! Or, William McGonagall Jr.,' for he would probably shrewdly change his Christian name. . . .

He did, in fact, eventually change his name—the McGonagall part, glad to dissociate himself.

It didn't work out for Jock, although he was to persist for a while yet.

'Twas in the month of December, and in the year 1883,
That a monster whale came to Dundee . . .

CHAPTER TWELVE

THE year 1881 was notable for terrible storm periods of extraordinary length. Scotland escaped the first, the great snowstorm of January 18th. The Thames overflowed, by evening every southern railway was blocked; at one time during that day 113 trains on the Great Western were stuck at various stations.

In the first week of March, Scotland was hit by the worst snowstorm since 1827. It lasted three days, and by the Saturday all railways in the north and east were completely blocked. Mountains of ice froze across the Caithness line.

In between times, there was still space to mention McGonagall. 12*th February*, 1881.

McGONAGALL AT ARBROATH

"In the Trades Hall, Arbroath, the Poet made his appearance on Saturday evening. Mr Scott, conductor of a star company of vocalists and company, secured the Trades Hall Theatre for that night, had issued bills on which the name of this popular author appeared, the result being a full house. The other members of the company, including Mr Boyack, a comic singer, were fully up to the mark in their varied departments, but it was evident that the Poet was an attraction, as repeated calls were made for him previous to his appearance.

"At length the time came, and also the man, McGonagall, clad in 'the garb of Old Gaul' with a claymore at his side . . . after graceful acknowledgment of the applause . . . he burst out with the sublime and patriotic composition, 'The Bruce of Bannockburn' . . . some fine passages were inaudible from the vehemence with which they were delivered. In his ardour he seemed to be under the impression that the 'Proud Usurper' with his bows and spears was about to cross the Brothock . . . drew his claymore with which he commenced a vigorous onslaught on the foe. While doing so he ceased speaking for a few minutes during which he walked majestically from side to side of the stage, making ferocious sweeps with his claymore, each of which was intended to do for a southern. From a minute observation and tally kept we are assured that had Edward's forces been there, 128 of the flower of his army would have 'bit the dust.'

"At first the fiddles made their escape from the front or got down under their seats, and the little boys who were clustering behind the orchestra also retired to a safe distance.

"When the onslaught was over, and the battle won, Edward now being at Dunbar, the Poet resumed his narrative, much of which was lost, however, amid cries of 'Tay Bridge' and so on. On the whole, McGonagall had a warm, though somewhat boisterous reception. His 'Rattling Boy' was a success, the whole gallery joining in the elegant and expressive chorus."

Undoubtedly a success; soon to be followed by another. Off he went again—

From the *Brechin Advertiser*—

"A DUNDEE BARD AT BRECHIN.   The renowned 'Bard of the Silvery Tay'—Mr McGonagall—honoured Brechin with his presence on Thursday evening (April 28th, 1881), when a large and enthusiastic meeting—called by tuck of drum—welcomed him in the Crown Hotel Hall.

"A local gentleman of well-known histrionic powers occupied the chair. The programme consisted of original readings, including 'Bannockburn,' the 'Burns Statue,' 'Living in London,' 'History of Wallace,' and selections from Shakespeare. Here is a fine morsel from the 'Burns Statue'—

This Statue, I must confess, is magnificent to see,
And I hope it will long be appreciated by the people of Dundee;
It has been beautifully made by Sir John Steel,
And I hope the pangs of hunger he will never feel.

The Statue is most elegant in its design,
And I hope it will defy all weathers for a very long time,
And I hope strangers from afar with admiration will stare
On this beautiful Statue of thee, Immortal Bard of Ayr.

Fellow-citizens, this Statue seems most beautiful to the eye,
Which would cause Kings and Queens for such a one to sigh,
And make them feel envious while passing by
In fear of not getting such a beautiful Statue after they die.

"The pieces were introduced in a racy manner and altogether the entertainment was unique in its way."

He was touring the little towns of the county of Angus on the crest of a wave. And then, on the following Monday, at Montrose—

"THE McGONAGALL. The illustrious man of whom Dundee is so justly proud gave one of his famed entertainments in the Masonic Hall on Monday night . . . which was attended by a number of young gents, who in a certain sense, properly designate themselves 'the chosen spirits of Montrose.' It would be difficult to say who was in the chair, as the occupation of that position during the evening varied so much from their respective anxieties to relieve the unbearable intensity of their feelings by an indescribable combination of zoological cries.

"Still the McGonagall went on. He sang a song of his own about bonnie Montrose which was so rapturously received that a 'choice young spirit' in a state of great cerebral excitement declared that the mighty genius before them ought to be Poet Laureate, and that Tennyson should be called upon to resign. The climax was reached, however, when the McGonagall sword in hand, was singing a terrific battle piece. The bump of combativeness became so simultaneously roused in the heads of all the 'chosen spirits' that they commenced attacking the lecturer and each other from a bag of flour in the possession of one of the choicest spirits. To add further to the effect of the blinding, mealy battery, the lights were put out, and confusion reigned supreme. On their being relighted, the appearance of the McGonagall and the flour bag combatants was ghastly in the extreme; but all except the great man before them seemed to be wildly delighted with the ordeal which they had so gallantly passed through.

"The McGonagall, shaking the dust off his coat, departed, and was most honourably escorted to the model lodging-house by a considerable number of the 'chosen spirits' who, on their way, were

132

loud in their protestations of the great admiration which they entertained for him."

Show business? That's how it goes.

As far as available records go he seems to have laid low for some time after this.

In May 1881 was passed an Act of Parliament authorising the construction of a new Tay Railway Bridge at a reduced height of 77 feet.

He had been reciting his "Tay Bridge Disaster" for some time now. There was to be a new bridge; there would be new lines.

In July terrible gales swept Scotland, the Shetland Isles suffering particularly; sixty fishermen losing their lives, leaving families destitute. Dundee subscribed generously to a fund organised; alas! McGonagall had not risen high enough in his chosen profession to be able to give an entertainment for charity!

In 1881 Disraeli and Carlyle died; President Garfield was shot in America to later die.

It was also the year of the Wet Review in Edinburgh. Neil Munro, who was there, describes in "The Brave Days," how it bucketed down from the first rendezvousing at 6 a.m. until evening "when the last battalion marched past the saluting-base ankle-deep in mire. . . .

"So many soldiers died as the result of this pageantry that medals were half-expected . . ." and Queen Victoria relates in her Letters that she had to strip to the skin afterwards.

McGonagall, who was not there, also wrote about it—

THE ROYAL REVIEW
August 25, 1881

All hail to the Empress of India, Great Britain's Queen—
Long may she live in health, happy and serene—
That came from London far away,
To review the Scottish Volunteers in grand array;
Most magnificent to be seen,
Near by Salisbury Crags and its pastures green,
Which will be long remembered by our gracious Queen—

And by the Volunteers that came from far away,
Because it rained most of the day.
And with the rain their clothes were wet all through,
On the 25th day of August, at the Royal Review.
And to the Volunteers it was no lark,
Because they were ankle-deep in mud in the Queen's Park,
Which proved to the Queen they were loyal and true,
To endure such hardships at the Royal Review. . . .

God help them—they had no choice!

These were the verses McGonagall enclosed when he wrote to the Queen in October, receiving in reply from Sir Henry F. Ponsonby, Private Secretary to the Queen—

"General Sir Henry F. Ponsonby has received the Queen's commands to thank Mr McGonagall for sending the verses which were contained in his letter of the 10th instant, but to express Her Majesty's regret that they must be returned, as it is an invariable rule that offerings of this nature should not be received by the Queen.

| | Privy Purse Office, |
| 17th October, 1881. | Buckingham Palace, S.W." |

Despite this polite rejection, the verses still retained after the title "Patronised by Her Majesty."

The effusion is dated September 23rd. . . . From October to the end of the year almost unbroken storms swept the country. Two hundred fishermen drowned between Berwick and Dunbar; the steamer *Clan Macduff* was lost, etc., etc.

In November the engineers made preliminary arrangements for building the new Tay Bridge, and in December the Sailors' Home was opened. McGonagall appears to have let these events pass him by.

Perhaps after all he *was* beginning to get discouraged?

No, he wasn't.

*   *   *   *   *   *   *   *

He seems to have kept out of the news for almost a year after the return of his verses from Buckingham Palace.

General Sir Henry F. Ponsonby has
received the Queen's commands to
thank Mr. McGonagall for sending
the Verses which were contained in
his letter of the 10th inst., but to express
Her Majesty's regret that they cannot
be received, as it is an invariable
rule that offerings of this nature
should not be received by the Queen.

17th October 1881.
Privy Purse Office.
Buckingham Palace. S.W.

Mr. William McGonagall
19 Smith's Buildings
Paton's Lane
Dundee

H.F. Ponsonby

From Sir Henry Ponsonby at the Privy Purse Office, Buckingham Palace,
returning verses sent to Queen Victoria.

Photo by kind permission of Dundee Public Libraries (Copyright).

Perhaps it would be more accurate to say *was kept out*, editors having decided he had gone out of fashion as a target. And/or this could have been a period when the magistrates put a ban on his entertainments on the grounds of their being rife causes of public disorder, encouraging hooliganism, etc.

If he was prevented from making public appearances, then he would assuredly still compose, publish and push his effusions, relying on this and such money as the family, including his wife, brought in from working to support him while "resting."

A piece from this period is "A Tribute to Mr Murphy and the Blue Ribbon Army—

> *All hail to Mr Murphy, he is a hero brave,*
> *That has crossed the almighty Atlantic wave,*
> *For what purpose let me pause and think—*
> *I answer, to warn the people not to taste strong drink.*

At times, when McGonagall is holding forth on something he feels sincerely and deeply about, it comes through . . . at such times his muse is like a beautiful, wise woman, who has drunk a little too much, sufficient to slur her speech somewhat—and to be honest, more than somewhat at times; enough to make her stumble, comically catch a heel in her dignified skirts now and then. . . .

A few stanzas later we have—

> *And he exclaims in the agony of his soul—*
> *Oh, God, I cannot myself control*
> *From this accurs'd cup!*
> *Oh help me, God, to give it up!"*

We are hardly aware of the slurring and stumbling, for this is something deeply felt. Alas, the unsteadiness of the muse the next moment is such that we cannot seriously pay attention to its sermonising—

> *And causes the drunkard with pain to groan,*
> *Because it extracts the marrow from the bone.*

Of the same year is "The Battle of Tel-el-Kebir."

This McGonagall sent to Sir Garnet Wolseley; and in the *People's Journal* 18th November 1882—

"Among the many poets who have celebrated the victory of Tel-el-Kebir, none has attracted a higher distinction than the Dundee minstrel Mr McGonagall. The subjects was one fitted to stir the

135

'muse' of that most patriotic poet, and the result has been a production which has elicited the following comment dated from the War Office and addressed to Mr William McGonagall, Poet, 19 Smith's Buildings, Paton's Lane, Dundee.

" 'Sir Garnet Wolseley has to thank Mr McGonagall for his letter enclosing some verses on the battle of Tel-el-Kebir, which he is much pleased with:—Horse Guards, War Office, 13 November, 1882.'

"We have been favoured by Mr McGonagall with a copy of the poem from which we give the following extracts for the benefit of our readers—

> *Ye sons of Great Britain come join with me,*
> *And sing in praise of Sir Garnet Wolseley;*
> *Sound drums and trumpets cheerfully,*
> *For he has acted most heroically.*
>
> *He has gained for himself fame and renown;*
> *Which to posterity will be handed down;*
> *Because he has defeated Arabi by land and by sea,*
> *And from the battle of Tel-el-Kebir he made him to flee.*
>
> *With an army about fourteen thousand strong,*
> *Through Egypt he did fearlessly march along,*
> *With the gallant and brave Highland brigade,*
> *To whom honour is due, be it said.*
>
> *Arabi's army was about seventy thousand in all,*
> *And, virtually speaking, it wasn't very small;*
> *But if they had been as numerous again,*
> *The Irish and Highland brigades would have beaten them,*
>   *it is plain.*

Surprisingly, the assassination of the Russian Czar did not "stir his muse," nor did the death of President Garfield of America through wounds received months earlier from an assassin—or that of Sir Thomas Bouch the previous November, the designer of the first Tay Railway Bridge, who had retreated into a kind of quiet insanity after the Court of Inquiry laid blame at his door.

"The Sunderland Calamity" was something he did get his teeth into—

'Twas in the town of Sunderland, and in the year of 1883,
That about 200 children were launched into eternity
While witnessing an entertainment in Victoria Hall,
While they, poor little innocents, to God for help did call.

In a stampede at a giving-out of presents the victims were trampled to death. He goes into considerable macabre detail in the fifteen verses which follow; but for all the bathos, lumbering metre, his considerable horrified compassion comes through.

Less dramatic is "The Inauguration of the University College, Dundee," which includes the memorable lines—

I hope the ladies and gentlemen of Dundee will try and learn
  knowledge
At home in Dundee in their nice little College,
Because knowledge is sweeter than honey or jam,
Therefore let them try and gain knowledge as quick as they
  can.

But the choicest composition of this period was "The Famous Tay Whale"—

'Twas in the month of December, and in the year 1883,
That a monster whale came to Dundee,
Resolved for a few days to sport and play,
And devour the small fishes in the silvery Tay. . . .

An eye-witness account in the *Dundee Advertiser*, Monday, December 10th—

"The whale still continues its pleasant gambols in the river and affords a lively subject of conversation to passengers between the Ferry and Dundee, as well as a desultory excitement to a few whalers, professional and amateur.

"On Saturday morning he was seen somewhere off Newport, and again down by the beach shortly after . . . enough to bring out a couple of steam launches, each fully manned with a daring and determined crew of hunters, and accompanied with all the necessary apparatus for butchering the noble leviathen now playing such havoc among the sprats. They had guns, harpoons, lances, and fish-knives aboard, and all they wanted was a whale on which to operate."

It was still at large at the end of the year—

137

"During the week the whale has afforded additional exercise to several crews of Dundee whalers.

"Repeated attempts were made to capture it, but the shots, as on former trials, did not find a lodgment in any part of the body. . . .

"Yesterday afternoon, between one and two o'clock, a splendid sight, and one of the most unusual character in these latitudes, was witnessed at Broughty Ferry. About 400 yards from the shore, right abreast of the Harbour, the whale leaped clean out of the water. The movement, which was repeated twice at brief intervals, is described as similar to a salmon's leap, only a little slower.

"It rose at first almost perpendicularly, and when clear of the water, fell forward on its side, causing a terrific commotion as it alighted heavily in the river, which at the time was as calm as a loch.

"After disporting itself for some time, it proceeded down the estuary, rising to the surface and blowing at intervals."

A correspondent commented that the whale had obviously known it was Sunday, and that the blubber-hunters would be in church.

From the point of view of its own good, the whale could not have chosen a more unsatisfactory river in which to flaunt itself.

Dundee had been a celebrated whaling port for a long time, and was helped to keep going through the happy chance of whale oil being just the medium for softening jute fibre to make it workable.

(In that year, 1883, thirteen vessels were engaged in the whale and seal fishing; six vessels at Newfoundland accounting for 92,000 seals (!), seven at Greenland for 20,000, between then 1,500 tons of oil. From Davis Straits six vessels brought seventeen whales; and from Greenland two vessels brought 101 bottle-nose.)

So what of the whalers' tales of deadshot harpoonists in icy, pitching seas? This one was laughing at them, and *had* to be got.

Did they get it? Well, like in so many fishermen's tales, *nearly*.

The whale having disported itself so flagrantly on the last day of the year would lead to midnight jests from first-footers—the custom of bringing in the New Year by the first foot to cross the threshold after midnight bringing a small present. . . . *Hoagmanay* in Scots; a time for friends to get together over a dram and wish each other luck in the years to come. . . . A popular first-footing present was a red herring; and so—

"Come in, come in—Happy New Year——"

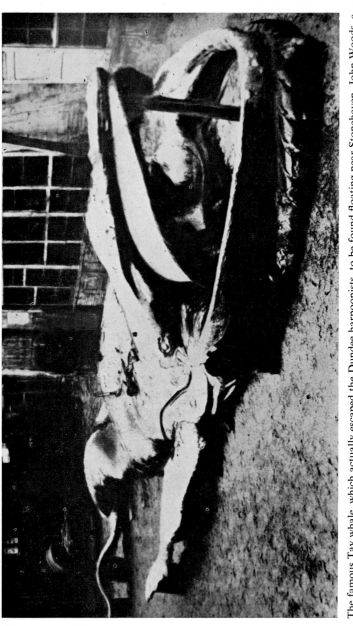

The famous Tay whale, which actually escaped the Dundee harpoonists, to be found floating near Stonehaven. John Woods, a Dundee showman, bought it for exhibition in the city, the bones eventually going to the museum, where they may still be seen. McGonagall's wish to have his stanzas on the whale shown alongside has now been granted.

"Same to you; here; I *was* going to bring you a *whale* but they wouldn't let me on the tram with it!"

And—

"Come in, come in, Tom; where's the wife—oh, there she is; a Happy New Year——"

"Give us your hand, Willie; Happy New Year. Here; I *was* going to bring you a *whale*, aye? She'll tell you, Willie; but we were afeard it would get stuck in the close! Ha, ha, ha. . . . You'll have to be writing poetry about the whale, eh?"

"He's waiting till they catch it—eh, Jean? My, you wonder how they ever brought any at all back when they can't get near one right on the doorstep——"

"Aye; Willie's been reading me bits about it from the paper—maybe the whalers are like an awful lot of men—great men away from home——"

"You're right, Jean; they're all the same if you ask me. I hope it gets away, anyway——"

"And so do I—what harm's the poor beast doing anyway, just playing itself——"

"Aye, just enjoying itself, and they can't let it be——"

"Ah, now, wait a minute—it's golloping up the sprats by the thousands isn't it, Willie?"

"I should imagine it would take some filling, right enough, Tom."

"Sprats? Hear them, Jean? *Sprats?* Go down to the docks any morning of the week you like and you can take them away by the basinful—they're glad to *give* them away! Well, Jean and me hopes it gets away, anyway——"

"Aye, poor thing, too."

"Och, to hell with the whale then—broach the whisky—it's Hoagmanay, isn't it?"

Well, the whalers who went many a hundred miles pursuing whales failed to get the one that came to them. Can we, in fact, even believe them about the size of this one that got away?

We can believe *McGonagall*; as always, the figures are there—

Which measures forty feet in length from the snout to the tail.

Evading the harpoonists the whale dived and escaped, and

Sped on to Stonehaven with all his might;

139

And was seen by the crew of a Gourdon fishing boat,
Which they thought was a big cobble upturned afloat.
But in the long run, Dundee did get the whale—
So Mr John Wood has bought it for two hundred and
twenty-six pound,
And has brought it to Dundee all safe and sound. . . .

Then hurrah! for the mighty monster whale,
Which has got 17 feet 4 inches from tip to tip of a tail!
Which can be seen for sixpence or a shilling,
That is to say, if the people are willing.

Among disasters of the year which McGonagall's muse let pass
by—

The *Dunstaffnage* left Dundee under tow; the hooks parted in a
storm; drifted onto rocks; 23 drowned. (In the same gale the Dundee
whaler *Mazinthien* was driven ashore at Peterhead Bay, but the crew
were saved by rocket apparatus).

As for deaths—Karl Marx, Turgenev, Gustave Dore, Wagner, and
Victoria's John Brown, whom the Court Circular described as "an
honest, faithful and devoted follower, a trustworthy, discreet and
straightforward man."

I wonder that McGonagall let his passing at least go without a
few lines.

This was a year in which in Dundee, it is recorded, employment
was never more abundant. The price of jute was extra low, and there
were many more ships than in any previous year bringing it in.

One particular ship took a cargo *out* from Dundee—to Queensland; the *Duntrune* which departed in September with 400 emigrants,
the first shipload of emigrants to leave for many a year.

Now you would think *that* a theme strikingly suitable for McGonagall; but God knows, there may well have been local pressures to
actually get him off with the ship! There is indeed some evidence
that by now there were citizens who thought the town should be rid
of him; citizens who, while they would never give him a copper for a
broadsheet or dream of going near his entertainments, would readily
if not eagerly subscribe to a fund that provided in some way for some
form of deportation. He was later to turn this to his advantage.

Incidentally, since the year 1883 appears to have been outstanding in the increase in employment, increase in wages, were the emigrants doing the right thing?

They probably were. The *boom-depression, boom-depression* labouring of the economy's heart with which we are so familiar was not unknown to the Victorians. 1883 was an outstandingly good year; but 1884 was outstandingly bad, with employment becoming scarce and wages being lowered.

And everything around seems dark and drear,
And fills the timid mind with an undefinable fear.

CHAPTER THIRTEEN

LOWDEN Macartney, who sold broadsheets in a little shop in the Overgate called "The Poet's Box,"writes in his Commentary in the sixpenny edition of "Select Poems of McGonagall" that as a boy he often met the poet, and retained a vivid impression of him.

"He was a strange, weird, drab figure, and suggested more than anything else a broken-down actor. He wore his hair long, and sheltered it with a wide-rimmed hat. His clothes were always shabby, and even in summer he refused to discard his overcoat. Dignity and long skirts are considered inseparable, and a poet is ruined if he is not dignified.

"He had a solemn, sallow face, with heavy features and eyes of the sort termed fish-like (I don't know why). Slow of movement, with a slight stoop acquired at the hand-loom formerly, but latterly at the desk, when he left off weaving cloth to take up the more congenial task of weaving dreams, leaning as he walked on a stout stick, he moved about the street, from shop to shop, from office to office, and from house to house in the residential parts of the town, vending his broadsides."

Fish-like eye? Others have described his eyes as black and sparkling, even in age. *Sallow*—others say "well-kippered." Perhaps Macartney recalls him on an off-colour day.

He goes on to state that 1884 was his most productive year, but unfortunately does not list any of the productions other than the Whale piece.

But "The Death of Prince Leopold" was likely to have been composed soon after the event—

> *'Twas on Saturday the 12th of April, in the year 1884,*
> *He was buried in the royal vault, never to rise more*
> *Until the great and fearful judgment day,*
> *When the last trump shall sound to summon him away . . .*

> *The coffin was borne by eight Highlanders of his own*
>   *regiment,*
> *And the fellows seemed to be rather discontent*
> *For the loss of the prince they loved most dear,*
> *While adown their cheeks stole many a silent tear.*

And "The Clepington Catastrophe"—

> *'Twas on a Monday morning in the year 1884,*
> *That a fire broke out in Bailie Bradford's store,*
> *Which contained bales of jute and large quantities of waste,*
> *Which the brave firemen ran to extinguish in great haste.*

A wall collapsing killed four firemen. As usual, in trying to express his obviously sincere compassion and horror, McGonagall verges on the macabrely comic—

> *But brave James Fyffe held on to the hose till the last,*
> *And when found in the debris, the people stood aghast.*
> *When they saw him lying dead, with the hose in his hand,*
> *Their tears for him they couldn't check nor yet command.*

> *Oh heaven! I must confess it was no joke*
> *To see them struggling in the midst of suffocating smoke,*
> *Each man struggling hard, no doubt, to save his life,*
> *When he thought of his dear children and his wife. . . .*

> *But accidents will happen, by land and by sea,*
> *Therefore, to save ourselves from accidents, we needn't try*
>   *to flee,*
> *For whatsoever God has ordained will come to pass;*
> *For instance, ye might be killed by a stone or a piece of glass.*

There is no record of his again going off at the Dundee Holiday Week.

Could be that wives then, having much the same temperaments as wives demonstrate now, Mrs McGonagall nagged him out of it—complaining bitterly of being left to drudge at home while he jaunted off enjoying himself—blundering exhausted with blistered feet through torrential storms, the rumbling of his empty belly

143

competing with the peals of thunder, to destinations where nine times out of ten the welcome mat had been taken in out of the rain. . . .

Since, according to Lowden Macartney, this was his busiest writing year, did an illness keep him at home? as possibly explained in—

A TRIBUTE TO DR. MURISON *

Success to the good and skilful Dr. Murison
For golden opinions he has won
From his patients one and all,
And from myself, McGonagall.

He is very skilful and void of pride;
He was so to me when at my bedside,
When I turned badly on the 25th of July,
And was ill with inflammation, and like to die.

He told me at once what was ailing me;
He said I had been writing too much poetry,
And from writing poetry I would have to refrain,
Because I was suffering from inflammation on the brain . . .

. . . And I wish him success for many a long day,
For he has saved me from dying, I venture to say;
The kind treatment I received surpasses all
Is the honest confession of McGonagall.

Without a doubt a tribute from the heart—although, being McGonagall, he tells us in rhyme that he must give up rhyming! Good lad, Willie; long may you carry on—as, of course, he did.

Or perhaps this was the year of the Fowlis Adventure. . . . Or the Liff Adventure; he has left two accounts of this, naming different, although admittedly close, hamlets, not far from the town.

A mixture of both versions—

"Being out one day at the little village of Fowlis, about six miles from Dundee, and being in rather poor circumstances, I thought of

*May not have been composed until later. First published in 1886.

trying to get a schoolroom to give an entertainment. But when I applied for the schoolroom I met with a refusal. . . .

"Well, being near to a smithy at the time I refer to, I resolved . . . to ask the smith's permission to give an entertainment . . . in the smithy that same night.

"Then I went all over the village, or amongst the people, inviting them to my entertainment, chiefly from my own works and from Shakespeare. The prices were to be—Adults 2d., boys and girls 1d., and the performance was to commence at eight o'clock precisely. . . . To while away the time, I called at the smith's house. The family had just sat down to supper, and the smith bade me draw in a chair and take some supper, which consisted of tea and plenty of oaten cakes and loaf bread; also ham, cheese and butter. . . . I fared very sumptuously, because I had got no refreshment since the morning before leaving Dundee.

"When it drew near to eight o'clock there was a very respectable audience gathered to hear me . . . so I told (the smith) to take the money at the door and I would begin . . . he took his stand at the door, and I addressed the audience as follows—'Ladies and gentle- men, with your permission I will now make a beginning by reciting my famous poem "Bruce of Bannockburn." ' Before it was half- finished I received a great applause; and when finished they were all delighted. Then followed the 'Battle of El-Kebir' and a scene from 'Macbeth'; also the 'Rattling Boy from Dublin," which concluded the evening's entertainment . . . they all felt highly delighted with the entertainment I had given them, many inviting me to hurry back again and give them another entertainment.

"The proceeds taken at the door amounted to 4s. and 9d., and of course I was well pleased with what I had realised, because it is a very poor locality in that part of the country.

"Well, I thanked the audience for their patronage; also the smith for allowing me the use of his smithy, and, bidding him good-night, I came away, resolving to travel home again straightaway. Well, as I drew near to *Fowlis* Schoolroom . . .

". . . and had left and had drawn near to *Liff* Schoolroom . . . I heard the pattering of feet behind me, and the sound of men's voices. So I was instantly seized with an indefinable fear, and I grasped my *stick* firmly in my right hand. . . .

"Having my *umbrella* with me I grasped it firmly, and waited patiently until three men came up to me at Liff schoolroom, and there they stood glaring at me as the serpent does before it leaps upon its prey. Then the man in the centre of the three whispered to his companions, and, as he did so, he threw out both his hands, with the intention, no doubt, of knocking me down, and, with the assistance of the other two, robbing me of the money I had realised from my entertainment. But when he threw out his arms to catch hold of me, as quick as lightning I struck him a blow across the legs with my *umbrella*. . . .

". . . but no sooner were his arms thrown out than my good oaken *cudgel* came across his body with full force . . .

". . . which made him leap backwards, and immediately they then went away round to the front of the school-master's house, close by the road-side and planted themselves there. And when I saw they were waiting for me to come that way as they expected, I resolved to make my escape from them the best way I could. But how? Ah, that was the rub. However, I went round to the front of the school-master's house, and reviewed them in the distance.

"My dear friends, I cannot describe to you my feelings at that moment. The cold sweat started to my forehead . . .

". . . if I could manage to get away from their sight they would give up the chase, and go home to Lochee without satisfying their evil intentions . . . the plan I adopted was by lowering my body slowly downwards until my knees were touching the ground, and, in that position I remained for a few seconds; then I threw myself flat on my face in the road, and I remained that way, watching them in the greatest fear imaginable. But, thank God, the plan I had adopted had the desired effect of saving me from being robbed, or perhaps murdered. . . .

"I took a back road, which leads up to the village of Birkhill, five miles from Dundee, and when I arrived at the village it was past eleven o'clock at night. I went direct to the constable's house and rapped at the door . . . he opened the door. . . . 'Oh, it's you, Mr McGonagall. Come in. Well, sir, what do you want at this late hour?' "

He told the constable what had happened, and explained he was now "rather afraid to pass through Lord Duncan's woods, which are

146

Paton's Lane, where McGonagall was living at No. 19 in 1877 when the muse descended upon him. He also lived at No. 31 before moving to Step Row, a neighbouring street, where he lived until evicted in 1894.

rather dreary and lonely, and the night being so dark, I want you, sir, to escort me through the woods. Then he said he couldn't do that, looking to the lateness of the night. 'But,' said he, 'just you go on, and if anyone offers to molest you, just you shout as loud as you can, and I'll come to you.' 'But, my dear sir,' I said, 'three men could have me murdered before you could save me.' 'Well,' he said, 'I'll stand at the door for a little to see if anyone molests you, and I'll bid you goodnight, Mr McGonagall, and safe home.' "

And in the great Camperdown Estate of Admiral Duncan, the hero of the Battle of Camperdown, the ears of stags twitched, squirrels opened their eyes in alarm, hunting owls silently altered course as the homing McGonagall bolstered his courage declaiming

> *Though I walk through death's dark vale,*
> *Yet will I fear none ill,*
> *For Thou art with me, and Thy rod*
> *And staff comfort me still,*

on his late night-march through the woods.

"Well, thank God, my dear friends, I arrived safe home . . . after twelve o'clock, and my family were very glad to see me safe home again . . . when I told them . . . they were astonished . . . and said I should thank God that had saved me from being murdered. However, the four shillings and ninepence I fetched home with me— I gave all to my wife, and she was very thankful to get it, for the wolf was at the door."

One of his more ambitious efforts in 1884 was his effusion on "The Great Franchise Demonstration, Dundee, 20th September."

This was a grand political march in favour of the Franchise Bill. Upwards of 20,000 walked from Esplanade to Magdalen Green, which, as one report put it, "more than maintained Dundee's reputation for robust and outspoken Liberalism."

One verse from the fifteen—

> *The reason why the Lords won't pass the Franchise Bill*
> *They fear it will do themselves some ill;*
> *That is the reason why they wish to throw it out,*
> *Yes, believe me, fellow citizens, that's the cause without*
> *a doubt.*

Those who know his work fairly well will probably be the littlest bit surprised at this coming from McGonagall who had hitherto—

and afterwards—showed himself to be one who loved a lord to the point of sycophancy. Still, he deserves to be congratulated that when it came to the point of a material decision being required he came down on the side of democracy.

However, I cannot see him actually *joining in* the march—unless he was allowed to lead some section of it, probably dressed in a version of his more arresting stage costume, as he is reputed to have appeared at Gilfillan's funeral. No; I imagine he watched the march past from his own or one or other of the steep streets leading from the Perth Road down to the Magdalen Green rendezvous, or more theatrically from the airier vantage point of a footbridge over the railway that ran along that way, standing like a prince taking the salute.

No records are available of entertainments put on by McGonagall in 1884.

Obviously, of course, his son had completely given up the business after the last attempted appearance. . . . Wrong. You won't believe this—*his son went solo*!

On the 22nd of July in the Argyle Hall, Jock had what the papers described as *A Noisy Entertainment*. The idea was to give readings from the works of his father, Shakespeare, Tennyson, etc.

There was an audience of about 200, mostly young men; and they brought home to Jock that before another appearance he would be well advised to study the art of nimble footwork and ducking and dodging from a pugilist rather than taking elocution lessons from his father. Bags of whiting, flour, rotten eggs sailed towards him unerringly. A member of the audience who ascended the platform and appealed for a chance to be given—a pal no doubt—was met with such a volley of pancake ingredients he was glad to make his escape again. . . . But certainly a friend indeed!

After an interval Jock tried to resume, but it was completely impossible; the marksmen had really got the range now; their accuracy was too deadly for even Son of McGonagall to try and face up to.

And with regards to New York and the sights I did see,
Believe me, I never saw such sights in Dundee!

CHAPTER FOURTEEN

IF 1884 was a bad year economically, 1885 was even worse. For
McGonagall, it started more or less the way it was to go on—
"January 20th 1885.   19 Paton's Lane,
                                                                    Dundee.

To Mr Alex. Hutcheson, Architect.

Mr. Hutcheson,
    My dear friend I write to inform you that I am well again thank
God for it, but still I am in great difficulties at present. I thank you
for the 26/- in stamps you sent during my illness, but by dear friend
I ask you again for the last time for gods sake to lend me one pound
to bring me out of my present difficulties and I promise I will pay it
back 2 fold before I die if not I will take it to be a great insult, and I
will never look you in the face again my modesty will not allow me.
Therefore my dear and best friend I entreat of you for Gods sake for
to comply with my request for fear I relapse again and die. believe me
                                        yours truly,
                                        William McGonagall, poet.
                                        write soon."

    In February he received acknowledgment from an aide, of poems
sent to Lord Wolseley at Camp Korti, and in March further acknowledgment from the same place of verses on the Battle of Abu Klea;
nineteen verses which, even if not poetry, reveal a close following of
the battle from afar which manages to have a considerable if crude
immediacy about it, causing there to rise in our minds a surreala-
istic vision of McGonagall, grotesque in his Rob Roy tinsel, looming
through the smoke of battle, his stately plume dipping and rising
in the whistling exchange of fire, the sound and fury of battle dying
to a background to his commentary and minute-by-minute analyses
of the action—as if in modern times some lounge-suited television

announcer suddenly appeared among astronauts on the moon to point out details of their operations and impedimenta.

In March, in Dundee, the President of the Chamber of Commerce stated millworkers wages were the lowest for five years; factory workers' wages were the lowest for eleven years.

(Referring to this, another spokesman near the end of the year said that "More than one abatement of wages has been made since that time, but the workers have wisely submitted to them after only a brief protest. On all sides privations are being endured—heroic privations which, let us trust, will enable the ship to weather the storm, and exercise a bracing, sweetening influence. . . ." Well, you can imagine the rest of it!)

The year 1885 was a year for closing accounts rather than opening new ones.

When they could get the work, the wives of unemployed, intemperate and layabout men, sewed jute sacks at home. That is, they collected the opened-out shapes to stitch into sacks at home—many saying that the carrying of the bundles was the worst part of the work. With children helping, a woman could manage a bundle of twenty-five a day. Payment varied over the years from 4½d. to 6d. per bundle; probable income about two shillings and sixpence a week. McGonagall's wife may well have gone in for this, may well have had to.

Meat, apart from what scraps clung to the bones the broth was made from, was unknown in the poorer households. Soup, oatmeal, bread and butter, "stovies" when the butcher threw in a bit of suet or other fat with the bones. . . . "Stovies," potatoes, and perhaps an onion, cut up and cooked with a lump of fat in a pot with just enough water in the bottom of the pot to be boiled away when the dish was ready; a greasy, flavoursome, satisfying feed. When there was a glut, enough herring could be got for a penny or tuppence to feed a family.

McGonagall had sent his "General Gordon, The Hero of Khartoum" to the slain hero's daughter, the Lord Mayor of London, and to the Duke of Cambridge, receiving thanks and acknowledgment from them severally in March . . . and nothing more. . . .

He felt compelled to turn again to the form of writing that paid better—a letter to a sympathetic friend, like Alec Lamb, proprietor of Lamb's Hotel and Restaurant in Reform Street, asking for loan of £1 to pay rent and offering him several of his MSS. or the letters acknowledging the above verses.

On the 5th May he sold eleven MSS. to a Mr Crawford for £1. 2s.

With such deals, and appeals for help, and with no record of public appearances (although the last was chancy indeed from the point of view of profit-taking), this was obviously a bad time for him.

Whether his output fell off is impossible to say, through the difficulty of dating most pieces. There were sixteen verses on "The Rebel Surprise Near Tamai." . . . Even so, to be turned into profit, broadsheets had to be printed, and that would normally cost money (although at least in the later years the printers of this book often obliged gratis); and then in hard times people would not be in the market so much for doggerel. Shopkeepers, for instance, would not welcome this persistent eccentric with something to sell when they were weary of watching for the door to open on someone wanting to *buy* something. He must have got many a brusque refusal.

There would have been bitter words in the home. No matter how easy-going Jean was—and, basically, she must have been—no woman will put up with continuing failure without eventually complaining.

The most fortunate among labourers and tradesmen were at work on the new Tay Bridge, of which 77 of the piers were now founded, or had been building the Her Majesty's Theatre and Opera House in the Seagate. Some public work was put in hand; in the winter the Police Commissioners spent £7,000 on laying out new streets for which (one guardian of the public purse complained) there was no immediate demand. As for a housing programme—well, there were over fifteen hundred unoccupied houses in the town.

A certain amount of charity, both publicly and privately financed, was available to the more destitute, and the McGonagalls may have qualified here. And there was always the poorhouse—if you could get in either of them, for not for many years was employment so scarce and destitution so great by the spring of 1886. So many applied for admittance to the poorhouses that the accommodation was insufficient and overcrowded (even at midsummer there were more in these institutions than the previous year). Trade was to get

151

a little better this year—but not much; wages were lowered another five per cent in June.

Still nothing of public appearances in town or tours being undertaken; difficult to say if his output of verse was great or small.

"*Next year*," the experts confidently predicted; "Next year the improvement will be substantial."

For one thing, the new bridge over the Tay should come into operation, helping trade.

Meantime, in the doldrumish years, did McGonagall never wish he had gone off with the emigrants to Queensland? Could he not have done well off their and other ex-patriates' nostalgia—an outrageous mascot? New opportunities in a new land, was this not something he would consider?

Oh, it *was*, it *was*!

In March, 1887, in the tenth year of his self-proclaimed poethood, he sailed away to conquer the New World.

Doubtless this super-ambitious excursion originated in a joking remark from someone—telling him that's where the money was for entertainers, that his talent would surely be richly rewarded.

Taking this at face value McGonagall decided to visit New York, and got enough friends, not forgetting enemies who hoped to rid the town of him for good, to subscribe (barely) sufficient funds for a one-way ticket. . . .

"Ah, you'll make the money in America!" Tom assured him at the little celebration the night before departure. "By God, I envy you. Had I a tenth of your talent I'd have been away there years ago; there's nothing here, Willie——"

"Nothing except your wife, that's all—eh, Jean?"

"If I was single, tomorrow I'd——"

"Don't let *me* stop you——"

"No, but honestly, Willie, Jean, it's a wonderful chance . . . you'll not forget your old friends, will you, eh?"

"I could never do that, Tom, and you know that . . . and as soon as I've made enough—and that should not be that long—I'll be back to see you all, and to take Jean back with me——"

"Maybe Jean's like me, Willie, as feared of the water. *You* wouldn't get ME on a boat all that distance——"

"Heavens woman, he isn't *wanting* YOU on the boat——"

152

"And *you* wouldn't get me on it, either; not any man . . . the storms; and there's great big lumps of ice, they say, bigger than this house. . . . Not me! *Would* you go, Jean?"

"Better wait until I get the chance; I think I wouldn't *like* the going, but I'd like to see what it's like there, too; for a wee while anyway. . . . Oh, the laddies would go in a minute; they're just *dying* to go."

"Their chance will come, as soon as I've made my mark; you'll all come out."

From "My Trip To America" (*The Autobiography of Sir William Topaz McGonagall*).

". . . before I left I went among all my best friends and bade them goodbye, but one particular good friend I must mention, the late Alexander C. Lamb, proprietor of the Temperance Hotel, Dundee.

Well, when I called to bid him good-bye, and after we had shaken hands warmly, he asked me if any of my pretended friends had promised to take me home again from America if I failed in my enterprise. So I told him not one amongst them had promised. 'Well,' says he, 'Write to me and I will fetch you home.' "

He spent a night in a hotel in Glasgow near to Broomielaw Bridge, but "didn't sleep very sound, because my mind was too much absorbed by the perilous adventure I was about to undertake."

Embarking on the *Circassia* next morning he found something of a chaos with everyone running about trying to secure berths, having himself considerable trouble in doing so. (He travelled steerage).

The anchor was weighed, the sails hoisted, and the ship left the Clyde with more than 500 on board, bound for New York. . . .

"Some were crying, some were singing, some were dancing to the strains of the pibroch."

Soon the vessel ". . . sped on rapidly through the deep blue sea, while the cooks on board were preparing the passengers' tea. . . ."

(Notice how rhymes creep in every now and again. Becoming an involuntary process through much striving after them?)

He enjoyed the meals. It would certainly have been a long, long time since he had fared so well.

They encountered a heavy swell, causing the ship to pitch and heave dramatically, and many of the passengers to heave as well, but

". . . I didn't feel sick at all. Well, the next day was a beautiful sunny day, and all the passengers felt gay" (there goes that rhyming) "and after tea was over it was proposed amongst a few of them to get up

A CONCERT ON BOARD

that night. I was invited by a few gentlemen, and selected as one of the performers for the evening, and was told to dress in Highland costume, and that I would receive a collection for the recitations that I gave them. The concert was to begin at eight o'clock. Well, I consented to take part in the concert, and got a gentleman to dress me . . . and when I entered the cabin saloon I received a hearty round of applause from the passengers gathered there. Among them were the chief steward of the vessel. He was elected as chairman for the evening, and addressed us as follows:—

" 'Ladies and gentlemen—I wish it to be understood that all collections of money taken on board this vessel at concerts go for the benefit of the Lifeboat Fund. . . . As Mr McGonagall, the great poet, is first on the programme, I will call on him to recite his own poem, 'Bruce at Bannockburn.'

"So I leapt to my feet and commenced, and before I was right begun I received a storm of applause, but that was all I received for it. Well, when I came to the thrusts and cuts with the sword my voice was drowned with applause . . ." but when he retired that night it was with the resolve that he would not dress up and perform on the homeward voyage. He continues—

"Well, my friends, the vessel made the voyage to New York in twelve days—of course night included as well."

He did not, however, disembark with elation; the reverse, in fact; the reason being he had only eight shillings.

Unlike Oscar Wilde, who on being asked if he had anything to declare on *his* arrival in America, languidly admitted "Nothing but my genius," McGonagall concealed his genius—

". . . and, of course, I told them I was a weaver, whereas if I had said I was a poet, they wouldn't have allowed me to pass."

Regarding his extremely pecuniary circumstances—

"I took from my purse the eight shillings, and laid it down fearlessly, and said—'Change that! It is all I require in the meantime.' So the man looked at me dubiously, but I got past without any trouble after receiving the American money."

Here he was, then, in the land of opportunity. . . . The America of spectacular Wild West Shows. . . . The America of Casey Jones and the vast proud network of railways—and carrying ten thousand comics, hoofers, baritones and tenors and others vaudevillians which included a generous unleavening of Shakespearean hams and dramatic monologuists on a ceaseless permuting of Opera Houses, Bijou Burlesques, flashy Saloon stages and Smalltown halls. Yet surely one more recruit could be absorbed, and in the Home of Entertainment itself, New York?

First of all he took a street car to Forty-ninth Street, where he rang the bell of an old Dundee acquaintance—who recoiled as if confronted with an apparition from the dead; as much, in fact, as if he had been in costume, a garish Macbeth haggardly seeking asylum or Bruce or Rob Roy come bizarrely to demand the blood of a traitorous deserter. It was not his garb, which was his normal frock-coat and wide-brimmed hat; nor, having fed better in the past twelve days than he had for many a long month previously, was it that his appearance was unduly cadaverous. Just, well, although McGonagall was not one of the things they had left Dundee to specifically get away from, it was like looking out of the window one morning and seeing instead of Brooklyn Bridge the Bridge Over The Silvery Tay in the final stages of completion. Venture on lesser excursions as he might occasionally do, McGonagall was a fixed part of the Dundee scene, the buffeted, unpaid, extremely parochial buffoon, who, though seeking inspiration in the despatches from many a foreign field, was, could never be anything other than, much of Tayside's constant smug reminder to themselves how normal and sensible *they* were.

But it *was* him, sure enough.

"In the name of——! Hey, look who's here! Willie, how on earth?"

And over tea—

"You mean you've nobody out here at all? Nobody sent over for you, or the like? A big heart, eh, Bella?"

"He has that . . . but where do you plan to stay? How long? Right enough, there seems to be any amount of work here. . . ."

Entertaining? Looking for engagements on the halls, *here*? Man and wife were both very pessimistic about his prospects in *that* direction, though.

They proved to be correct. And so he then sought to bring the second string to his bow into play—

"I thought I would try and sell some of my poems I had fetched with me from Dundee. Well, the first day I tried to sell them it was a complete failure, for this reason—When they saw the Royal Coat of Arms on the top of the poems they got angry, and said, 'To the deuce with that. We won't buy that here. You'll better go home again to Scotland.' "

Now regretting he had ever come to New York he—

". . . resolved in my mind to get home again as soon as possible."

His friend advised cutting off the Royal Coat of Arms and trying again—

". . . I was astonished to hear him say so, and told him. 'No!' I said, 'I decline to do so. I am not ashamed of the Royal Coat of Arms yet, and I think you ought to be ashamed for telling me so, but you can think as you like, I will still adhere to my colours wherever I go.' "

At the end of three weeks in New York he had not made one cent; so taking Alec Lamb at his word he wrote home, beseeching him—

"For God's sake to take me home from out this second Babylon, for I could get no one to help me, and when writing it the big tears were rolling down my cheeks, and at the end of the letter I told him to address to the Anchor Line Steam Shipping Company's office, to lie till called for."

Had he had the wherewithal to hire a hall, would he have made anything of it? Who knows?

As it was, New York and its wonders was not for him; the collossal department stores where you could buy anything up to a grand piano, if you had the money; the five and ten cent stores where you could buy an amazing variety of things. . . if you had the money.

He wrote home to Lamb on Saturday. Next evening, the neighbours were invited in for a musical get-together, naturally McGonagall was expected to perform. He waited until his friend had been elected chairman, and everyone was seated, waiting for the concert to start; then when he was called upon to open with "Bannockburn"

"I leapt to my feet and said, 'Mr Chairman, Ladies and Gentlemen—I refuse to submit to such a request, because I believe in God, and He has told us to remember the Sabbath day to keep it holy, and I consider it an act of desecration to hold a concert on the Sabbath. Therefore I refuse to recite or sing.'

" 'Oh, but,' the Chairman said, 'it is all right here in New York, quite common here.' "

There followed a bit of an argument, then the friend's wife said that if he wouldn't perform he had better leave; he had affronted her before her neighbours, and ought to be ashamed of himself—

"Then I said, 'But I haven't affronted God.' "

This led to another altercation, with someone asking if he had ever seen God—

" 'Not in this company, at least,' I replied. And then I arose and left the company, considering it to be very bad, and retired to my bed for the night, thinking before I fell asleep that I was in dangerous company, because, from my own experience, the people in New York in general have little or no respect for the Sabbath. The theatres are open, also the music halls, and all of them are well patronised."

Extracts from "Descriptive Poem—Jottings of New York"—

Oh mighty city of New York, you are wonderful to behold—
Your buildings are magnificent the truth be told—
They were the only thing that seemed to arrest my eye,
Because many of them are thirteen storeys high. . . .

Then there's the elevated railroads about five storeys high,
Which the inhabitants can hear night and day passing by;
Of such a mass of people there daily do throng—

No less than five 10,000 daily pass along;
And all along the city you can get for five cents—
And, believe me, among the passengers there's few discontent.

And the tops of the houses are mostly all flat,
And in the warm weather the people gather to chat;
Besides, on the housetops they dry their clothes;
And also, many people all night on the housetops repose. . . .

And as for Brooklyn Bridge, it's a very great height,
And fills the stranger's heart with wonder at first sight;
And with all its loftiness I venture to say
It cannot surpass the new railway bridge of the Silvery Tay.

He deprecates the "ten thousand rumsellers" and the men carrying tins of beer on the Sabbath, and his disgust at the singing and dancing that also went on then—

And with regards to New York and the sights I did see—
Believe me, I never saw such sights in Dundee;
And the morning I sailed from the city of New York
My heart it felt as light as a cork.

For Alex Lamb kept his word; and handsomely—

". . . when about three weeks had expired, I called at . . . the office. . . ." Yes, a cablegram had been received, authorising passage home in a second class cabin, and *six pounds*—

"I felt overjoyed, and thanked him and my dear friend Mr Alexander C. Lamb." His passage would be again on the *Circassia*, to sail in about a fortnight. The clerk bade him look after his money till then, for there were many bad characters in New York.

With the other passengers he embarked to the pibroch's skirling " 'Will Ye No' Come Back Again?' and other old familiar Scottish airs, and the babbling of voices, mingling together with rather discordant music ringing in my ears. The sails were hoisted and steam got up, and the anchor was weighed, and the bell was rung. . . . The stout vessel sailed o 'er the mighty deep, and the passengers felt delighted, especially when an iceberg was sighted . . . a very big one, about ten feet high, which in the distance had a very ghostly appearance, standing there so white, which seemed most fearful to the passengers' sight. And some of the passengers were afraid it might come towards the vessel, but it remained immovable, which the passengers and captain were very thankful for.

"Well, on sped the vessel for a week without anything dangerous happening until the sea began all of a sudden to swell, and the waves rose up like mountains high; then the vessel began to roll from side to side in the trough of the sea, and the women began to scream and the children also. The big waves swept o'er her deck, so much so that the hatches had to be nailed down, and we all expected to be

Lamb's Hotel, Reform Street, Dundee. Proprietor, Alec Lamb, helped McGonagall financially many times, including sending the money to bring him back from New York in 1887.

Photo by kind permission of Dundee Public Libraries (Copyright).

drowned in that mighty ocean of waters. Some parts, the steward told me, were five miles deep. . . ."

The passengers' worries were not yet over, for—

"The vessel all at once gave a lurch, and slackened her speed, and the cause thereof was owing to the piston of one of the engines breaking in the centre, which rendered it unworkable, and it couldn't be repaired until the vessel arrived in Glasgow. By that break in the engine we were delayed three days longer at sea, and, strange to say, as I remarked to some of the passengers, 'Isn't it wonderful to think that the sea calmed down all at once as soon as the piston broke?' And some said it was, and others said it wasn't, and I said in my opinion it was God that calmed the sea—that it was a Providential interference. . . .

"Well, my friends, after that I was looked upon as a prophet and a God-fearing man, and very much respected by the passengers and the chief steward . . . next day the sea was as calm as a mirror, and the vessel skimmed o'er the smooth waters like a bird on the wing, and the passengers felt so delighted that some of them began to sing."

(Are you continuing to note the involuntary couplets, by the way?)

There was a concert that evening, and he agreed to appear, seemingly having succumbed to the "all one big happy family" atmosphere of the ship, commenting that the brotherly and sisterly feeling so much more evident than on land was no doubt due to being in more fear of losing their lives.

As on the outward voyage, the chief steward was chairman, and announced that all monies collected would go to the Lifeboat Fund.

McGonagall's turn was preceded by that of an actor, who, with a lady assisting him, made a hash of the parts of Claude Melnotte and the Lady of Lyons from the play of that name. They got applause when announced, but—

". . . that was all the applause they received during their recital, for she stammered all along in the reading of her part, and as for the actor, he wasn't much better. All the difference was he remembered his part, but his voice was bad."

McGonagall followed this with *Othello's Apology* "which was received with great applause." For an encore he gave them the "Rattling Boy" and "received thunders of applause. When I had finished, several of the passengers shook hands with me warmly, telling me I had done well."

Asked to do the final number he complied with "Tel-el-Kebir" to more applause. He slept well that night (he does seem to have been something of an insomniac, incidentally). And to cap his success completely—

"I was awakened from my sleep by someone knocking at the door of my berth, gently, and I asked who was there . . . 'a friend' . . . one of the gentlemen who had heard me recite at the concert, and he asked me if I was open to receive from him a few shillings as A TOKEN OF REWARD and his appreciation of my abilities as a reciter, telling me he considered it a great shame for passengers to allow me to give so much for nothing."

The ship arrived at Glasgow after 14 days at sea—

"The next morning I took an early train bound for Dundee, and arrived there shortly after one o'clock noon. When I arrived . . . my family were very glad to see me; and also some of my old friends; and as I had written a diary regarding my trip to New York I sold it to a newspaper reporter who gave me 7/6d. for it."

So let the beautiful City of Glasgow flourish
And may the inhabitants always find food their bodies to nourish.

CHAPTER FIFTEEN

HE had missed a grand parade in New York through still being at sea—the St. Patrick Day celebrations, which, since he was of Irish descent, would have roused his muse to perhaps another winner like the "Rattling Boy"—and surely, had he arrived in time, he would have found somewhere to render that number profitably.

Never mind, he was back in plenty of time to celebrate big events at home.

The new Tay Railway Bridge was opened in June with much less fuss than might have been expected, seeming to the cynical like a holding of breath to see if *this* particular structure would remain in service for any length of time.

McGonagall in "An Address To The New Tay Bridge" gave his approval of the design—

> *Beautiful new railway bridge of the Silvery Tay,*
> *With your strong brick piers and buttresses in so grand array,*
> *And your thirteen central girders, which seem to my eye*
> *Strong enough all windy storms to defy.*

Also—

> *With thy beautiful side-screens along your railway*
> *Which will be a great protection on a windy day,*
> *So the railway carriages won't be blown away. . . ."*

And, aha!—

> *The New Yorkers boast about their Brooklyn Bridge,*
> *But in comparison to thee it seems like a midge. . . .*

> *And as you have been opened on the 20th day of June*
> *I hope Her Majesty Queen Victoria will visit thee very soon.*

The Jubilee Celebrations on Saturday, 18th June, now, that was different.

A day of feasting—

Provost Ballingall entertained 2,500 poor children to hot pies, lemonade, cakes, and a take-away packet of sweets from Lindsay & Low, a local manufacturer of confectionery. They also took away commemoration jugs used at the picnic (in Barrack Park) and Jubilee medals.

The inmates of the two poorhouses were served up mince and potatoes (what did they *usually* get, if this was "special"?) followed by rhubarb tart and milk, and a present of snuff and a new shilling.

Every person on the Poor Roll, adults and children, were presented with a new shilling. 300 aged and infirm were given provisions.

The full-belly-and-shilling-in-the-pocket may well have had something to do with the fact that crime was less that day than on an ordinary Saturday, only 32 being apprehended; 12 at Central Office and 20 spread over the stations.

A bonfire lit on The Law on Friday night burned until four o'clock on the Saturday afternoon. Balloons made from thin paper in the shape of animals, operated by cotton wool soaked in spirits of wine, were released from the river to drift over the crowds . . . upwards of 50,000 watching the firework display on Magdalen Green, the McGonagalls certainly among them, since this was at the foot of their street.

In his commemoration McGonagall leaves the local aspect out entirely, justifiably, no doubt, since he would be aiming at a national public, not to say the royal ear. He gained, at the time anyway, neither.

One couplet from "An Ode To The Queen On Her Jubilee Year;
> *And as this is her first Jubilee Year,*
> *And will be her last, I rather fear.*

Tennyson, of course, wrote "On The Jubilee Of Queen Victoria"; and for once at least he and McGonagall appear to have been in step—in that many critics scoffed at his verses, complained they could not understand them; others parodied them wickedly. However, they delighted the Queen, who wrote to Tennyson to say so. It is not known whether she ever saw McGonagall's, and if so her comment.

Somewhat uncharacteristically McGonagall does not even give the year of the Jubilee in his stanzas, but there were later compositions featuring *'Twas in the year of* 1887. . . .

162

'Twas in the year of 1887, which many people will long
    remember,
The burning of the Theatre at Exeter on the 5th September.
Alas! that ever-to-be-remembered and unlucky night,
When one hundred and fifty lost their lives, a most agonizing
    sight.

Lines of pathos and horrific detail, full of pitiful shrieks, devouring flames, weeping orphans, charred bodies. The last verse—

I am very glad to see Henry Irving has sent a hundred pound,
And I hope his brother actors will subscribe their mite all round;
And if they do, it will add honour to their name,
Because whatever is given towards a good cause they will it
    regain,

strikes a touching chord. How McGonagall himself would have gladly contributed to such a cause had he been a success. Poor soul, he could only ever give sympathy, and what compassion he could manage to get into his lumbering rhymes.

Fire, then flood—

'Twas in the year of 1887, and on the 28th September,
Which many people of Honan, in China, will long remember,
Especially those that survived the mighty deluge,
That fled to the mountains, and tops of trees, for refuge.

In the next verse he extremely untypically fails to achieve a rhyming couplet—

All over the province of Honan, which for its fertility
Is commonly called by historians, the garden of China.

He draws a moral—

The Chinese offer sacrifices to the water spirits twice a year,
And whether the water spirits or God felt angry I will not aver;
But perhaps God has considered such sacrifices a sin,
And has drowned so many thousands of them for not worshipping
    Him.

And after rushing torrents bearing along scores of corpses, watery graves, etc., he ends—

Therefore good people at home or abroad,
Be advised by me and trust more in God,
Than the people of Honan, the benighted Chinese,
For fear God punished you likewise for your iniquities.

One more time—

> *'Twas in the year of* 1887, *and on a Saturday the* 12*th of*
> *November,*
> *Which the people of Aberfeldy and elsewhere will remember,*

from lines on the unveiling of the Black Watch Memorial.

He had now spent ten years labouring in the vineyards on the uttermost outskirts of Parnassus, labouring in the most lowly labouring capacity. . . . No real Muse, but an impudently impersonating leprechaun lured him on to usually end up floundering about in quagmires—a leprechaun which boldly looks out from his eyes in the more lively portraits and which at times in some performances seems to have taken over completely and blatantly, and not always to his disadvantage; in "Rattling Boy from Dublin," for instance. But at the final count, it was always the leprechaun who had the good time. Having emboldened its host to then launch forth into *Macbeth* or *Bannockburn* it faded away and left him the target. . . .

Ten years of almost total rejection. Spurned in the world's two greatest cities, guffawed at or completely ignored by the rustics; his great odyssey for regal patronage brutally terminated in one minute after at last reaching the castle gates; hoaxed and pelted by his fellow-townsmen, even jeered at by little boys in the streets which he thought to dignify with his promenading.

After ten years of that, what do you do?

If you are McGonagall you carry on for another ten years.

*   *   *   *   *   *   *   *

Had he been less pre-occupied with fire, famine, flood, bloody carnage, and been able to take a look at the contemporary scene in the shrewd manner of pop purveyors of more recent times, he would have been writing in the following year, 1888, the Victorian equivalant of bluebirds ousting the hoodie crows; would have been pointing out the rainbows settling round the weather-stained shoulders of his own Inverness cape and the mutton sleeves and short high lapels of his fellow citizens—not forgetting the shawls and plaids of the mill women and the scraggy boas of the would-bes. For there was a marked revival in trade, and wages were twice raised in that year.

Perhaps he could only look around him through glasses dimmed too long with his own straitened circumstances. In February he was offering his "Bannockburn" sword to Lamb for money to pay the printer. Perhaps, after all, there were not that many rainbows despite the optimistic journalist-economists. For instance, here is how a labourer working long hard hours in the shipyard made out in that year. He had a wife and five children—

For a start, no meat on a wage of 15/6. And little of anything else when unemployed; even when in employment, for unemployment had to be expected and prepared against as much as possible—

Tea 9d., sugar 8d., bones 2d., fish 3d., herrings 1d., butter 3d., milk 7d., potatoes and veg. 6½d., meal 4½d., bread 2/7½d.=6/3½d. Rent was 1/9d. On this they managed to exist during out-of-work periods. Coal and light? As much as they could do without.

Clothes for themselves and the children? Well, someone better off might take pity on them and pass on cast-offs enough to hide their nakedness, and the children's patch-accumulating misfits were handed down regardless of sex until they finally disintegrated into their component rags and tatters.

Working girls, say two single girls sharing a single room, had to manage on very little. A "low mill hand" had 8/9d. wages—which in earlier years had been 10-11/- for the same job; no doubt the increasing effect of mechanisation; earlier, handloom weaving had paid better still.

The girl's share of the rent would be about 9d. And a steady-working young girl must have *some* clothes . . . maximum annual clothes budget 30/-. There was, of course, 4½d. for a weekly one-and-a-half ounces of *snuff*. Away with such extravagant luxury? Actually a necessity in the raging jute-dust storms that filled the mills of that time.

Sack-sewing was still going on, for which 6d. per bundle of 25 might be obtained. Yet, in 1874 a bundle was worth 1/3; mechanisation again, a recurring pattern in the lives of generations of jute operatives.

Should not McGonagall have recorded such things? (A later poet of Dundee, Mary Brooksbank, certainly did).

Well, Tennyson also ignored the squalor, unfair exploitation, grinding poverty of even many of the fully-employed. Classically, such was not looked upon as being within the province of the poet.

But Tennyson's circumstances and way of life insulated him to a considerable extent from the realities of the slums, while McGonagall was a pauper more or less all his days. And if Tennyson can be thus excused—and, after all, every age needs a writer of fairy tales, and in this field he was superb, it can only be assumed that the undoubtedly kindly and compassionate McGonagall was so inured that he did not really notice the squalor, apart from probably in any case being horrified at the idea of taking the Muse by the hand to tip-toe round the edge of an open communal midden.

The best muck-rakers come from outside, anyway. It took Jack London, a successful American, to disappear into the east end of London and emerge with "People of the Abyss."

Meantime—

> *'Twas on a Sunday morning, an in the year of 1888,*
> *The steamer 'Saxmundham' laden with coal and coke for freight,*
> *Was run into amidships by the Norwegian barque 'Nor,'*
> *And sunk in the English Channel, while the storm fiend did roar.*

And—

> *'Twas in the year of 1888, and on the 17th of January*
> *That the late Rev. Dr. Wilson's soul fled away."*

A liberty is taken with spelling to get a closer rhyme—

> *The coffin containing the remains was brought on Tuesday*
> *   evening from Edinboro,*
> *And as the relatives witnessed its departure their hearts were*
> *   full of sorrow.*

And again—

> *'Twas in the year of 1888, and on October the 14th day,*
> *That a fire broke out in a warehouse, and for hours blazed*
> *   away,*
> *And the warehouse, now destroyed, was occupied by the Messrs*
> *   R. Wylie, Hill & Co.,*
> *Situated in Buchanan Street, in the City of Glasgow. . . .*

> *And in the spectators' faces were depicted fear and*
> *   consternation;*
> *While the news flew like lightning to the Fire Brigade Station.*

This is entitled "The Miraculous Escape of Robert Allan the Fireman," under whom a floor gave way—

He thought he was jammed in for a very long time,
For instead of being only two hours jammed, he thought 'twas
  months nine,
But the brave hero kept up his spirits without any dread,
Then he was taken home in a cab, and put in bed.

Moral—

> And all those that trust in God will do well
> And be sure to escape the pains of hell.

Near the end of the year the town lost a prominent citizen whom
McGonagall much admired, and he wrote—

The Funeral of the Late Ex-Provost Rough of Dundee

'Twas in the year of 1888, and on the 19th of November . . .

As President of the Dundee Temperance Society, and Vice-
President of the Scottish Temperance League for many years,
during his Provostship he certainly seems to have been rough on the
publicans—

Because while Provost he reduced the public-houses to three
  hundred.
Wheareas at the time there were 620 public-houses in the town.
But being a friend of the temperance cause he did frown,
Because he saw the evils of intemperance every day
While sitting on the bench, so he resolved to sweep public-
  houses away. . . .

And when the good man's health began to decline
The doctor ordered him to take each day two glasses of wine,
But he soon saw the evil of it, and from it he shrunk,
The noble old patriarch,* for fear of getting drunk.
And although the doctor advised him to continue taking the
  wine,
Still the hero of the temperance cause did decline,
And told the doctor of wine he wouldn't take any more,
So in a short time his spirit fled to heaven, where all troubles
  are o'er.

Difficult to know if he was under some kind of restraint from
performing in public at this period, no records survive. One function

---

* The licensed trade would have another name for him!

he was certainly not invited to was the banquet given by Lord Provost and Mrs Hunter in the Albert Hall to 300 in commemoration of the Queen's elevating the town to the rank of City.

The seven-course dinner lasted two hours, to an accompaniment of a band playing Scottish airs, alternating with a couple of pipers.

Trade in the town was now getting into a really thriving state; but could McGonagall even afford the 1/- three-course dinner offered by the Dundee Arms Restaurant, or the fish or meat tea for 8d.? Still, there were hot pies for 2d. and sandwiches same price.

But, too long had he tarried!

From a newspaper cutting, September 27th, 1894:—

"*McGonagall as Actor.*

A correspondent sends us a copy of a poster which some years ago drew much attention in Brechin, and resulted, we are informed, in hostile demonstrations against the poet, in which rotten eggs played an important part.

The Mechanics' Hall, Brechin.
*Wednesday First, 27th March.**

The management have much pleasure in intimating to the inhabitants of Brechin the appearance of the world-renowned Actor, Author and Poet

WILLIAM MCGONAGALL, ESQ.

After a lengthy and most successful tour of the United States and no less unsuccessful appearances in the towns in the east of Scotland, the Unexampled and Incomparable Career of this Eminent and Versatile Literrateur is a chapter in the history of Scotland's greatest men that is without parallel, His transcendant genius shines, the brightest star in Scottish poetry.

Through casting into deep shadow the lesser lights of Poesy [*sic*]; through the calumny of rapacious and unscrupulous rivals, he has marched with triumphant strides to discomfiture and despair.

The efforts to dwarf the growth and expansion into matured fruits the glorious beauties which emanate from his poetic powers have met with a defeat which his giant mind and intellectual strength has alternately blasted.

* 27th March landed on a Wednesday in 1889.

His life, writings and doings are the theme of Old and Young
... hope and belief in his own powers is urging him on in his
sacrificial career of enlightenment and uselessness.

All who would hear and witness this alpha and omega of
Literature should not fail to embrace this opportunity.

The Programme, which cannot fail to amuse, will consist of
Selections from his Inspired and Prolific Pen, and from several
less-important authors, such as Shakespeare, Walter Scott,
Tennyson, Longfellow, Moore, Hemans, Montgomery, etc. Come
and see the Perfection of Poetic Purity! Come and hear the Paragon
of the Declamatory Clans!

Come in your hundreds and drink deep from this most marvellous well! Come One, Come All, and hear The Great McGonagall!

Special Notice: No one with black bags and wide-awake hats
admitted!

Tickets: Front seats 1/-, Back seats 6d. Doors open 7 o'clock.
Commence 7.30. Carriages may be ordered for 10."

April, 1889, saw his first public appearance in Glasgow (not in
1897 as Neil Munro erroneously states in "The Brave Days").

From the "Dundee Courier" 4th April, 1889:—

"The gifted McGonagall has been in Glasgow, and has been
received with becoming honour. A Glasgow contemporary devotes
half a column to his performance from which we quote the following—

'At a select smoking concert in Ancell's Restaurant on Tuesday
night, McGonagall, laureate, or rather doggerel laureate, of
Dundee made his first public appearance in Glasgow. His reception was of the most flattering description, although the audience
refrained from any enthusiastic ovation such as the great bard
has drawn forth during the past four months in his native town by
the Tay' (no record of these ovations).

'He was only one of the items on the programme, but he was
the *piece de resistance* and he seemed to realise it. McGonagall
wore a fearful and wonderful Highland costume. Future generations may contend for the custody of his sword, which is decidedly
McGonagallian, having been made by the gifted bard's son.

'A Glasgow literatteur, who was in the chair, introduced
McGonagall in a very complimentary speech in which he com-

169

pared the works of McGonagall to those of Shakespeare, very much to the disparagement of the latter. Then the poet took some lemonade, tightened his belt, sought the centre of the room and recited his famous epic lay "Bruce of Bannockburn." This poem, he admits himself, excites the patriotism of his countrymen more than any other that he has written. When he recited it in a Dundee hall the place had to be fumigated afterwards. He generally prefers to recite at Easter, for eggs at that time are very dear, and even bad ones are not to be obtained cheaply. "Tel-el-Kebir" which he also read is, however, considered to be one of the finest creations of the poet. Its construction is somewhat peculiar. It presents the appearance of having been written without the aid of a footrule, for the lines are very irregular. In this respect the style is somewhat Walt Whitmanesque. To see McGonagall recite this poem is a liberal education in dramatic action. It is a performance necessitating a considerable vacant area, and precautionary measures for the safety of the furniture. McGonagall's best-known work, however, is the *Tay Bridge*. According to the Chairman, the bridge would never have fallen if this poem had not been written. The poet's works were sold to a large number of his admirers present, and his valued autograph was in great demand.' "

There were quite a number of events in 1889 seemingly worthy of McGonagall's pen, which (unless the effusions have been lost) do not appear to have inspired him. For instance, there were two murders in Dundee; one by a lunatic, the other (quoting a contemporary report) committed by "a Londoner, who apparently selected Dundee as the theatre of his crime quite by chance. He expiated his crime on the scaffold, no execution having occurred in Dundee during the 42 years previously."

Dundee M.P., Mr Firth, died in Switzerland on holiday. John Leng was urged to stand, and was elected without a contest, the first time this had happened in 25 years.

Three new schools were opened, Morgan Academy, Blackness Road and Cowgate schools.

In the summer, shopkeepers successfully organised a weekly half-holiday on Wednesday afternoons. And the traditional Fast holidays were officially abolished and replaced by the magistrates by the second Mondays of April and October as statutory holidays.

In September the Trades Union Congress met in Dundee, the largest assemblage in its history, and a visit which greatly increased the strength of the local trade unions.

The train in which the Shah of Persia was returning from Deeside halted for a few minutes at Dundee, and the Shah received an address from the Lord Provost and Magistrates.

(Incidentally, on the way up to Deeside, the driver, seeking to impress the Shah, had the train tearing along in the nineties. On his arrival, the shaken Shah, when asked about the journey, demanded of the Queen that the driver be beheaded!)

Two marble busts of Queen Victoria and the Prince Consort, presented by ex-Provost Ballingal, were placed in Victoria Art Galleries.

Mr W. Arroll, Engineer-in-Chief of the new Tay Railway Bridge, was made a Freeman of Dundee in the Albert Hall.

Another railway was attracting the young bloods and the more daring of the girls, the Grand Scenic Railway beside the Gymnasium and Skating Rink at the People's Recreation Ground in Lochee Road.

There was work in plenty and wages to spend, and prospects looked bright for most people. Yet, four years previously, a Dundee manufacturer had stated, crossing in the Newport ferry, with the utmost seriousness, "Mark my words, in six months you'll not see smoke coming from a single chimney there!"

He was a little out with six months. It was more than sixty years before the smoke showed any considerable abatement—through the introduction of smokeless zones.

McGonagall would surely be a fringe benefitter in the general prosperity, people would more readily spare a copper for his verses.

He probably wasn't in the mind of the local critic who declared that during the year "In the domain of literature, no work of outstanding value has been added to the world's stock of books."

But even if Willie took this personally, at least he was in good company; both Tennyson and Browning published volumes in that year. (And Browning died in 1889).

171

CHAPTER SIXTEEN

FOR a while in 1889 it began to look—from where McGonagall stood, and that was in a circus ring at the receiving end of a cornucopia of decaying fruit and veg., rotten eggs, off-colour ham and cheese—as if he was at last achieving some solid success; for he was getting 15/- a night and it looked like being as regular as he was prepared to stick it.

Then the magistrates stepped in. Certainly, there is no doubt there was rowdyism; hooligans attended specially loaded with the discarded debris of the local greengrocers to unload onto the struggling sage of Step Row. Baron Zeigler was told "No More McGonagall," not by McGonagall, but by the Authorities, sometimes known as They, or Them.

Of course this put the peter on *all* public appearances.

Protests being of no avail, there was only one answer—(here appearing for the first time since it was composed in September 1889)—

Fellow citizens of Bonnie Dundee,
Are ye aware how the magistrates have treated me?
Nay, do not stare or make a fuss
When I tell ye they have boycotted me from appearing in
  Royal Circus,
Which in my opinion is a great shame,
And a dishonour to the city's name.

Fellow citizens, I consider such treatment to be very hard;
'Tis a proof for me they have little regard;
Or else in the circumstances they would have seen to my
  protection;
Then that would have been a proof of their affection,
And how Genius ought to be rewarded,

But instead my Genius has been disregarded.
Why should the magistrates try and punish me in such a cruel
form?
I never heard of the like since I was born.
Fellow citizens, they have taken from me a part of my living,
And as Christians to me they should have been giving;
But instead of that they have prevented Baron Zeigler from
engaging me,
Which certainly is a disgrace to Bonnie Dundee.

Who was't that immortalised the old and the new railway
bridges of the Silvery Tay?
Also the inauguration of the Hill of Balgay?
Likewise the Silvery Tay rolling smoothly on its way?
And the Newport Railway?
Besides the Dundee Volunteers?
Which met with their approbation and hearty cheers.
And has it come to this in Bonnie Dundee?
But, fellow-citizens, I will not submit to such an indignity
For I am resolved to leave the city
And bid the city a long farewell,
For I cannot get protection in it to dwell,
Therefore I'm resolved from it to flee
For a prophet has no honour in his own country,
And try to live in some other town
Where the magistrates won't boycott me or try to keep me
down.

No more shall the roughs of Bonnie Dundee
Get the chance of insulting or throwing missiles at me
For I'm going off to the beautiful west
To the fair city of Glasgow that I like the best,
Where the River Clyde rolls on to the sea
And the lark and the blackbird whistles with glee
And your beautiful bridges across the River Clyde,
And on your bonnie banks I'm going to reside.

In "Brief Autobiography" (*Poetic Gems*) he states that he went to
live in Glasgow for a month, where he gave three entertainments "to

crowded audiences, and was treated like a prince by them, but owing to declining health I had to leave the city of Glasgow."

In a letter to Alec Lamb dated 7th November, 1889, address c/o Mrs Hendry, 3 stairs up, 40 Rose Street, South Side, he says he is not selling many poems; complains about the din of Glasgow, and as for the climate—"I fear it will soon put an end to my existence." He enclosed two copies of "a new song . . . *Beautiful Glasgow*" of which the chorus is—

> *Then away to the West—the beautiful West!*
> *To the fair city of Glasgow that I like the best,*
> *Where the river Clyde rolls on to the sea,*
> *And the larks and the blackbirds whistle with glee.*

He added that he did not want anything for the verses, but if Mr Lamb wished he could give the payment to Mrs McGonagall at Step Row.

Poor McGonagall was made to suffer as if he was the sole cause of hooliganism in Dundee; yet the newspapers of that period are full of reports of vandalism, brawling, drunkenness, cruelty to children, the rowdyism of youths in public places—incidentally, in London, Jack the Ripper's eighth female victim had just been found in Whitechapel with her throat cut, and still warm; and no reporter today would wallow in the gory details as did the unpermissive Victorians—but back to Dundee. . . .

Pitch and Toss, cards and other gambling games in Mid Kirk Style on Sundays. . . .

On a short walk in Lochee one Saturday evening a correspondent counted 37 drunk women. . . .

"Is it not time the police were taking sharper measures with the ruffians who prowl about the direction of the Hawkhill molesting people on the streets? The sentences imposed this week are, to say the least, inadequate, seeing that those implicated were the ringleaders."

"I would again call attention to the Esplanade on Sunday evenings. Gangs of young men parade the whole length of the Esplanade evidently for what they term fun. I wonder if the females they interfere with, or those who are compelled to listen to the choice language they utter, enjoy the sport too?"

174

A Rechabite Parade was joined by a drunk, who eventually fell out and lay in a drunken stupor as the Parade went on.

"The streets of the city presented a lively scene last Saturday night—full drunks, half drunks and quarter drunks being all the fashion," and this writer goes on to remark on the crowds hanging about unofficial drinking establishments next day, Sabbath.

"There seems to be an unlimited supply of able-bodied beggars in the city just now, I trust the police will keep an eye on them. I have heard several complaints about the manner in which they solicit charity."

"It is to be earnestly hoped that those who destroyed the railing of the bandstand (newly-erected at Magdalen Green, a public park at the foot of the street where McGonagall lived) will be caught and severely punished, and also that the police should be empowered to carry a good hazel stick to keep the young rowdy element in order when a band is playing in the stand. A good thrashing is far better than some of our Bailie's admonitions." (And you thought a softness on the bench was a phenomena of *our* time?)

At a rural flower show the winning scones in the baking contest were discovered to be the product of the "Carse of Gowrie Co."— a commercial dairy, whose stamp they bore.

"Some of the streets in the Maxwelltown area have the appearance on a Saturday night of a first-class menagerie. It is disgraceful to see men and even women fighting like cats with one and other. . . .I wonder if anything can be done to put a stop to these Saturday night orgies? . . ."

This, then, was Dundee entering the gay nineties, with one of it's gayest adornments forced to turn his questing melancholy histrionic gaze to the west.

No account of his Glasgow entertainments of this period survives.

But when he returned to Dundee—

A friendly gossip-writer describes in April 1890 what happened when he went to the doctor with head noises—which he had suffered from for a long time, but had recently worsened; the doctor, "Put a tube up his nose and blew in it as if he were performing solo on the trombone. The pain was excruciating and McGonagall danced and roared and writhed in a sensation of agony worse than when in the throes of poetic fancy."

The trouble was diagnosed as an air cavity blocked by intense mental activity.

"Now, poor McGonagall must do something to earn a crust . . . we cannot see a poet and a son of genius starving by the roadside like an old horse." Now was the time to collect his fugitive poems into, say, a shilling edition; and this was done—

"A publisher has been found, and the poet is canvassing for subscribers, and as soon as the list is filled up the volume will be issued from the press. Those who wish to possess a copy cannot do better than put down their names at once."

By the end of the month 200 subscribers had been found, and the book was announced to appear in a fortnight. Meantime, to head noises had been added another and lightning affliction; he woke up one morning to find his neck seized up, immovable in any direction. Medical treatment consisted of ironing with a hot iron.

Whether this was efficacious or not is not recorded, but at this time McGonagall did say that he proposed to change to a lady doctor, whether or not we can take this to imply that he was finding the cures he was being assaulted with by the current practitioner just that little bit too heartily unorthodox. . . .

Then on May 10th—

"McGonagall is out at last in yellow covers!" The slim volume cost a shilling, and was peddled by himself, with gratifying success.

Did he make enough to be able to spare the money for a visit to the one-night appearance at Her Majesty's Theatre of Henry Irving and Ellen Terry doing a reading of Macbeth on June 21st? This was a sell-out at prices from 2/6 to 10/6. Ellen Terry took the part of Lady Macbeth, and Irving all the other parts . . . a *tour de force* according to the critics.

It was in June that McGonagall brought out what he undoubtedly intended to be his most ambitious effort, the "Crucifixion of Christ" no less. From the friendly columnist—

"It is his ambition to deliver the last three verses from the pulpits of our city churches, when he would outshine all your prosy, humdrum, namby-pamby divines, who only 'mouth the Gospel' he says.

"We have seen Mac on the stage in Giles' penny gaff, but to see him with black gown and bands, wagging his pow in a pulpit would make the groundlings stare."

The verses suffer from his usual technical deficiencies; but if they cannot be hailed as epic, at least they are, perhaps surprisingly, an unpretentious attempt to translate St. Luke into verse narrative.

H. M. Stanley, the eminent explorer's visit to speak in the Kinnaird Hall in June brought from fellow-footslogger the sympathetic

> *Welcome, thrice welcome to the City of Dundee*
> *The great African explorer, Henry M. Stanley,*
> *Who went out to Africa its wild regions to explore,*
> *And travelled o'er wild and lonely deserts, fatigued and footsore.*

(Stanley appears to have spoken at length and with some bitterness about the operations of the Germans in Africa—declaring that whenever an Englishman cast his eye on a coveted spot, and found he could make something of it, he was always sure to find a German saying that he was there first).

Andrew Carnegie, the millionaire and Republican, also gave an address in Dundee, in the newish Gilfillan Memorial Hall, on the 1st of September—which McGonagall did not celebrate.

Republican is the key word here. . . . A Royalist could hearken with nothing but disfavour to such as—

"The cost of Government under Monarchy is four times as great as under a Republic (*Hear, hear, and applause*).

"The American pays to his President £10,000 per annum, and has nothing to do with his brothers and sisters, and cousins, and grand-cousins (*cheers*). Nor had the Americans anything to do with a foreign German contingent that took the great places under them and over the heads of veterans who had fought for their country (*applause*).

"The total cost of the American Government—administrative, executive, and legislative—including payment of 413 public servants —is £425,000 per annum. The cost you here pay to one family is £900,376, and what is that family? They are denied all political power; they are the fifth wheel of the coach as far as the governing of the country is concerned (*hisses and applause*).

"The last thing an American would do would be to remit anything to people who were only fit to lead the mad and extravagant race of fashion."

In August, it had looked as if McGonagall was to once more entertain in Dundee, but—

"The circumstances, which are causing no little sensation, are as follows:—Last week the dead walls and wooden fences were one morning plastered over with large posters announcing that the Great McGonagall was to appear in the circus for one night only. The patrons and admirers of the unmatchable poet and tragedian were in ecstasies at the prospect of witnessing a 'scene' in the ring. But to the astonishment and disgust of all classes, the announcement was withdrawn on the following day. We tried to fathom the mystery, but no one could explain it till we stumbled across the poet in our wanderings, and he enlightened us and opened our eyes to a knowledge of one of the most scandalous and dirty tricks ever perpetrated on a poor, struggling genius.

"McGonagall was as mad as a March hare when he learned that the engagement was cancelled. Professionally and pecuniarily, it was a serious loss, more particularly the latter, as fifteen shillings was not to be picked up every day. What did he do? Just what any sensible man would do—put it in the hands of his solicitor. . . . To the credit of the circus people they paid Mac his fee. . . ."

He thought that his life-long crusading against drink had more than a little to do with his being banned—

"In fact it is Mac's firm belief that the publicans have put the screw on the Magistrates and made them their cat's-paw to do their dirty work. Bailiedom had better take care lest their fingers are not burned with this business. . . .

"What is McGonagall's offence, that he should be so hardly dealt with? I do not think the Bailies have any personal ill-feeling towards the poet, but they are afraid of a row. Now who is it that makes the rows? Not McGonagall but the rowdies, and he is not responsible for them by any means. Where are the police? Always absent when wanted, of course. McGonagall is a peaceable citizen, pursuing a legitimate business, and the Magistrates are bound to protect him. . . .

"Now I hope, after this exposure, our worthy Magistrates . . . will do simple justice to the poet. If they are bent on depriving him of the means of earning an honest living, in justice they are bound to find him bread and butter in some other way.

" 'The Poorhouse,' I hear someone whisper. Perish the thought! It must never be said that Dundee allowed the most extraordinary man she ever produced to drift to that receptacle for waifs and strays of humanity.

"A word in your ear, my worthy Lord Provost. Mr Gladstone is coming. There is such a thing as the Civil Pension List—you understand? Push the G.O.M. into a quiet corner, hold him tight by the button of his coat, and whisper the sad tale of McGonagall in his ear. Tell him when next he takes the helm of state, he must ask the Queen to confer a pension on our long-suffering and neglected poet. She will remember how he visited her at Balmoral, and was kicked from the gate by officious lackeys. Do this—get him a snug pension and he will lie quietly on the shelf, and trouble the city no more forever."

Unaccountably, McGonagall seems to have seen no need to seek to ingratiate himself with Gladstone by the production of an effusion. The Grand Old Man's visit to Dundee in October went unmarked as far as the Muse was concerned. Yet, it was a considerable occasion. . . .

No such crowds had ever gathered in the city; flags were hung out as if in preparation for royalty. By daybreak, barricades were in position, and by 9 a.m. Bank Street, Reform Street, Commercial Street, High Street and all the main thoroughfares were packed.

Mill and factory hands showed a disinclination to return to their spinning frames and looms after the breakfast break, and so many did not that several factories did not operate after this.

Young men clambered onto such roofs and balconies as would afford a vantage point, even climbed lamp-posts, some to remain "up the pole" for an hour-and-a-half until the arrival, scheduled for 11.35 a.m.

All the windows along the route from the station to the Kinnaird Hall were crowded as the procession of carriages passed, Gladstone's carriage being escorted by mounted policemen.

The Kinnaird Hall where he was to be presented with the freedom of the city had been packed since the doors were opened shortly after 9 a.m., some having been waiting since daybreak to make sure of a good seat.

The ladies in the hall crocheted, embroidered, sewed, knitted and chattered; the men read the morning papers, discussed Gladstone and the things he stood for; a few sketched with pencil. They

179

whistled—and sang; unled, spontaneous community singing; "Ye Banks and Braes," "Poor Old Jeff," "Cockles and Mussels," "Ole Virginny," "True Till Death," and "Bonnie Dundee."

In the streets, before, while waiting, youths had marched along singing "in the absence of an original song for the occasion," as one commentator put it, "the refrain 'Home Rule For Ever, O'."

Had he taken thought beforehand, and, inspiration responding, McGonagall might have set appropriate lines, laudatory lines, to some old familiar air and had a big hit. What a market for broadsheet copies, the thousands in the streets!

Yes, yes; agreed, agreed; it's easy to have hindsight eighty-odd years after!

We do not know if he managed, or even tried, to get into the hall. Perhaps he did, and was one who, when the Gladstonian carafe was being passed back to the platform after being sent to the aid of a swooning lady, also swigged from it—in his case it would be with approval to find it unalloyed *aqua pura*. . . .

"As the vessel was returned . . . toll was levied on its contents by various thirsty souls, and as each wight took his waught shouts of merry laughter rang through the room."

A selection on the organ was given from eleven o'clock, culminating in "Conquering Hero" as the orator of the people finally entered to tremendous cheers. After receiving the freedom, Gladstone opened a Fine Art Exhibition at the Albert Institute, where lunch was served to 360.

It could well have been that McGonagall was too sick at heart as well as having the physical torment of the roar of trains rushing in one ear and out the other to pay much attention to the most extravagant public show. His friend the columnist continued to publicise his difficulties—

"Every feeling-hearted individual must pity the sorrows of poor poet McGonagall. The injuries he has suffered at the hands of our magistrates is enough to make all hearts boil with holy indignation. One would think he had a good case for damages against them, but alas! it is not easy to set the legal wheels in operation. McGonagall has put the case in the hands of his solicitor, but his legal adviser, like most of his class, has a strong liking for filthy lucre. He believes Mac has a good case, but declines to move unless current expenses are guaranteed—a ten pound note or so to oil the spring would be a godsend. But McGonagall lacks the needful, and there the matter will have to rest, unless some kind friend and patron sends him a cheque. . . .

"In his despair he has been advised to apply to the Home Secretary. Not a bad idea. The Marquis of Lothian is the highest authority in Scotland, and is bound to listen to the appeal of the meanest citizen. I understand that a humble memorial and petition will in due course be drawn up by the poet, and transmitted to his Lordship setting forth the plain, unvarnished tale of his wrongs. We may expect to hear of a public inquiry or a Royal Commission being appointed to sift the matter to the bottom. Failing that, the question should be brought up at the forthcoming municipal elections, heckling the candidates as to their opinions on the McGonagall case. That subject—to the poet at least—is far more important than the Lord Provostship."

And he *did* write to the Home Secretary, the Marquis of Lothian. Thus—

"48 Step Row, Dundee.   August 30th 1890.

"Honoured Sir,—I take the liberty of writing to you to let you know how I have been boycotted by the Magistrates of Dundee. My dear Sir, I have been prevented by them from appearing in Baron Zeigler's Circus, Nethergate, or Circus of Varieties since 20th August 1889 up till the present year 1890, and which holds good against me for some months to come. Unless the Magistrates change the License to allow me to perform, and as it deprives me of my living comparatively so, besides being hurtful to my feelings and detrimental to my character, I appeal to you to see me righted, and to see this wrong towards me requited, and I will feel delighted. My dear Sir, I only ask the same liberty any other actor has got to be allowed to display my abilities when I get the chance to do so. If not, in my opinion it is an act of injustice. Whoever heard tell of a Poet being prevented from reading his own works? See copies enclosed, from such I make my living by selling and giving recitals when I get the chance. Queen Elizabeth in her time allowed Shakespeare to read his Plays before her, and I have no doubt Her Majesty Queen Victoria would allow me to do the same if I were only properly introduced to her. Hoping you will be so kind as to

181

see me righted and your humble petitioner will ever pray for your welfare.—Believe me Sir, yours truly, William McGonagall, Poet."
He got a reply—
"Office of the Secretary for Scotland,
Whitehall, S.W. 29th August 1890.

Sir,—I am directed by the Marquis of Lothian to acknowledge receipt of your letter of the 27th inst." (presumably the date on McGonagall's letter was wrong) "and to inform you in reply that the matter of which you complain is not one for the interference of the Secretary for Scotland.

I am, sir, your most obedient servant, (signed) W. G. Dunbar."
Hardly satisfactory. Ah—but in a corner of the letter—
"Any further communication should be addressed to the Under-Secretary for Scotland, Whitehall."
And so he further communicated, enclosing selection of works which included *Tribute to H. M. Stanley*. There was a reply by return—
"Whitehall S.W. 2nd September 1890.

Sir,—I am directed by the Secretary of State for Scotland to acknowledge the receipt of your letter and enclosures.

I am, sir, your obedient servant.
                    (Signed) R. W. B. Cocharan Patrick."
When his champion on the newspaper saw this he wrote—
"Was there ever such a mockery and a sham as this last reply? Twenty words printed in the centre of a sheet of paper 12 × 6 inches— a waste of public money on paper. . . . Red tape is still as rampant in Whitehall as ever. That is a pretty revelation of the way in which our high paid State officials discharge their duties. That's the return they make for their big salaries. Typewriters and printer's devils do their work, and they roll in their carriages and fatten on the blood and sweat of the toiling millions.

"Now what is to be done for our friend McGonagall. . . . The voice of the people must be heard, and if the people will but rise in their might they will make the Provost shiver in his robes and the Home Secretary shake in his shoes. . . . A great meeting ought to be convened on the Magdalen Green. There are Demosthenes in plenty in Dundee, who, if once mounted on a lorry, would make the welkin ring with their eloquence . . . electors should make it one of

182

the burning questions to blister the fingers of would-be candidates for Municipal honours."

McGonagall did, himself, in fact, address the electors, via the columns of the *Weekly News*—
Saturday, September 13th, 1890—

"Fellow citizens of the city of Dundee, I now lift my pen to ask of ye if ye are all willing to aid me in the present fight against the Magistrates of the city of Dundee. Perhaps you may not be aware of how I have been treated by them. If not, I take the liberty of letting ye know. Well, my fellow citizens and fellow electors of Bonnie Dundee, I have been prevented by them for more than a year past now—from the 20th August 1889, up till this present year of 1890, from appearing in Baron Zeigler's Circus of Varieties, whereby I lost a deal of money, besides being detrimental to my character, also hurtful to my feelings and against me getting engagements elsewhere, and depriving me of my living, comparatively so; and in the name of justice, fellow electors of Dundee, I ask ye if such a base inhuman action toward me is to be tolerated or not? Fellow citizens, it is for ye to decide—'to be or not to be?' that is the question—whether I am to be permitted to perform in public places of entertainment or not. If ye allow the Magistrates to treat me so, wherein is your respect towards me? Therefore I appeal to ye for to see me righted. In the name of all that's good and just, fellow electors, in ye and God I put my trust. 'Man's inhumanity to man makes countless thousands mourn'—*Burns*. 'Vain man, dressed up in a little brief authority, plays such fantastic tricks that make the angels weep'—*Shakespeare*. Therefore ye electors of the city of Dundee, I hope ye will all rally around me, and aid me in this Magisterial fight, and Heaven will defend the right."

And the closing sentence rhymes as well as anything he ever sought to encompass in stanzas—

> *Therefore ye electors of the city of Dundee,*
> *I hope ye will all rally around me,*
> *And aid me in this Magisterial fight,*
> *And Heaven will defend the right.*

Note also the use of "ye."

His journalist friend heartily seconded this—

"Electors and non-electors, citizens and aliens that have your habitation in Dundee, Lochee, and even Newport and Broughty Ferry, can you resist such an earnest appeal? You all know McGonagall, personally or by reputation. You know his worth, and his powers to please, amuse, and edify both by pen and voice. His works are with you, and will remain forever. Verily, are they not written in a book, which, if it has not yet been catalogued in the Free Library, ought to be without delay. But what are his writings compared to the living voice of the great man himself? His eloquence, and attitudes on the boards, whether rendering the immortal Shakespeare or reciting his own matchless effusions, is a feast for the gods.

"For a year and more our modern Roscius has been silent in Bonnie Dundee. Are we, the free citizens of a great city and a great nation, to be deprived of such a treat at the autocratic behest of a few paltry Bailies, who are nothing but a set of drapers, bakers, and duffers? Rise in your might and put your foot on this injustice, and the poet will bless you."

Genuine sympathy here; and if the following paragraph seems somewhat cruel, even sarcastic perhaps; considering McGonagall's history of public appearances and his now long-established role of buffoon-at-large, it is not so much a kick at the fallen as a somewhat exaggerated—slightly embarrassed even?—form of friendly banter—

"McGonagall is not ungrateful for past favours. He cannot and never will forget the meat offerings, the bouquets of flowers, the savoury eggs and ham you were wont to shower around him so profusely in the Argyle and other halls in the city. At times he may have seemed put out a little at your rough and random generosity, but he gave you credit for goodness of heart and the exuberance of spirits raised under the power of his eloquence.

"And are those days, or nights I should say, never to come again? McGonagall loves Dundee, and Dundee ought to respect him in return. As an illustration of the warm feelings the Bard cherishes for the city, and its surroundings, I take the liberty of culling a few lines from one of his latest——" Then follows the first and last verses of "Bonnie Monikie."

But now it seemed another door onto serious recognition was opening, a crack at least; it was headlined in the *Courier*—

Poetic Gems, selected from the works of Mr William McGonagall, with biographical sketch by the author, and portrait was accepted by the Free Library—

'Mr William McGonagall,

I am instructed by the committee to acknowledge receipt of the donation named below, and also to tender you their grateful thanks for the same.

Yours respectively,

(Signed)   J. McLauchan,

Chief Librarian and Curator.' "

On the flyleaf of the donated copy he had inscribed: "I, William McGonagall, poet and tragedian, present this book of Poetic Gems to the Dundee Free Library for the benefit and edification of the readers. Hoping they will derive pleasure and profit from its pages. Believe me, yours sincerely, William McGonagall, poet, September 10th, 1890."

However, since it was McGonagall, the press could not let it go with a simple announcement of this tiny, but proud, step towards respectable acceptance, but must postscript it with—

"We understand that Mr McLauchan has informed the donor that the book will be adorned with a grained morrocco cover, with gold bars across it."

185

Pity the sorrows of the poor poet when he wants bread;
Help him living, for he requires no help when dead.

CHAPTER SEVENTEEN

McGONAGALL sent his new "Bonnie Monikie" to the Lord Provost and to Jas. Watson, the town's Water Engineer. (Monikie was a source of Dundee's water supply). The Lord Provost did not even acknowledge, but Watson sent a letter of thanks.

The bones of the whale that had sported itself in the Tay were now on display in the museum; and this gave him an idea. He offered a copy of his "Tay Whale" to be exhibited alongside; but this was not taken up; some said because the museum had on sale a penny booklet which told about the whale, and if McGonagall's description could be read free no one would buy the booklet!

A door had opened a crack; but acceptance by the committee of the Free Library was not enough to raise him into the ranks of the quality who glittered at the Kinnaird Hall on the occasion of the appearance of Madame Adelina Patti (*Prima Donna of the World*; *will make her first and probably only appearance in Dundee. . . .*).

The prices, too, were a little out of his reach: 21/-, 10/6, 7/6.

In the same week as Patti's triumph before the gentry, there appeared in the Sheriff Court a fourteen-year-old boy charged with allowing his six-year-old brother to sell newspapers at midnight in the Murraygate. It transpired that the mother was in jail; and her paramour, who was found unconscious drunk on the floor of their hovel on the night in question, had wanted to put the children in the poorhouse. This the fourteen-year-old boy was fighting against by organising his brothers in newspaper selling in order to support themselves. The case against him was dismissed.

In October 1890 McGonagall had a new photograph taken; a "cabinet" size was presented to the gossip writer, who commented—

"In all other pictures of the poet . . . he wears an expression of timid distrust" (not true, but columnists have to aim at a certain humorous liveliness) "that seems to suggest he was listening to the approach of the house factor, and wondering what he was to say."

186

The photograph, by Gavin T. M'Coll, was entitled "McGonagall Defying His Enemies" and showed him in proud stance, staff in hand, etc.

The columnist does not say whether he himself so titled the photo.

The photograph was not a parting gift, although nothing was heard of William for a few weeks—

"Weekly News," November 22, 1890—

"McGonagall is still alive, though he was nearly a goner the other day. His old complaint still goes on, the roaring in his head like the roaring of the sea. The idea of being in a perpetual seastorm with no prospect of a calm is somewhat horrifying. But this is not all. One day he was seized with sudden spasms which nearly carried him off. He felt that his hour was come, but with a superhuman effort he grappled with the enemy and conquered.

"If Dundee had lost her poet, how would she have mourned the loss of the Grand Old Man? I believe Dundee will weep and howl when the poet shuffles off this mortal coil. Probably he will be honoured with a public funeral and a sculptured bust in the Victoria Art Galleries half a century after this; but what good will that do the poor man now? Dundee does not appreciate its most wonderful citizen, but other people can and do. If the citizens do not behave a little better to a poor genius, they may, and in all probability will not have the satisfaction of attending his funeral."

There is no record of his having been inspired in this year by the opening of the Forth Railway Bridge, two major colliery disasters, the wreck of H.M.S. *Serpent* off the coast of Spain, the opening in London of the first electric railway; and it is surprising that the attempts to get publicans to agree to close on New Year's Day did not make him feel obliged to bring his pen into support.

Not all the publicans kept to the agreement finally reached to not open. Those who did open did phenomenal business, as was to be expected; and there were stories in the papers of poor drouthy citizens roaming the town looking for such oases. One publican interpreted the agreement in a peculiarly individual way. The doors were opened, the bar was immediately crammed and the doors closed. Then after those inside had been adjudged to have had a fair session at the trough, the doors were opened again for a change of patrons.

At the beginning of 1891 the effects of a railway strike were being felt everywhere. . . .

"That's the last of the coal, Willie; you'll just have to keep your coat on if you're cold. And you shouldn't go wandering about so much in this weather, it can't be doing you any good."

"I've got to keep trying to bring in a copper some way or another; but people are not inclined to part with even a penny or tuppence with so much uncertainty——"

"Oh—there's some old palings round at the back; Charlie bought them from some old property; but we couldn't find the hatchet to break them up."

"Eh? Ah, for the fire. . . . I'll soon break them!"

"You're not going to use your sword, Willie?"

"Do it no harm—and there's little other use being made of it these days anyway. Soon as I've broken a few I'll bring them in and you can be boiling the kettle while I break the rest. . . . If my new book could be got out it would take us out of our difficulties; but the subscribers *are* coming in, a bit slow, that's all."

The *Weekly News* drew attention to his poor health and circumstances, and publicised the forthcoming new collection. It also drew attention to the fact that the uncertain times were doing nothing to reduce drunkenness and disorderliness in some districts— *January 31st, 1891*—

"I think it would be productive of good if the Chief Constable would detail an officer or two to travel with the tram-cars between Lochee and Dundee on a Saturday night to endeavour to put a stop to the disgraceful language used by that genus of society—the Lochee rough. These characters are a disgrace to the city. Instead of sending missionaries to the heathens, there is far greater need of them in Lochee.

"An independent observer taking a circular tour round this suburb by way of Tipperary* to the Bog, thence by Quarrymill round to Burnside Street, returning by Whorter Bank and High Street, would be nearly paralysed by the amount of lawlessness going on. What is wanted is a few more hardy policemen driving out from the city in the interests of the respectable part of that district."

*So named because of Irish colony settled there.

188

In February, McGonagall received a letter which cheered him greatly. He took it along to his champion at the newspaper office.

"What do you think of this, eh?"

"Well! It's nearly as big as a page of the paper . . . *Glasgow University*, eh? '*Dear Sir, We the undersigned beg to send you herewith Ode we have composed in your honour. We have had the extreme pleasure of reading your Poetic Gems, and have embodied our sentiments in the poem referred to. We do not hope to receive a very favourable criticism upon our small effort, but as young men desirous to imitate the master of poetic art we have discovered in you, we trust you will be as lenient as possible with your enthusiastic disciples. We do not wish to rival your splendid achievements, as that would be as presumptuous as it would be futile, but if we can, afar off, emulate the performance of the Poet of Dundee, or in a remote way catch any of his inspiration, our reward will be truly great. We beg, therefore, that you will write us, and inform us what you think of our poem. You might also reply, as far as you are able, to the following questions* . . .

"Aye, Willie—and are you going to give away your secrets to them? And what do you think of the last question?—'*If we should resolve upon going to Balmoral, which route would you recommend? Also, name any models that may be known to you in that direction; stating landlady's name, and if married or single.*' "

"We must allow for something of the exuberance of youth, of course. Certainly, I'll answer it—and encouragingly. What do you think of their poem? It *is* very good, isn't it?"

"Hmmm; it's certainly in the true McGonagallian style—the imitation is almost perfect; especially in that peculiarity of centipedian lines which undoubtedly distinguishes your work from all who have gone before you. Twelve verses of fulsome praise. . . . Aye, well may you slap your knee and rub your hands with glee, Willie, I can see you ending up in Poets' Corner in Westminster Abbey, yet!"

"Oh, and what do you think—the printer says I should put it in the book."

"I think you should. And won't the young fellows open their eyes when they see themselves in print!"

"Yes, I'll write them a very encouraging letter right away."

189

"Well, they certainly seem to have studied your work very thoroughly . . . line after line recounts your matchless effusions, from the 'Tay Bridge' to 'Death of the German Emperor.' "

"I'll certainly put it in the new book. You know, it's made me feel a great deal better——"

"But, of *course*, Willie; we writers—if I may mention my own humble scribblings in the same breath as your own—we need to know that we are read, and better still, appreciated."

"It's given me heart to go on with the 'Execution of Montrose.' "

By March the book was in the press, and as his friend aptly remarked, McGonagall was eager to get it out of the press so that he could get some groceries into his kitchen press. And then came an invitation from the Dennistoun Literary Club to visit them in Glasgow.

The secretary met him at the station and escorted him to a hotel in Broomielaw, from thence by cab to the club's own rooms in the rear of a Duke Street pub.

He was received with a great ovation from an audience of more than forty, and performed for two hours to thunderous applause. He was called the "Grand Old Man" and carried in triumph shoulder high after the meeting; and then escorted to his hotel by the committee; had his bill and railway fare paid, and was sent home to Dundee with a pound note in his pocket.

Reporting his triumph in the paper, his friend added—

"What do you think of that, you hard-hearted, scoffing, miserable jute-spinners? Will you never think shame for your hard-hearted neglect of poor McGonagall?"

His first book had yellow covers; now, at the end of March, his second came out, in red covers, with a frontispiece portrait considered a striking likeness, and much better than the one in the first book. Contents included two new pieces, "Battle of Sherrifmuir" and "Battle of Culloden." The price was one shilling, and a copy of this was also donated to the Library.

So things were getting better?

Alas! Not very much. The book went very slowly. The *Weekly News* did its best to help by urging templars and teetotal folk in general to buy copies, if it were only for the way he exposed the publicans in "Reminiscences." "Is it not one of the great contributions to their cause? I am astonished that passages are not read out at evening tea and cookie meetings got up by grand lodges."

The book was certainly not setting the Law Hill on fire as the writer had previously predicted.

Even worse; a letter from McGonagall dated May 6th, 1891—

"My Dear Friend, I write to inform you that I am resolved to leave Dundee owing to the shameful treatment I meet with daily while walking the streets. No farther gone than today a cab-driver called me an imposter and a pauper imposing on the people of Dundee. Moreover, I was attacked in Reform Street by a young man while entering a shop to sell my new poem 'The Battle of Langille.' He drove up against me full force, and almost drove me through the shop door, and as he ran he kept shouting 'Poet McGonagall! Poet McGonagall!' as loud as he could bawl, which I consider, sir, a great grievance to put up with. But I am resolved, my dear friend, not to submit to such uncharitable treatment any longer, because I can get no protection in Dundee. . . . I am resolved to leave when my own time comes.

> 'No boasting like a fool
> This deed I'll do before the purpose cool.'
> —*Shakespeare.*

Believe me, yours truly, William McGonagall, Poet."

This was published, with a suggestion that his friends should get together to arrange a benefit entertainment for him before his departure.

He was not to leave Dundee, yet, however, although a few days after writing the letter his hat was knocked off by a workman who shied something at him as he passed a new pub in the Nethergate.

By the middle of June, things were so bad financially that he felt forced to act on a suggestion his friend had once made . . .

"And now, gentlemen, we come to something unusual, not to say rare, and for which I have no doubt connoisseurs amongst you have come especially to bid for. I refer to the very valuable original manuscripts of Mr William McGonagall, Poet Laureate of our city.

"Here we have nothing less than the very valuable original in the poet's own handwriting—the manuscript of 'The Silvery Tay' no less. Now, what am I offered; shall we start at five pounds; who will offer five pounds for this manuscript—'The Silvery Tay' remember. . . . Well, name your price, where do you want to start?"

"A penny."

"My dear sir, a *penny*? Come, come now, gentlemen!"

"Tuppence."

"Gentlemen, surely I do not have to tell you again that these are valuable original manuscripts in the poet's own hand. As time goes by they will increase enormously in value. These manuscripts are an *investment*—and an investment which can only increase in value— they will be worth a considerable sum of money to the fortunate owner in years to come. . . ."

With considerable cajoling a bid of sixpence was arrived at and stuck at.

"No," said McGonagall proudly to the auctioneer's questing gaze, "I look on that as an insult. I'll burn the manuscripts rather than part with them for a paltry sixpence!"

Little consolation when it was said to him later that, it being a market day, the bidders were mostly country clod-hoppers who knew nothing of literature. There was only, at this time, the consoling letter he had recently received from a Dundonian, Andrew D. W. B. Proctor, now resident in Brazil, congratulating him on his work.

His friend on the paper was writing about the soot and ashes deposited on passengers on the open-topped steam cars, comparing them to Etna and Vesuvius; and about the prevalence of horse-drawn vans rattling through the streets with drivers lying asleep on top; about a well-dressed young woman kicking her hat along the street in drunken hilarity egged on by the shourts of a gang of youths; about the squads of youths playing cards and pitch and toss every Sabbath, as well as uproarious games of football—all this within sight of the Northern Police Station—the noise being such that it must ring through the premises. And an interesting story about one of a party of merrymakers who wandered into the Overgate and fell foul of one of the touchy denizens. On being invited to remove his jacket and fight, he was about to comply—until one of his pals counselled him against this—"If you take your coat off you'll never see it again!"

But poor William . . .?

192

He had applied to the Queen for a Civil List pension; appealed to the Lord Provost, the Earl of Strathmore; and all he got was the cold shoulder.

Now he drew up a memorial to the First Lord of the Treasury. The sheet, headed by the Royal Arms, set forth—

"William McGonagall, who has been enlightening us with poetic effusions for the last fourteen years, is now in failing health, and has been forbidden by the doctors to compose any more pieces; he is now 62 years of age, and in poor circumstances; he has been a loyal and respectable citizen, and he prays that his Lordship will be generous enough to grant him a small annuity."

The appeal concluded with "God Save The Queen" and the stanza—

> *Pity the sorrows of the poor poet*
> *When he wants bread;*
> *Help him living*
> *For he requires no help when dead.*

Many people willingly signed, although the further up the social scale he went the more reluctance he met with. The Lord Provost, for instance, to whom he had offered the first space, told him to come back when the sheet was full—and then he would sneak his signature in at the bottom? Or as likely refuse point-blank? William had had more than enough experience of magistrates and such to now put much trust in them.

That was in September. By October he had obtained more than 400 signatures, and he was now hopeful that, say, £50 per annum, would not be denied him. And as he said at this time, "I have been forbidden to compose poetry; I have been forbidden to recite or to act on the stage. I have been told to live on the most nourishing food and take as much care as I can, and how can I do so without money? These pensions are for men of genius, and I should like to know where there is a greater genius than myself. The argument is unanswerable; McGonagall must have a pension!"

And then the despatching of the petition was delayed. W. H. Smith, of the Treasury, died.

He now printed in broadsheets for the first time his early lines on Gilfillan and Prince Leopold, and peddled these. Then at last, in November, he got off the signatures, to Balfour, Smith's successor.

At Christmas he received a complimentary letter purporting to come from a professor, or was it the *Principal*? of Glasgow University; and he had this printed for sale at a penny a time.

Stalking through the town on New Year's Day, noting with satisfaction that nearly all the pubs were closed, and dwelling on the pleasurable prospect of a pension in the pipe-line, he could not be blamed for thinking that 1892 could well be a good year.

CHAPTER EIGHTEEN

"IN *Lochee*, Willie? Do you think you should go? You've always had bother there."

"Ah, but these are respectable people, Jean—and they've invited me, it is not like me choosing to go out at my own risk."

"But *Lochee*, Willie—and according to what they say has been in the papers it's a place that's getting worse all the time. Oh, Willie, they would just have to *see* you in the streets of Lochee to start trouble! Would you not be better to refuse——"

"Not at all! I couldn't disappoint this club; the *Dundee, Lochee and East of Scotland Society of Poets* will hardly be a gang of ruffians bent on mischief."

"Do you know them?"

"Well, no—but I *know* they are genuine—hooligans wouldn't have the brains to think up such a name for a hoax; they will perhaps be a fairly new body—maybe even newly formed, want me to give an inaugural address. I can't disappoint them; I'm going! and the money's needed. Anyway, I'm not dressing for it; I'm not risking another chill just yet; I won't be noticed."

The entertainment was a great success. His heart was lifted right away on entering the clubrooms with a large sign on a wall "WELCOME McGONAGALL."

The members entered from another room one at a time to shake hands with him and take their places. Strangely, though all quite young, they nearly all wore spectacles or eye-glasses.

After he explained he had no props with him, he was offered a bayonet or rifle for the performance of "Bannockburn"—but since such weapons were unknown at the time of that battle he declined, and contented himself with his stick, and a couple of handkerchiefs tied round his waist; and when the stick began whistling past those nearest him, they were thankful he had declined.

195

So pleased was his audience with him, they secretly put back the clock hands an hour the longer to enjoy him; and at the end he was rewarded with a handsome collection.

Close on the heels of this triumph he was invited to Brechin.

Ah, but here he was cautious. Here he required some kind of guarantee.

He hadn't forgotten the last time he had appeared there.

His hat, for instance. First it went missing, then when found it had been cut in pieces. He would only go to Brechin if they sent on his fare and half the fee beforehand, and sent proof that a clergyman or other respectable citizen would be chairman.

A piece of doggerel in the Doric appeared in a newspaper advising "Dinna Gang Tae Brechin" and reminding him of incidents on the previous occasion.

"No" to Brechin—but "Yes" to Perth.

"Weekly News," March 19th, 1892.

POET McGONAGALL IN PERTH.
Enthusiastic Reception.
Presentation of Address.

"The other evening, Poet McGonagall of Dundee was entertained to a supper in Campbell's Restaurant, St. John's Place, Perth, by the members of the 'Waverley Shakespeare Club.' The chair was occupied by a well-known local gentleman, and a large enthusiastic audience was present. After supper, the Secretary read a number of apologies received, among them being one which read as follows:—

" 'All hail McGonagall,

Shakespeare the Second.

'Honoured Bard,—Greeting! I regret that I cannot be present tomorrow night to get at first hand your valuable words, but I hope you will get the reception your poetry deserves.'

"The Chairman in the course of his opening remarks said that they had a programme before them which would astonish all. His knowledge of Dundee enabled him to say that it was perhaps the most poetical city in the British Empire. (Laughter.) Almost every fifth man met on the street was a poet; in fact they were as stars in the firmament that could not be numbered. (Laughter.) But like the stars they too had a great centre, and when he spoke of that centre they would at once understand to whom he referred. (A voice— 'McGonagall.') (Loud cheers which were again and again renewed).

"But his poetic influence was not confined to Dundee, for wherever the English language was spoken, the name of McGonagall was known. (Loud cheers.) Many a time when he (the Chairman) felt harassed and annoyed by the cares of this life he turned to the poems of McGonagall and in them found that consolation which restored the vitality to his languid spirits. Long may poet McGonagall continue to manufacture poetry. (Loud cheers and applause.) He was sorry to hear from the poet that he was troubled by a 'ringing' in the head, but he believed that a 'bee in the bonnet' was a common complaint among poets, and they could not expect him to be an exception to the rule. (Laughter.) He trusted, however, that the ringing would soon pass away, and leave the poet in vigorous health to add to his many powerful works, and still further prove himself worthy of being named 'Shakespeare the Second.' (Great applause and ringing cheers).

"The Poet briefly thanked the company for the enthusiastic reception he had received, and proceeded to read his able exposition entitled 'Shakespeare Reviewed' in such dramatic style that it called forth loud cheers, and bore evidence to his great histrionic abilities. McGonagall next gave a recital from 'Macbeth,' beginning at the lines

'Hang out your banners on the outer walls;
The cry is still they come,'

which he delivered in such a powerful manner that a crowd, attracted by the sound, gathered in the street below, and cheered him over and over again.

"McGonagall's conception of 'Macbeth' is certainly an original one, and it may be questioned if any other living tragedian could speak the part with the same effect. His intonations of the voice, his dramatic positions, and his facial expressions all marked him as one who had formed his own idea of the part. On the advice of his medical adviser, however, the Poet did not appear in Highland costume. He got a couple of handkerchiefs, which he tied round his waist, and his stick did service for a sword.

"The Poet at this stage was presented with the following address from the members of the Club—

" 'Most Noble Poet,—We welcome you tonight with all the fervour we are capable of possessing, for we see in you the man who is to raise the poetry of our day from the present level to a platform far above the capabilities of any other poet—past, present or to come. Your purity of diction, your correctness of metre and your limpidity of verse all stamp you as the brightest poet of the Victorian era. You shine out with all the brightness of the Polar star. There is no end to your beautiful thoughts, which, expressed in the 'once-heard-never-to-be-forgotten' poetry you alone can manufacture, thrill the hearts of all who may hear you. You are indeed the brightest gem in the poetic crown, and we long to see you raised to that position which you are justly entitled to and which ere long, you will, we are sure, occupy. Who has not been cheered by your stirring 'Battle of Bannockburn'? Who has not felt the scalding tears run down their cheeks in hearing your beautiful 'Ode to Prince Leopold'? You stand alone in your power of expression. You have no peer, and we have determined to-night to give you your proper place in the poets of this, the nineteenth century. You are, like Gulliver among the Lilliputians, shoulders and head above them all, and yet you are poor. Fear not, McGonagall, money could not purchase your brains; and as to-night we gaze in your placid countenance, see your flowing locks, we are apt to exclaim—

'Gallus noster ego,
Et ignis via.'

" 'Work on, dear soul, shine on, bright star, a pension is yet in store for you. Be not dismayed at the rebuffs of men who are jealous of your powers, but ever keep your eye on the 'Waverley Shakespeare Club of Perth' which to-night welcomes you to its first annual supper in the hope that you shall eat and drink in order that you may recite and sing.' (Great cheers, again and again renewed).

"The poet next delivered what we consider the masterpiece of the evening, viz., his poem 'The Battle of Bannockburn.' He began by giving a graphic description of the Scottish army before the battle; then, warming to his subject, he impersonated King Robert riding along the ranks, making his staff serve as a horse! He also showed the manner in which the Scottish army prayed before going to fight, winding up with a description of the battlefield and of the English flying in all directions. Seldom has the patriotism of any audience

198

been raised to such an extent as on this occasion. Even the reading of the poem is soul-stirring, but when read by an elocutionist such as the author the effect is electrifying. His imitation of the slaying of the English was highly exciting, and his powers of imagination were brought into full play, the way he wielded the sword being

'. . . wonderful to be seen
Near by Dundee and the Magdalen Green.'

"A number of appropriate patriotic pieces were then played on the piano by a city musician, after which the poet gave his poem on 'Tel-el-Kebir' in a manner which turned the room into a very battlefield, the whole company being incapacitated through lack of power to restrain their merriment. The climax was reached when the poet in his enthusiasm inadvertently hit the Chairman a stunning blow on the head which, however, did not prove fatal. Our city musician then rose and said that McGonagall had inspired his powers of musical composition, and asked to be allowed to play 'The McGonagall March.'*

"The Chairman then intimated that the march would be published some time next century, price one shilling and sixpence."

The evening continued on similar lines, the Chairman saying that McGonagall's verses should replace the trash in the school-books; that he had never seen an actor equal McGonagall's delineation of Shakespeare's characters; that they could proudly tell their grand-children that on the night of 9th of March, 1892, they had spent a night with the famous poet McGonagall . . . to whom a brass plate would surely be erected at Step Row.

After being made an honorary member of the club, McGonagall said that he had been in many places, but he never experienced so much gentlemanly treatment as he had done at their hands that night. He would have the greatest pleasure in appearing before them again at any time they required his services.

He was accompanied to the station by a large group who sang as they marched along "Will Ye No' Come Back Again?"

"When the poet got seated in his saloon he spoke a few words of professional advice, and so rapid is his power of composition that what he said was in rhyme. He lingered at the window, apparently

* This "inspiration" was to be repeated at another entertainment in Perth some years later.

199

loath to leave his friends of that night, and when at length the train steamed away it was seen that a poetic tear streamed down his classic features."

*   *   *   *   *   *   *   *

"DUNDEE, LOCHEE & EAST OF SCOTLAND POETICAL SOCIETY.
Diploma of an Associate.

"These lines testify that William McGonagall, Poet and Dramatist, has been enrolled as an Associate of the Dundee, Lochee & East of Scotland Poetical Society on the recommendation of a quorum of the members in the Year of Our Lord One Thousand Eight Hundred and Ninety Two. The said William McGonagall hereby undertakes to devote his abilities to the furtherance of the Poetic Arts and study of the Dramatic Muses.

In witness, whereof, we, the above-named Society do hereby at our hand and seal at Dundee, aforesaid, the day, month and year above written. . . ."

Before this was passed on to him by his gossip-writer friend, there had been talk of a semi-public presentation; that more than fifty people, some of them prominent citizens, had applied for tickets.

Then a letter was published claiming that a group had broken away from the Society because money which had been intended for a bust had been spent on the ornate seal the diploma had been decorated with—the breakaway group to found the City & Suburban Art, Drama & Literary Club, with McGonagall giving the inaugural address.

However, the schism did not happen, and an entertainment took place, reported thus—

"DRAMATIC RECITAL BY MCGONAGALL.
A Rival In The Field.   Horseplay By The Rowdies.

"As our readers may remember, the great Dundee poet was recently made an Associate . . . in their private chambers.

". . . it was arranged to bring the poet more prominently before the public under the wing of the Society . . . in the hall of the Imperial Hotel, Commercial Street.

"As a set-off to the genius of the poet, and by way of contrast, Sandy Paice, the poet-bellman of the Ferry, was invited.

200

"McGonagall took the largest share of the programme, and opened with a new poem specially composed in defiance of doctor's orders. (This was 'Black Beard').

"Sandy Paice sang an original song about a cup of tea . . . well received, and he had to respond to an encore. The programme was going on swimmingly, when a gentleman at the back near the door started to sing a doggerel ditty all about a misadventure that befell McGonagall in New York . . . how he fell into a bucket of lime and burned his nose. The audience laughed, and seemed to relish the joke, but the poet could not see the fun. In the middle of the song he sprang to his feet, and in a loud, stern voice denounced the vocalist as an enemy. It was not true, and the author of the song ought to be ejected. A storm of indignation arose among the audience and the ribald ballad-monger made a dash for the door in time to escape being lynched on the spot. This unfortunate interlude ruffled the poet's feathers and damped his ardour. He threatened to resign from the Society, but was mollified and came to the front with the 'Battle of El-Teb,' which roused the patriotic fire in the breasts of his admirers. Sandy Paice was very obliging, and though he could only play second fiddle to McGonagall, he was ever ready to take the floor to give him a breather. One peculiar feature of the meeting was the number of telegrams that were continually arriving.

"The first that was read was from Wilson Barrett. Then came one from Dion Boucicault, who regretted that distance prevented him from being present. This was too much for the poet's credibility. 'That man's dead!' he cried; 'it's an undeniable fact.'

"The Chairman came to the rescue and assured McGonagall that he had made a mistake in the name.

"As the evening went on, the audience began to show themselves rather *too* lively. Peas came rattling over the floor, but the poet went on to the end of the programme, reciting 'Tel-el-Keber,' 'Bannock-burn' and 'The Rattling Boy.' But the poet had got disgusted at the business, and at the close he loudly announced that he would never give another entertainment in Dundee. The Philistines had been set upon him, he believed, and he was not far wrong.

"The greater portion of the audience dispersed, but a knot of too ardent admirers remained behind. They made an effort to carry the poet shoulder high, but he had no ambitions for the honour. On the stair an attempt was made to seize him, but he struck out with his stick. The roughs got desperate, and in the scuffle the poet was dragged down the stair in a rough and reckless fashion. He rushed to the street, complaining that he had been thrown downstairs, and his head bumped against the steps. A crowd gathered on the High Street, some shouting 'It's McGonagall!' A sergeant of police made his appearance, and under his escort the poet was conveyed to the Nethergate and sent home on the car."

The entertainment had taken place on the evening of All Fools Day. Next day he resigned his Associateship of the Dundee, Lochee & East of Scotland Poetical Society.

Despite such tribulation, and continuing noises in the head, not to say medical advice against composition, he completed another piece during that month; not to Walt Whitman, whose death at seventy-five occurred, but about Black Beard, a pirate.

His spirits were raised by another letter with Glasgow University heading, praising his "Review of Shakespeare";* and on the heels of this he heard through the newspaper that "The Waverley Shakespearian Drama Club" of Perth planned to present him with a vellum diploma.

Meanwhile, another piece composed, printed and peddled—"The Bonnie Lass o' Ruily." . . . This beautiful village girl was loved by Donald McNiell, but longed for wider horizons. A ship arrives, and redcoats disembark, and then one day—

". . . *as Belle was lifting peats a few feet from the door*
She was startled by a voice she had never heard before.

The speaker wore a bright red coat and a small cap,
And she thought to herself he is a handsome chap;
Then the speaker said, "Tis a fine day,' and began to flatter,
Until at last he asked Belle for a drink of watter. . . .

watter not being a misprint, for he uses the same rhyme again, later.

Now read on ("More Poetic Gems.")

* Which he had printed as a pamphlet. While the piece says nothing very original, it is sensible enough within its modest limits. A footnote offers lessons in elocution.

Next, a piece titled "Too Late" about a couple called Willie and Florence, composed in August, the same month in which a man took out a patent for signalling to Mars in the manner of a heliograph with mirrors and a telegraph key; and also the month in which McGonagall received, again via the newspaper, an illuminated address—

"THE WAVERLEY SHAKESPEARIAN DRAMA CLUB, PERTH.
Address
Presented to William McGonagall, Poet
(Shakespeare the Second)
On the Occasion of His First Professional Visit
To the Fair City.
Most Noble Poet

There followed the address which had been read to him when he had appeared before them. It was signed George Watson, Hon. Pres., Matthias Goldnorthy, Pres., James Guidn, Sec., Henry Gosporth, Treas.

"I thought you had an awful high opinion of them gentlemen, Willie? And that's a lovely piece of work; maybe Tom could frame it for you—he's handy at——"

"No. It's going back. I've had enough of diplomas. And why didn't *they* have it framed, if they think so much of me? And presented properly, and instead of leaving it with the *Weekly News* for me to collect, like—like a laddie that sells papers. No, my eyes have been opened, lately, Jean."

"But, they say that nice things about you; what you read out to me was beautiful——"

"Aye, Jean, aye; nice things—*too* nice. When they read this to me, it was maybe easier to believe then; well, when you have been performing it's like your blood is up, and no praise can seem too much. But seeing it now, and especially after that last experience in Commercial Street . . . I *know* it's false; it's too fulsome, too flattering; I could not honestly keep it. And look at the way the poems were returned 'Not Known.' "

"But how would the man give you a wrong name?"

"Shame, Jean—shame they should all feel. I knew he'd been introduced to me as Mr Nicoll in Perth; but when I met him in

Reform Street he insisted it was Speedie, to send the poems I promised him to that name at High Street, Perth; and here they are back again."

"But they treated you so well; you have always said it was the best entertainment you ever gave——"

"Aye, they did treat me well, like a prince . . . but—they are not genuine, and I am not going to be the butt of their hoaxes."

And a few weeks later, when he was invited to the Club's Second Annual Meeting, terms same as before, he took the letter to a friend before replying. The letter was signed "The Secretary," without an actual signature. His friend confirmed his suspicions, and he wrote— the only address given was Perth—to say that he took no notice of anonymous letters.

Was this an indication, then, that it was *not* to be a case of "no fool like an old fool" with McGonagall?

October saw him selling "The Troubles of Matthew Mahoney"; and in October Tennyson died, a certain theme for his pen; but first he celebrated the Great Lifeboat Demonstration which had taken place in Dundee on the 28th of September. He took the lines in to the gossip writer—

"In his very latest poem, McGonagall gives a vivid description of the procession, varied by characteristic observations, and seasoned with imaginative touches. . . . From the minute details presented the reader might think that the venerable Poet, perched on a lamp-post, had jotted down in a note-book everything that came under his eagle eye. . . . Startling as it may appear, the Poet did not see the procession. At the time it was passing he was in his home in Step Row reading the story of *Lizzie Munro* in the "Weekly News.' "

(This story was advertised as "A Story of Pathos and Peril.")

The verses quoted are all that survives of "The Lifeboat Demonstration"—

'Twas in the year of 1892, and on the 24th September,
Which the inhabitants of Dundee will long remember,
The Great Lifeboat Demonstration
Which caused a great sensation. . . .

The Mars boys were there with their band
Leading the van, which looked very grand.

There were a body of sailors all in a row,
And Firemen, Brassfounders, and Operative Masons also,
Besides Carpenters and Joiners and Manchester Oddfellows
And Boilermakers and Blacksmiths that can blow the bellows . . .

Pattern-makers and Painters most beautiful to be seen
All marching in the procession towards the Magdalen Green. . . .

The bakers carried a monster loaf—
Such as a big loaf of over fifty pounds,
And the cheers of the spectators had no bounds,
When they saw it held aloft with a sheaf of corn
They declared they never saw the like since they were born.

His friend continues—

"McGonagall showed an exuberance of spirits not usual with him. Was it the boom in the local poetry market, or was it due to another cause—the disappearance of a rival? 'So your friend is gone,' said a gentleman alluding to the death of Lord Tennyson. . . . McGonagall made the end of his stick come down on the floor with much force, and, striking a picturesque attitude, he said, 'He was no friend of mine, sir! I once communicated with him, and got no answer. He never replied to me; do you believe that, now?'

"With one less rival in the field, McGonagall's star once more appears to be rising."

"The Death and Burial of Lord Tennyson" was finished about a fortnight later, and a copy sent to the Marquis of Lorne who was staying at Glamis Castle, who replied—

Glamis Castle, N.B.   October 23rd, 1892.

Sir,—I thank you for your enclosure, and as a friend would advise you to resolve to keep strictly to prose for the future.
Believe me, Yours in faithful dealing,
(Signed)   Lorne.

But wait! Who is this important-looking person come to his door in Step Row? A messenger from none other than the Earl of Camperdown seeking three copies of the very same verses!

William charged him one shilling, which was no more than double what an ordinary customer was asked to pay.

And when washing the most dirty clothes
The sweat won't be dripping from your nose . . .

CHAPTER NINETEEN

Welcome! thrice welcome! to the year 1893,
For it is the year I intend to leave Dundee,
Owing to the treatment I receive,
Which does my heart sadly grieve.
Every morning when I go out
The ignorant rabble they do shout
'There goes Mad McGonagall'
In derisive shouts as loud as they can bawl,
And lifts stones and snowballs, throws them at me;
And such actions are shameful to be heard in the City
  of Dundee.
And I'm ashamed, kind Christians, to confess
That from the Magistrates I can get no redress.
Therefore I have made up my mind in the year of 1893
To leave the ancient City of Dundee. . . .

Only he did not leave. A letter from a rival doggerelist was published, referring to his schauchlin' form,* his blue nose, his long locks, to which he came back with "Lines In Reply To The Beautiful Poet, Who Welcomed News Of McGonagall's Departure from Dundee."

And in conclusion, I'd have him to beware,
And never again to interfere with a poet's hair,
Because Christ the Saviour wore long hair,
And many more good men, I do declare.

Therefore I laugh at such bosh that appears in print,
So I hope from me you will take the hint,
And never publish such bosh of poetry again,
Or else you'll get the famous "Weekly News" a bad name.

* He was most indignant about this; claiming he was well-known for his majestic gait—the result of his military training when a private in the Perthshire Militia! No record of this service remains.

The *Scottish Leader* said—

"Dundee is threatened with a serious calamity, to wit, the departure from its gates of the Poet McGonagall.

"McGonagall is a very good poet for Dundee, with limitations—such things as a lack of ideas, a trivial shakiness about spelling, and a want of familiarity with syntax, for which doubtless his parents are more to blame than himself. He is never at a loss for a rhyme, and when he discovers the full value of the circumstance that Dundee rhymes with 1893, he may be induced to reconsider his decision and stay for yet a year. As it is, he finds the iron of another's rhyme entering his poetic soul, namely that the citizens of Dundee 'disrespect him.' Alas for Dundee!"

And in the *Piper O' Dundee* February 22nd—

"Juteopolis must take care for its fair name and fame is not filched away by the hoodlums of the city who insult the one and only city poet, McGonagall. Wherever Scots gather the name of McGonagall is as familiar as that of Burns, and Juteopolis has shone in the refulgent glory which shines round the Laureate of the city. True it is—and pity 'tis true, 'tis true—that the poetic prestige which the poet has won has not brought him treasure of gold and silver; but that is no reason why the hoodlum should jeer, and the gamin and the street arab ally themselves to attack and annoy the only poet which the city harbours. The poet who has sung of the Bridge of the Silvery Tay must be protected. Dundee cannot afford to permit him to shake the dust off his feet, and unhook the West Port and let him go free.

"There is yet another important point to consider. The looms of Hawick have been busy weaving a special spring suit for the poet, and though it is true that it is not the coat that makes the poet, yet Dundee cannot afford to make a present to any rival city of a poet like the McGonagall clad in resplendent raiment, and looking quite an Old Worthy."

The suit, reputedly supplied in exchange for verses extolling the quality of the tweed, etc., inspired the "Lines in Praise of Mr J. Graham Henderson, Hawick," according to contemporary reports was striking to say the least. An extremely loud large check made up in the style he favoured—frock coat and square-cut waistcoat, was said to be easily picked out half a mile off in the busiest street. With

207

this he wore his usual poetic hat, and on occasion lambskin gauntlets with the wool lining outside.

. . . Owing to the treatment I receive.

He told his newspaper friend how he buttoned his coat up tight and then steeled himself to go out into the fray every time he left the house. He got no satisfaction from the police, and they would not adopt his suggestion to post bills around the town announcing that anyone giving evidence of any person interfering with Poet McGonagall could claim £1 reward.

One thing in particular he did not like, he said—"And mind you there are married men cry it as well as boys. You know what it is? Get your hair cut! But I gave one fellow a sharp reply today—it is not often I take notice of such remarks—but I said to him, 'Yes; then I would be more like Jack Sheppard!' And you know, in ancient times only thieves wore their hair short."

And his friend, who as it happened had just returned from the barber, ran an embarrassed hand over his shorn neck.

In March, the Dundee, Lochee & East of Scotland Poetical Club said they had decided to give him a new hat, of his own choosing, and a new walking-stick mounted with a silver engraved plate, to go with his new suit.

As for his vow never to entertain in Dundee again—

> *'Twas on the 31st of March, and in the year of 1893,*
> *I gave an entertainment in the city of Dundee,*
> *To a select party of gentlemen, big and small,*
> *Who appreciated my recital in Reform Street Hall. . . .*
>
> *Because they showered upon me their approbation,*
> *And got up for me a handsome donation,*
> *Which was presented to me by Mr Green,*
> *In a purse most beautiful to be seen.*
>
> *Which was a generous action in deed*
> *And came to me in time of need.*
> *And the gentlemen who so generously treated me*
> *I'll remember during my stay in Dundee.*

He was back in the old routine, the ups, but mostly downs, of a show-biz career.

Alas! After this it appears to have been a case of "all dressed up and nowhere to go." No more is heard of him until August, when he is beset with troubles—domestic, physical, mental, as well as the seldom-absent financial trouble. The doctor is attending him, he writes to an old friend; and there is no food in the house. He asks the friend to get in touch with two clergymen whom he thinks might be able to help him.

Then within a few weeks there is talk from the borders of inviting him to the next Common Riding. This results in a further effusion to Mr J. Graham Henderson who had presented the tweed for his spring outfit.

Early in November, Keir Hardie spoke in Rosebank Hall, but called forth nothing from William—nor had he recorded the four-day strike in May of 15,000 mill-workers against a five per cent cut in wages (the mill-masters capitulated).

The closing weeks of the year saw him peddling "Little Popeet"; and he had not left Dundee.

His health continued to improve, according to a rhyming letter sent to wish his borders benefactor a happy New Year—

> *My health is improving fast,*
> *Better than for some time past;*
> *All that I need is nourishing food*
> *Which will do my body good.*

March saw the production of the "Kessock Ferry Boat Fatality" and this was followed by what he considered a much more ambitious piece, "Nora, The Maid of Killarney," which he considered had possibilities for developing into a dramatic work. It is noteworthy for America being written *Amerikay*, thus combining a nod in the direction of the brogue with a useful rhyme with "day," "delay" and "dismay." This work was inspired, not by a yearning for the land of his fathers, but by a picture of Killarney on a grocer's calendar.

In turn, however, the verses might have been responsible for his next statement about leaving Dundee. . . . He planned to go to Ireland, and put a sizable stretch of water between him and his tormentors.

Occasionally he answered back. Like when passing a group of joiners, and one shouted "Burns is the man!"

"Aye—and if he was living today you wouldn't give a damn for him either!"

"Very true, Mr McGonagall," from a sympathiser who happened to be passing.

The outlook in Dundee at that time was not encouraging. The jute trade was suffering a depression; mills were on short time. The masters were again trying to get wages reduced by five per cent; one section of the local press took a poor view of their tactics—

"To say the least, it was not the clean thing for a firm who re-started a work that had been standing to send for the old hands, then reduce their former wages by five per cent. No doubt they can find plenty of poor half-starved creatures glad enough to accept work at these terms. . . . The prospect for operatives is very disheartening, for they are at the mercy of the capitalists."

And if McGonagall planned to settle in a country famous for its pigs, at least one Dundee woman had had enough of these animals. Her landlord kept a pigsty right under her tenement window; and when she complained of the smell of the "clorty" pigs she was put out of the house.

Opter-out as he already was to a marked degree, it looked as if William was wise in opting even further out of Dundee at times like these.

But now his health again deteriorated; the emerald lure faded into the greyness of faint possibility. He did cross water, though.

Probably with a recuperative change of air in mind, he spent a couple of days at Tayport in August, rewarding that village on the Tay with an effusion.

Then, to Step Row came the mysterious visitor from Edinburgh. The Laureateship was still vacant since Tennyson's death; McGona-gall's "friends" had been urging him to apply. . . . Some had warned him of strong opposition—Osburn Blackburn of Auld Reekie, for instance. So! This was surely he!

William did not confront him with his suspicions, but it was obvious to him the way the fellow quizzed and quizzed.

He told him his honest attitude to applying for the Laureateship. Certainly no trying to pull strings by getting some big bug to put in a word; merit alone, etc. The curious visitor went off apparently well-pleased at what he'd learned.

However, William had a more immediate material end in view at this time.

There seemed to be distinct possibilities in *commercialising* his talent. . . . Had not he received a splendid suit for a jingle?

So, he tried again—and got *two guineas* . . .! His friend pictured the scene in his gossip column—

"The poem may be taken to delineate a homely scene in Step Row, and it indicates that the operations of Mrs McGonagall amongst the family linen have engaged for some time the earnest attention of her poetic husband. As a result of this close, personal observation he is able to pronounce thus—

> *You can use it with great pleasure and ease*
> *Without wasting any elbow grease;*
> *And when washing the most dirty clothes*
> *The sweat won't be dripping from your nose. . . .*

He skips to the last verse then—

> *You can wash your clothes with little rubbing*
> *And without scarcely any scrubbing;*
> *And I tell you once again without any joke*
> *There's no soap can surpass Sunlight Soap;*
> *And believe me, charwomen one and all,*
> *I remain yours truly, the Poet McGonagall.'*

When he had this printed as a broadsheet, his friend was delighted with what might be termed the flip side—for there were two for a penny on this sheet—"The Beautiful River Dee," combining, as it did, soap and water!

On receipt of the two guineas he thanked the makers—

> *Gentlemen you have my best wishes, and I hope*
> *That the poem I've written about Sunlight Soap*
> *Will cause a demand for it in every clime*
> *For I declare it to be superfine.*
> *And I hope before long, without any joke,*
> *You will require some more of my poems about*
>   *Sunlight Soap.*
> *And in conclusion, gentlemen, I thank ye—*
> *William McGonagall, Poet, 48 Step Row, Dundee.*

Next he turned his attention to—well, here it is—

What ho! sickly people of high and low degree
I pray ye all be warned by me;
No matter what may be your bodily ills
The safest and quickest cure is Beecham's Pills.

They are admitted to be worth a guinea a box
For bilious and nervous disorders, also smallpox,
And dizziness and drowsiness, also cold chills,
And for such diseases nothing else can equal
    Beecham's Pills.

They have been proved by thousands who have
    tried them
So that the people cannot them condemn.
Be advised by me one and all
Is the advice of Poet McGonagall.

We now return to the mysterious person from the capital—now revealed as an Edinburgh journalist, whose interview with McGonagall was now in the *Dispatch*.

A letter arrived, supposedly from Lord Roseberry, inviting him to apply for the Laureateship. He was suspicious of this, but sent off a bundle of poems, which included "Railway Bridge of the Silvery Tay," "Newport Railway," "Sunlight Soap," "River Dee" and "Tayport." He became something of a pet with the Edinburgh press about this time. So things were beginning to look fine again?

Not quite.

In the issue dated 6th October, 1894 of the *Weekly News* it was revealed that Mr Sibbald, McGonagall's house-factor, had obtained an order in the Sheriff Court enabling him to eject McGonagall and family from his house. The case was that the tenants above had threatened to leave, and that meetings at an adjoining mission were not only being interrupted but frequently brought to an abrupt termination by family disturbances in the McGonagall household.

"McGonagall! McGonagall!" echoed through the court several times, but there was no answer. This meant that 48 Step Row now had to be evacuated within three days. And so he did leave Dundee; not with a bang, as a later writer put it, but a whimper . . . although, perhaps that isn't really fair; there is no record of whimpering; he just stole quietly away.

From 57 South Street, Perth, he declared, "I will keep from the city of my persecution, so help me God!" and wrote a eulogy of the Fair City.

Perhaps he had previously spied out the land for this move, when in September he had been in Perth at the Lyric Club Banquet, which is celebrated in *Lines In Praise Of—etc.*, and where, if it wasn't exactly a feast of wit and virtuosity, at least remained memorable to the guest as a more timely kind of feast—to wit, a good "tightener," as—

> There was Beef, Fish, and Potatoes galore,
> And we all ate until we could eat no more.

Soon after he took up residence in Perth there appeared in the Edinburgh papers—

WAVERLEY HOTEL: SATURDAY FIRST
at 3 and 8 p.m.

THE GREAT MCGONAGALL will give his inimitable performance from MACBETH & c. Music, Songs, etc., by other Gentlemen. Admission 1/-. Reserved Seats 2/-, by tickets only, from Kohler & Sons, North Bridge. Mr MCGONAGALL & PARTY will appear in Morningside Hall on Monday, 5th November, at 8 p.m. Tickets at Morningside P.O.

Henry Irving and Ellen Terry were appearing in Edinburgh that week, and *they* called on *McGonagall*, who, according to the press, received them graciously.

Incidentally, he had it seems considered moving much further than Perth, or Ireland—even than America for that matter, for a letter to a Mr Wishart from Perth dated 30th October says he is keeping well, and encloses a letter from a mutual friend, Rev. Mr Alex. C. Henderson, Melbourne, advising him not to think of emigrating, telling of rows of empty shops, scarcity of work.

He and his wife stayed in the garret at 57 South Street for about eight months, according to "The Autobiography of Sir William

213

Topaz McGonagall," during which time he appears to have gone unmolested, and given successful entertainments there and in Edinburgh and Glasgow. It was from Perth, too, that he travelled to Inverness to star at the celebrated Heather Blend Club Banquet, described in some detail in the same autobiography, and which he also celebrated in eleven verses.

Perth, he felt, was too small, so off again, to live in Edinburgh some time about the middle of 1895.

In fact it had been put to him several times at entertainments he gave in the capital that he should take up residence there. An Edinburgh newspaper reported his arrival—

"He was met by a few admirers at the station. On reaching Princes Street, which looked extremely beautiful in the moonlight, one of the party ventured to remind him that if he cared to dip his pen into the poetical well, here was an excellent subject. With a magnificent gesture he replied, 'I immortalised this scene years ago!'

"His opinions regarding Shakespeare and Burns were vastly entertaining. He gravely informed those around the tea-table that he considered himself even greater than these celebrities.

"His entrance into the large room was an occasion for wild cheering. The Chairman introduced McGonagall, and the members of the gathering were in turn introduced to the poet. The entire company were patriarchs for the night, with fictitious titles. During the evening the poet condescended to allow one of his own efforts to be recited. The rendering was inimitable, and the poet complimented the Thespian confrere on his ability."

His rendering of "Bannockburn" was reported in the usual manner, with those nearest him ducking as his cudgel whistled through the air.

"The fun waxed fast and furious until midnight. Never throughout the entire proceedings was there the semblance of a smile on his sombre countenance. Perhaps he was no fool when he had our guineas in his pocket. Be that as it may, the money spent was a good investment.

"The Order of the White Elephant was conferred on him in the University Hotel. After the ceremony an illuminated address in latin was presented. Finally, a large drawing of the poet as the Genius of Poetry was placed on the steps of the throne. . . ."

214

(This "Order" was conferred on him by letter first of all in December 1894 while he was still in Perth).

Well, if in Edinburgh his audiences still came to "knock a rise out of him" at least they did it with better manners than in Dundee, and appear not to have thrown things at him.

Little news of him came through to Dundee, just the odd snippet.

But when the *Weekly News* reprinted from the *Montrose Standard* verses about the "New Town Hall" in Edinburgh from "Mr Usher's bounty" it brought a letter dated 11th July, 1896, from McGonagall at 12 Grove Street, Edinburgh, disowning the effusion, calling the author a *coward* and an *enemy* and thanking the columnist for bringing the counterfeit to his notice.

This gives the lie to some writers who claim that he was quite happy to see imitations of his efforts, and in fact incorporated them into his works as his own later on. He *did* incorporate the verses others had written *to* him, in supposed praise; but never passed such off as his own; always giving the author, or at least how they had come to him.

A further example of his attitude was when he wrote to an Edinburgh paper the following year, not only denouncing a piece supposed to be his, but enclosing a specially-composed effort to show "a genuine specimen of my muse so that the City of Edinburgh may see how immeasurably superior I am to the writer of the wrong counterfeit. These lines were composed on the spur of the moment *vita voce* and written down by one of the bystanders—

> *It was on a Wednesday and on the 15th September,*
> *A day which we all will do well to remember,*
> *And the city of Edinburgh will bear me no grudge*
> *When I tell of the day they suffered their Lord Provost*
>   *to open the new North Bridge."*

No doubt about *that* being the genuine article!

Incidentally, he was not offered the vacant Laureateship, which went to Alfred Austin (and who quotes *him* today ? but as a sympathiser consoled McGonagall, at least the job didn't go to Osburn Blackburn or The Loonie, his Edinburgh and Aberdeen rivals respectively.

215

Oh Dundee, Dundee, think of your treatment towards me
And blush for shame
For I fear I will never live amongst ye again.

CHAPTER TWENTY

H E wrote to his Dundee journalist friend, referring to the laying
of a wreath on the Burns Statue in Albert Square—
26th July, 1896.

'I will ever remember the day I walked in the Burns' procession
in Highland costume with the manuscript of the Burns' Statue poem
in my hand, which I willingly would have read had I been permitted,
but no! when I made the attempt for the third time, to get onto the
platform, I was told by the police to go away, just the same as if I
had been a dog. My dear friend, such was ever the treatment I
received in Dundee. the cause was Envy . . . and I am afraid it
would be the same treatment I would meet with if I was in Dundee
again. You are at Liberty to publish this letter or the poems enclosed.
I hope to find ye all well in the Office, as this leaves me at present
Thank God. . . ."

His friend comments—

"Well do I remember that memorable Saturday afternoon when
the great procession rolled along the streets to unveil the Burns
Statue. Of all the fine shows in that gorgeous display the majestic
and dignified figure of the poet, arrayed in the garb of Old Gaul, was
the most conspicuous."

McGonagall was refused permission to join on the grounds that
he was not a "representative body."

"McGonagall maintained his right. He was a citizen of Dundee.
Moreover, he was a poet, and therefore the true representative of a
brother poet. McGonagall demonstrated, and he was cheered all
along the line. . . ." But they still kept him out.

"He fears the same spirit still prevails, and would quickly be
manifested if he should again visit Dundee. . . . Perhaps it might.
I fear it would. But the poet will still live all that down yet, and his
figure may be set up in marble or bronze. . . ."

The verses enclosed were about the River of Leith.

216

Another letter was published on the 22nd August—

"Since I came to Edinboro, I must say I haven't felt sorrow. Such wasn't the case in Dundee, no my dear Friend, the Dundee folk have yet a deal to learn before they are an equality with the citizens of Edinburgh, namely, good mannerism, which is not to be found in Dundee. You said, in reference to the Burns' procession and if you remember aright that the Boss of the procession prohibited me from walking in the procession, you are right in your judgment in saying so, and moreover, I must tell you, my dear Friend, that I was prohibited from walking in the Franchise Demonstration. Which I will ever remember of me running along the line of processionists and trying to get a place amongst them, but it was in vain, and in my opinion the greater shame. And my dear Friend I was like to faint with shame to think I should be refused a place in that procession that I had composed a Poem about, why Sir, I look upon it to be one of the most degrading actions ever I met with while in Dundee; and only that Mr M'Givern, John Wood's Theatrical Manager, noticed me running about and took me into Mr Wood's little carriage I wouldn't have found a place at all such was the treatment bestowed upon McGonagall.

> *Oh Dundee, Dundee,*
> *Think of your treatment towards me*
> *And blush for shame*
> *For I fear I will never live amongst ye again."*

He enclosed his latest work, probably not published since then—

COLINTON DELL AND ITS SURROUNDINGS

Ye lovers of the picturesque, away! away!
To the bonnie Dell of Colinton, and have a holiday;
And bask in the sunshine and inhale the pure air
Emanating from the beautiful trees and green shrubberies there.
There the butterfly and the bee can be seen on the wing
And with the singing of the birds the Dell doth ring;
While the innocent trout do sport and play
In the river pools of water all the day.
Therefore, lovers of the beautiful and who are fond of
    recreation

217

Go, visit the Dell of Colinton, without hesitation;
And revel among the scenery on a fine summer day,
And it will elevate your spirits, and make you feel gay.

Had he been in Dundee the following January, he would certainly have been inspired. As the Bard of the Silvery Tay it surely could not have been otherwise. Had he not lived within sight and sound of the Bridge—nay *Bridges* for so many years, hailed their construction, lamented that calamitous fall. . . .? His interest in the Railway Bridge of the Silvery Tay being practically proprietal, with what zest would he not have seized pen to acclaim the marvellous feat of Tommy Burns?

He had turned back peaceably when the railway men apprehended him near the middle of the bridge; but Tommy was a persistent man, and eventually made it—no, not to achieve an ambition to walk across the bridge. As a matter of fact his success eventually was due to the fact that he went by train; and not right across either.

At a previously decided point he left the train—left the swaying *roof* of the train to clear the parapet flying past and curve head first into the Tay far below.*

One newspaper, hailing this incredible feat, said that Dundee was in need of such a sensation at the time; and that it was only to be regretted that he could not have obtained official permission to perform the dive publicly—what a gala day out for the town it would have been; the boats, and the thousands lining the river!

And within perhaps days McGonagall with a new broadsheet— "Tommy Burns' Wonderful Dive From The Bridge of The Silvery Tay."

But, it had to be a stolen feat; and McGonagall wasn't there.

McGonagall's life seemed now to have settled into something of an even tenor; and if he still was not getting any richer, at least he had peace from the hooligans of Tayside, and that was worth a lot to an old man surely. True, the better-educated class who in Edinburgh got up functions in order to have a laugh at him—students; aye, and doctors and professors, ought to have known better, but they didn't, and they were prepared to pay for their fun.

* Surely it was not a coincidence that Tommy did it on 29th January, namesake Rabbie's birthday? The previous December, at 3 a.m. on the 31st, he had leaped from the Forth Bridge.

Did he, by this time, realise what was afoot, and go along with it for the sake of the money, as some have suggested?

This seems hardly likely, since on the occasions when he *did* suspect leg-pulling he showed his displeasure—even with the Perth Waverley Club from whom he had received the finest reception in his career up to that time. The fact that he left the Fair City on that occasion with tears of happiness running down his cheeks did not prevent him seeing—or cause him to prefer not to see—through the diploma which followed.

No, without a doubt he was convinced of his own genius; and was so carried away with his own words, performances, that *any* noise the audience made apart from direct personal insults, was an ovation; an ovation, the illusion of which was destroyed when they erupted rotten fruit and eggs, etc., of course.

The patronage of the hoi-poloi was not to go on indefinitely; he was in vogue for a few seasons, then the invitations began to fall away. And a number of the students went on to be professors no doubt, and the professors went on to be heads of bigger and bigger departments and establishments; but, having exalted McGonagall— even to conferring upon him a "knighthood"—none of them seemed to feel the slightest responsibility for even seeing that he was let down gently, that some of his more essential needs should be met now and then, even if they no longer wished to pay him sniggering adulation.

When, after the turn of the century, things had began to get really desperate, it was to Dundee he had to turn, writing begging letters often enough from a sick-bed, pleading for a little money to buy food and pay the rent. Some time in June or July 1901 he changed his address from 26 Potter Row to 5 South College Street, and this could well signify a "moonlight" or an eviction through financial difficulties.*

Before leaving Dundee he had written to Sir John Leng, M.P., asking him to see if he could get him something from the Civil List, to see Lord Roseberry on his behalf—"don't think you need to be afraid to approach him," but no more was heard.

He had a "mailing list" of patrons to whom he sent his latest effusions; his champion on the *Weekly News* who often quoted from

* He had also published broadsheets with a Lothian street address.

them, and a Mr James Shand who worked in a Dundee bank, and to whom he often appealed to get him out of difficulties and to whom he was able to acquaint of a small triumph, the serialisation of his autobiography to start in the *Weekly News* 27th July 1901;* and a tragedy, the death of his daughter Mary in June, in her early thirties.

In June 1902 he wrote to Shand; he had been a fortnight in bed with bronchitis, and "I am in arrears 11s. and I have a hard factor, excuse me for letting you know this."

In September his columnist friend wrote—

"I remarked the other week that I had an idea that the Poet McGonagall had either been ill or had been at the Coronation. Well, he has been both. The influenza had laid him up, but in the midst of all his many infirmities he has produced the great Coronation poem. A copy came last week enclosed in a large envelope . . . the printing has been a triumph. The verses are produced on a folio sheet with headings, inscriptions, and copies of letters from Royal and other notorious personages, including His Majesty King Edward. The sheet is well adapted for framing, and with due regard to the subject and the illustrous author, it might grace any drawing-room in a setting of gold and glass. Here are some of the most striking passages" (all that survive)—

> '*Twas in the year of 1902, and on August the 9th, a beautifull day,*
> *That thousands of people came from far away,*
> *All in a statement of excitement and consternation*
> *Resolved to see King Edward the VII's Coronation.*

> * * * * * * *

> *The Coronation ceremony was really very grand,*
> *There were countesses present, and duchesses from many a foreign land,*
> *All dressed in costly dresses, glittering with diamonds and gold,*
> *Oh, the scene was most beautiful to behold.*

* "The Autobiography of Sir William Topaz McGonagall."

The Queen, from first to last, was the crowning glory of the
  ceremony,
Her beauty, her grace, her exquisite dress was lovely to see,
And her train of crimson and gold was borne by eight
  gentlemen,
Which certainly was a grand honour conferred upon them.
     *   *   *   *   *   *   *

King Edward throughout the ceremony seemed quite content,
And when the Archbishop administered the oath of good
  government
The King's response was "I am willing," must have been
  heard down the nave.
So said the King without fear, his courage was brave.
     *   *   *   *   *   *   *   *

When Queen Alexandra was being crowned she looked lovely
  and gay,
And the ceremony took only a few minutes delay,
And the King permitted the Archbishop to retire to his chair,
Because the Primate felt very weak, he was well aware.
     *   *   *   *   *   *   *   *

Then at the close of that solemn rite they both put on their
  crowns,
And take their sceptres in their hands, while neither of them
  frowns,
Then robed in purple and velvet, they prepare to take their
  departure,
The Queen goes first and the King follows after.
Then the King entered the beautiful coach, the sides were
  made of glass,
Especially made so that his subjects could see him pass,
And he seated himself by his Queen, most lovely and gay,
Then the Royal coach was driven by eight beautiful bays away.

This was the last piece he was to write.

He had not been well, but didn't seem to be so very bad, when
death came suddenly a fortnight later. The death certificate says
"cerebral haemorrhage," the name is spent McGonigal—his wife
(with him when he died) could not read. For "the poor poet" as he

sometimes when beset with difficulties described himself, no Poet's Corner in the Abbey . . . an unknown corner, unmarked; a pauper's grave, like his daughter. In a way, like an amusing, but cheap, toy, to be thrown out with other rubbish when broken.

*   *   *   *   *   *   *   *

And nowadays? If McGonagall were alive today?

Nowadays, when merely to be sufficiently extrovert and spot-light loving seems to be an almost certain passport to electronic fame and fortune, McGonagall would be a rich celebrity, most certainly not an impoverished worthy. How lovingly some astute TV producer would be exploiting his ripe eccentricities; how the agents would be manoeuvring behind each others' backs to carve themselves thicker slices from this gloriously succulent ham! Yes, as has been suggested, he could have risen high in the church; equally so in politics— providing. . . . *Providing* he had the right script-writers.

Paradoxically, the banalities, the soldier-on-until-you-get-there rhyming schemes which have ensured his survival, would have to be discarded in such a career. They have served their purpose; a link kept alive by gibers and mickey-takers, connecting McGonagall the man to us in the present day. . . . And it is this astoundingly most individualistic of men who will live, for a long, long time yet, and, another paradox, draw succeeding generations to his "Poetic Gems."

FINIS

222

THE BOOK OF THE LAMENTATIONS OF THE
POET McGONAGALL

On the 25th March 1886 McGonagall made by Deed of Gift to Alec Lamb the MSS of two autobiographies, one spurious by John Willocks.

Many, coming across this last, which does not bear Willock's name, would assume it to be the work of William.

He agreed to Willocks writing this, no doubt hoping to get something out of it. He did not bargain for what was published, and most understandably took grave exception to it, threatening legal action. The book was withdrawn, Willocks allegedly stating that it would be re-issued after McGonagall's death, and to the eternal shame of Willocks, it was; I have in front of me the 1905 shilling edition.

The book starts in the manner in which it is to go on, by libelling William's sober God-fearing parents as "poor but bibulous"; and ends—the 1905 edition—with mocking McGonagall even in death.

A conceited, immature, tasteless stringing together of gibes.

31. patons Lane. Dundee.
March. the 25th.
1886.

I do hereby
Certify,
that I have resigned to Mr. Alexander
C. Lamb.
the Manuscript. of an authentic
Autobiography, of myself written by
my own hand, also the Manuscript.
of a Spurious Autobiography,
written by John Willocks about me.

believe me yours.
Sincerely
William McGonagall.

poet.

The "spurious autobiography" is referred to in Appendix I.

By kind permission of Dundee Public Libraries (Copyright).

48. Step Row, Dundee.
May, the 22nd.
Mr Alexander C. Lamb. 1891.
my dear Sir, as I am thinking
of selling, all my Manuscripts.
which, in number, is
100. and 42. great, and small,
I will give you, the preference
of purchasing them, if
you, feel inclined to do so.
as I intend, to sell them,
to the first person. that gives
me a fair bid for them,
but looking to our long friendship. I would like, that would
be the purchaser... an answer,
will oblige. yours truly,
Wm. McGonagall poet.

Mr. Alexander Lamb Esq
Temperance Hotel Proprietor.
Reform St
Dundee.

Letter offering all his MSS., totalling 142, to Alec Lamb, antiquarian, owner of a Temperance Hotel. It is due to Lamb's interest that many McGonagall relics survive.

Photo by kind permission of Dundee Public Libraries (Copyright).

Unsuccessful appeal to his M.P., Sir John Leng, to obtain money from Civil List.

Photograph by kind permission of Dundee Public Libraries (Copyright).

No. 5. South College Street.
Edinburgh.
June - 1902 -

Dear Mr Shand.
I hope to find you
well, but I am in a very
poor state of health at present,
I am suffering from a severe
attack of Bronchitis. I am
very weakly, I have been
Confined to Bed. for a fortnight. but thank God I am able
to be out again. but I am in
arrears with my quarters
Rent. which troubles me.
very much it is due, on
the 2nd, of February, I am
in arrears. P.S. and I have
a hard Factor, excuse me
for letting you know this.
believe me yours truly
Wm McGonagall. poet.
Mr James Shand Esq -

James Shand worked in a Dundee bank, and befriended McGonagall even after
he had been living in Edinburgh for several years. This letter was written a few
months before McGonagall died.

Photo by kind permission of Dundee Public Libraries (Copyright).

"Jack O' The Cudgel," little more than the synopsis of a play, developed from the stanzas of the same title in July 1886, and never published or performed in his lifetime.

Photo by kind permission of Dundee Public Libraries (Copyright).